Humanitarian Intervention after Kosovo

Also by Aidan Hehir

STATE-BUILDING: Theory and Practice (*co-edited with Neil Robinson*)

Humanitarian Intervention after Kosovo

Iraq, Darfur and the Record of Global Civil Society

Aidan Hehir
Senior Lecturer in International Relations, University of Westminster, UK

palgrave
macmillan

First published 2008 by
PALGRAVE MACMILLAN

Palgrave Macmillan in the UK is an imprint of Macmillan Publishers Limited, registered in England, company number 785998, of Houndmills, Basingstoke, Hampshire RG21 6XS.

Palgrave Macmillan in the US is a division of St Martin's Press LLC, 175 Fifth Avenue, New York, NY 10010.

Palgrave Macmillan is the global academic imprint of the above companies and has companies and representatives throughout the world.

Palgrave® and Macmillan® are registered trademarks in the United States, the United Kingdom, Europe and other countries.

ISBN-13: 978-0-230-54221-1 hardback
ISBN-10: 0-230-54221-2 hardback

This book is printed on paper suitable for recycling and made from fully managed and sustained forest sources. Logging, pulping and manufacturing processes are expected to conform to the environmental regulations of the country of origin.

A catalogue record for this book is available from the British Library.

Library of Congress Cataloging-in-Publication Data

Hehir, Aidan, 1977–
Humanitarian intervention after Kosovo : Iraq, Darfur and the record of global civil society / Aidan Hehir.
p. cm.
Includes bibliographical references and index.
ISBN-13: 978-0-230-54221-1 (alk. paper)
ISBN-10: 0-230-54221-2 (alk. paper)
1. Humanitarian intervention. 2. Human rights. I. Title.

JZ6369.H44 2008
341.5'84—dc22 2008024819

10 9 8 7 6 5 4 3 2 1
17 16 15 14 13 12 11 10 09 08

Transferred to Digital Printing in 2010.

For Sarah, Esmé, Elsie … and Red

and

Hilda Marshall, Kieran McMahon,
Nick Webster and Bernadette Hehir

Contents

Acknowledgements

First I would like to thank Neil Robinson; his 'intervention' saved my previously aimless PhD and stagnant CV (thanks, Luke), and I have benefited enormously from his invaluable advice.

Thanks to my former colleagues at the University of Limerick – 'The Girls': Mairead Moriarty, Ide O'Sullivan, Jennifer Moore, and Chris McInerney, Martin Mullins, Louise Kingston, Marie O'Dwyer, Ed Horgan, Alina Georgescu, Gabrella Hanrahan, and especially Ger Downes and Barry Ryan – the perfect mix of cynicism and pessimism. Thanks also to all those current and former staff at UL who advised and helped me, especially Maura Adshead, Eoin Dexereux, John O'Brennan, John Logan, Alex Warleigh, Owen Worth, but not Eoin Reeves!

This book began at the University of Sheffield and I benefited enormously from working in such a great department; thanks in particular to John Hobson without whose help my book proposal would be mired in an endless cycle of rejection. Thanks also to the fantastic admin staff, Katie Middleton, Sarah Moga, Sarah Cooke, Sarah Archibald, Sue Kelk and Margaret Holder. Thanks also to Mike Kenny, Andrew Geddes, Andrew Taylor, Tony Heron, Tony Payne, Caroline Kennedy-Pipe, Katherine Adeney, Ian Bache, Dave Richards, Steve Ludlum, Sean Carey, Graham Harrison, Alistar McMillan, Gareth Brown, Adam White, Ben Richardson, Tim Montgomery and Andy Mumford.

Thanks to my current colleagues at the Centre for the Study of Democracy, especially Tom Moore, David Chandler, Liza Griffin, Paulina Tambakaki, Tara McCormack, Patricia Hogwood, Simon Joss, Giovanni Navarria, Rob McMaster and Suzy Robson.

My family, as ever, deserve huge credit; eternal thanks to my parents, Mary and George, for making everything possible. A big thank you to Nial, Niamh, Rita, Paul, Hazel, Ashling, Aran, Jay, Hannah and Katie for being so encouraging and supportive.

The following also deserve credit: Conor Barry, the editorial team at *The Journal of Intervention and Statebuilding*, James Gow, Vanessa Pupavac, William Bain, James and Kathlyn, Anne O'Dwyer, Kim Deal, Darren Atkinson, Mark E. Smith and, of course, the Far Canals for 'Way out West Past Rosaveal'.

This book would never have been written without the support of my wife, Sarah, and my daughters, Esmé and Elsie. I am privileged to have you as my family and will never be able to thank you enough.

1
Introduction: The Humanitarian Intervention Controversy

Introduction

'Humanitarian intervention', despite its positive rhetorical connotations, has become one of the key causes of contention and controversy in contemporary international relations. Each of the issues inherent in this debate – human rights, sovereignty, order versus justice, the role of the UN – constitutes seminal current concerns in itself; together the issues create almost limitless scope for discussion and dispute. This capacity for dissonance is unsurprising given that the fundamental question raised by this issue – 'when is it right to use force to protect those suffering in other states?' – interrogates humanity's moral values, challenges the composition of the international political system and questions the responsibilities and duties of all major international actors.

For some the necessity of humanitarian intervention is axiomatic; suffering should be stopped by those with the capacity to do so. Others raise concerns that complicate this simple moral imperative. While few are opposed outright to the principle of helping those in distress, many, sceptical that states will ever act without some self-interested motivation, highlight the potential to abuse the malleability of the terms employed in humanitarian discourse. Realists see humanitarian intervention as undermining the basic tenets of sovereignty and thus as posing a danger to international order, while relativists view such action as the unjustifiable imposition of values by the powerful onto the weak.

This book's underlying premise is that debate surrounding this issue has stagnated due to the restrictive theoretical parameters recently embedded in the discourse. The dominant pro-intervention perspective, described here as the 'normative thesis', clashes with the dominant counter-perspective articulated by the realist position. Neither perspective offers a viable solution to the penumbra presented by humanitarian intervention, and thus the discussion has effectively deteriorated into an otiose dialogue of the deaf.

This study seeks to circumvent this impasse by articulating a critique of the normative position that goes beyond the traditional realist and left-wing positions. The need for a means by which humanitarian crises are addressed is endorsed, but the prescriptions advanced articulate a solution premised on an acceptance of the nature of state interests but not the immutability of either contemporary state practice or the existing international legal regulatory framework.

This introductory chapter highlights the importance of humanitarian intervention in contemporary politics and outlines the sources of controversy inherent in the issue. It then locates this book within the existing debate contrasting the guiding hypothesis herein with the realist and normative theoretical approaches. It finally provides an overview of the book's structure.

The humanitarian intervention controversy

The end of the Cold War catalysed a renewed interest in humanitarian intervention. The removal of the constraints imposed by bipolarity ostensibly presented new opportunities for proactive international engagement for both the UN and Western states, and some heralded the dawn of a more progressive and humanitarian era.[1] The Security Council-approved action in Kuwait in 1991 and the subsequent imposition, through Operation Provide Comfort, of safe havens and no-fly zones in Iraq certainly appeared to confirm this new proactive disposition and the realization of President Bush's famous 'New World Order…where the United Nations, freed from cold war stalemate, is poised to fulfil the historic vision of its founders. A world in which freedom and respect for human rights find a home among all nations.'[2] The fact that this humanitarian vision was articulated by the leader of the newly dominant hegemonic power in a suddenly unipolar world contributed to the building sense of optimism. As Chapter 3 demonstrates, subsequent events, especially in the Balkans and Rwanda, diminished this optimism but redoubled the underlying conviction, and the pro-intervention lobby articulated calls for humanitarian action with increasing voracity and frequency throughout the 1990s. This tension between a vocal and well-organized human rights movement and those, especially the UN and Western states, implored to 'do something' shaped much of the political debate in the 1990s.

These calls for humanitarian intervention challenge the very basis of the international system. The issue has, at its core, four sources of controversy that have contrived to propel it to contemporary global importance.

Human rights

The evolutionary trajectory of international law in the twentieth century evidences a trend towards the codification of human rights and the creation of the individual as an inviolable rights bearer.[3] In reality, the plethora of legislation outlawing certain human rights violations, such as torture, detention etc., though indicative of the capacity of the human rights lobby to affect legal change, have not eradicated these practices.[4] While states may sign human rights treaties, compliance is another matter, and a state's assent certainly does not constitute the assent of all clandestine factions within that state. With the liberating structural changes newly extant in the post-Cold War era, humanitarian intervention ostensibly constituted one means by which compliance could be compelled and was thus embraced by those eager to enforce the existing humanitarian legal doctrine.[5]

Yet there has emerged a counter-perspective which rejects the very notion of universal human rights. Critics note that humanitarian advocates are overwhelmingly Western and that their perspective reflects a conception of human rights that is less universal and more Eurocentric.[6] The rhetoric of the humanitarian movement, critics argue, sounds all too similar to the colonial logic of the 'white man's burden'.[7] Humanitarian intervention is thereby viewed by some as the forced homogenization of societal and cultural values, or worse, a means by which dominance is exercised under the guise of humanitarianism.[8]

Sovereignty

According to Jarat Chopra and Thomas Weiss, 'One word explains why the international community has difficulty countering [human rights] violations: sovereignty.'[9] The legal rights afforded to states under international law, and the UN Charter in particular, have increasingly come to be considered the paramount barrier to universal human rights enforcement and the focus for much of the indignation voiced by the humanitarian movement.[10] In what Stanley Hoffman describes as a 'revolution against unfettered sovereignty',[11] champions of human rights have singled out sovereign inviolability as a concept that needs to be reconstituted, if not abandoned. The principle of non-interference is an anathema to the universalism inherent in the humanitarian perspective, and to respect sovereignty is, according to some, 'to be complicit in human rights violations'.[12]

The question of overriding sovereignty or making it conditional on the adherence to certain basic human rights legislation poses a clear challenge to the prevailing state-based system. While sovereignty was not consistently respected during the Cold War, the contemporary humanitarian challenge constitutes a concerted attempt to conclusively repeal sovereign rights rather than a situational, expedient suspension of sovereignty, as was generally the case during the Cold War.[13] Some claim that the present challenge to sovereignty has rendered the sovereign state 'arguably weaker than it has ever been since its first form was established in the Treaty of Westphalia in 1648'. [14]

Order versus justice

'Humanitarian intervention', Nicholas Wheeler notes, 'exposes the conflict between order and justice at its starkest.'[15] The humanitarian perspective has increasingly advocated the privileging of justice over order. Proponents of intervention often argue that the military and economic asymmetry characteristic of the post-Cold War era facilitates the union of justice and order, as the 'just' now possess the unrivalled power to act justly *and* maintain order.[16]

Theoretical opposition to the prioritization of justice comes most vociferously from the realist perspective which rejects morality as a guiding principle in foreign affairs and considers moral actors as invariably hypocritical and certainly a menace to order.[17] The behaviour of Western states in the post-Cold War era has evidenced a continued reluctance to jeopardize order regardless of the scale of unjustness occurring, and 'in-humanitarian non-interventions' have been readily evident.[18] There has, therefore, been an ongoing tension between conservative Western foreign policy and the radical agenda advocated by the humanitarian lobby.

The UN and international law

The controversy surrounding humanitarian intervention is, according to Julie Mertus, 'a debate about nothing less than the very purpose of the United Nations'.[19] The optimistic pronouncements about the UN in the immediate aftermath of the Cold War suggested that the coming era would see the organization's power and capacity grow. This vision of new vigour has been undermined by the power wielded by the P5 in the Security Council and the UN's inherent bureaucratic lethargy. Indecisive UN responses to the crises in Bosnia and especially Rwanda increased calls for the organization to be reformed, if not bypassed, and fed the increasingly vocal support for 'illegal but legitimate' unilateral interventions.[20]

NATO's intervention in Kosovo in 1999 witnessed the convergence of these seminal issues and 'brought the controversy to its most intense head',[21] highlighting the gulf between contemporary legal doctrine and evolving conceptions of human rights and ethical state behaviour. The conclusion reached by the Independent International Commission on Kosovo (IICK) – 'that the NATO military intervention was illegal but legitimate' – is succinctly illustrative of the central problem.[22]

Humanitarian campaigners rejoiced at this 'humanitarian milestone',[23] describing it as one of many 'hopeful signs that we are indeed entering the third age of the human rights revolution: the era of enforcement'.[24] The intervention was, to an unprecedented extent, justified by its instigators on humanitarian grounds. The violation of international law was excused as a moral imperative,[25] and the evident desire of the NATO leaders to win endorsement from the human rights community suggested that the moral guidelines articulated by the normative perspective could constrain state action. The normative thesis, therefore, had seemingly achieved a resounding endorsement and proven its vitality, establishing a template to be emulated in the subsequent era.

Events since Kosovo have not evolved according to the normative perspective, and Chapter 4 illustrates the extent to which the ambitious prescriptions outlined during and immediately after the intervention in Kosovo have demonstrably failed to manifest. This critique, however, does not simply highlight the practical illustrations of the normative position's failings; Chapters 5 and 6 outline the flaws inherent in the normative position, and Chapter 7 advocates a new approach to addressing humanitarian crises. The following section establishes this book's guiding hypothesis and locates this perspective in relation to the normative and realist positions.

Normative theory, realism and international law

The theoretical framework employed throughout this study proceeds from an endorsement of the basic premise that those who are suffering terribly should be helped if their host state is unwilling to do so. In the realm of international relations this translates into a belief in the need to contrive the means by which basic human rights are protected, if needs be, by force. Complete sovereign inviolability is therefore rejected in favour of a system whereby state sovereignty involves adhering to certain minimum humanitarian laws domestically with the potential for punitive action by a third party in the case of wilful violation.[26]

This initial assertion is, therefore, in coincidence with the foundational premise of the normative position and clearly differentiated from the mainstream realist perspective. However, the prescriptions advanced from this underlying view differ significantly from the dominant normative prescriptions and incline more towards the realist position on interstate relations. The following section briefly outlines the fundamental theoretical perspectives advanced by the normative and the realist positions and, finally, situates the framework offered here in comparative perspective.

The normative position

The historical lineage of the normative position and its resurgence in the 1990s is dealt with in greater detail in Chapter 2, and the following paragraphs seek to serve as a brief illustrative synopsis to facilitate the comparative framework.

The fundamental assumption inherent in the normative thesis[27] is that human rights are universal and state sovereignty must be made subordinate to these inviolable rights. As Deen Chatterjee and Don Scheid note, 'a state's sovereignty should not shield it from outside military intervention when it brutalises its own people.'[28] The prescriptions advanced regarding the diminution of sovereignty are thus clearly radical, described in fact by Michael Ignatieff as amounting to a 'revolution'.[29]

Given the perceived limitations inherent in international law, the impotence of international organizations and the naturally self-interested nature of states, the normative position increasingly determined that humanitarian activists should mobilize to affect a more humanitarian world order.[30] This mobilization has manifest as the establishment of humanitarian NGOs that aim to exercise sufficient moral pressure on states to respect basic moral norms domestically and uphold these 'natural laws' internationally. This perspective, therefore, essentially seeks to turn states into 'moral agents'.[31] Increased importance is thus placed on the role of 'global civil society' and its capacity to influence international affairs.[32] This position advocates the primacy of moral rather than positive law, explicitly endorsing 'illegal but legitimate' action.[33]

Given the inherent desire on the part of democracies to maintain internal and international support, they are, according to the normative position, more susceptible to acquiescing to moral pressure, and advocacy is especially targeted at these states. The values inherent in the West, and its military and economic capacity, provide it with 'a historic responsibility' to exercise 'global leadership' on the human rights issue.[34] In a bid to maintain some yardstick by which to judge the actions of intervening states, normative theorists have compiled the criteria necessary for a just intervention, with the tenets of the Just War tradition forming the basic template.[35] Through the safeguards provided by the mobilization of global civil society and the compilation of definitive criteria governing interventionism, 'states engaging in humanitarian intervention know that they have an extraordinarily high burden of justification.'[36] States which deviate from these principles, it is argued, can be readily identified, and humanitarian campaigners can thus 'confront the perpetrators with the unjustness of their actions in order to constrain potential abusers through normative pressure'.[37] The regulating role of global civil society and its capacity to judge the actions of states are thus paramount and the primary guard against abuse and inaction.

This prescription is supported by a long-term project that seeks to promote global democratization, which is seen as a means by which human rights will be more consistently protected and the need for external intervention lessened. More extreme proponents of this view advocate 'a larger project of creating a just and non-statist global order'.[38] Global institutions, as presently constituted, are considered ineffectual, but the idea of global governance is endorsed. The composition of the hypothetical global institutions is, however, more exclusively democratic.[39]

The realist perspective

The realist framework is fundamentally different from the normative position. 'The notion of common humanity and human solidarity is', as David Chandler notes, 'diametrically opposed to the statist paradigm which is predicated on the contention that state leaders and citizens do not have moral responsibilities or obligations to aid those beyond their borders.'[40] The essence of the realist perspective on the applicability of morality to international relations is, according to Jack Donnelly, contained in four key premises, relating to human nature, power, national interest and morality.[41]

Ego and self-interest are central to man's nature and compel him to compete with his fellow man both at individual and at state level, where ego and self-interest are transferred to national pride and national interest. Power is the overriding political goal and state action is, therefore, orientated towards its acquisition and maintenance.[42] Whereas domestically individuals are compelled by the judicial system to reign in their compulsion for singularly selfish action, in international relations there is no overarching authority with the power to impose the order that prevails internally in functioning states. The state is thus the sole guarantor of its own security and cannot rely on any other organization to ensure its survival; therefore foreign policy must be concerned only with the national interest. Governments 'do not have the right to launch their nation into large unfathomable military adventures...purely out of humanitarian feeling'.[43] While the pursuit of national security may have consequential moral effects, these moral goods should not be, and realists suggest they invariably will not be, the motivating rationale behind state action. Realists therefore oppose the application of morality in theory and maintain that in practice states do not act according to this precept.

The realist perspective is fundamentally opposed to the application of morality to international relations on the grounds that moral actors constitute a menace to international order. As Tonny Brems Knudsen argues, 'any right of humanitarian intervention represents a serious threat to the element of order constituted with international society.'[44] The breakdown of the system of sovereignty in favour of morality will lead to the wholesale abuse of moral imperatives and widespread disorder.[45] Far from advocating that states adopt an immoral, aggressive foreign policy, the realist tradition stresses the importance of respecting diversity and the rights of states to autonomous evolution.[46] Realism suggests an inherent symmetry between the dominant powers of the day and prevailing conceptions of morality. 'Theories of international morality are', according to E. H. Carr, 'the product of dominant nations or groups of nations.'[47] Morality is thus not an objective fact and certainly not the preserve of certain enlightened, benevolent states.

Codification

The perspective underpinning this study constitutes elements of both these contrasting views. It is held, in tandem with the normative position, that human rights are a valid international concern, that certain inviolable rights can be determined and that these rights should be respected and enforced. The disregard for humanitarian concerns evident in the realist perspective is held to be both morally and practically untenable. It is morally untenable because it serves, at its essence, to contrive a situation that enables the most appalling violence to be visited upon citizens by barbaric leaders. It is also clear that human rights do exist; states have signed hundreds of treaties outlining their duties to their citizens. The problem is not, therefore, that states cannot agree on human rights, but rather with enforcing these rights. Weak states will naturally resist larger states imposing rights or values, but do not necessarily oppose the qualification of sovereignty in principle, as many declarations and treaties attest. State sovereignty and human rights can be reconciled provided the enforcement of these rights is consistent and non-partisan. Additionally, it is simply unrealistic to suggest that morality is a domestic issue and not an international concern; this dichotomy is, in practice, no longer valid.[48] Human rights *are* an international political issue.

However, the normative prescriptions advanced as solutions to the need for action to halt humanitarian crises are rejected for the following reasons, which will be explored in more detail in Chapters 5 and 6:

- The theory does not proffer a viable adjudicating mechanism capable of definitively and objectively regulating interventions.
- It employs a discourse that is inherently malleable.
- It exaggerates the capacity of global civil society to influence Western foreign policy.
- It fails to investigate the symmetry between power and moral values.
- It ignores the positive effects of sovereignty.
- It undermines international law and the role of the UN.
- It creates a need on the part of the oppressed to titillate Western publics into demanding action, thereby leading to an 'escalation imperative'.

The dilemma of how to facilitate humanitarian action in cases of egregious human rights abuses without undermining the basis of the international system remains pertinent. The solution advocated in Chapter 7 is the creation of an independent, international judicial body charged with judging cases of abuse and imbued with the authority to sanction intervention. To overcome the problem of state reluctance to answer calls for intervention, it is further suggested that an independent means of enforcement, involving a standing military force, be created. Rather than seeking to influence what states do through fashioning moral guidelines which they 'should' follow lest they fall foul of the rhetorical wrath of global civil society, respect for human rights and the maintenance of sovereign equality can only be reconciled through legally binding doctrine, internationally conceived and objectively and consistently assessed.

Reconciling humanitarian intervention with state sovereignty 'represents a profound moral and political challenge'.[49] This proposal is clearly ambitious and is not proffered as a straightforward or even likely amendment to existing state practice. Additionally, international law is not reified and the scope for dissonance over positive law is acknowledged.[50] Yet the basic premise advanced endorses Michael Burton's view: 'A codified rule of intervention is less prone to abuse than is the current "sublegal" status accorded unilateral humanitarian intervention.'[51] The normative approach has failed to provide a framework for realizing the goal of basic humanitarian protection, and its strategy has, in fact, been counterproductive. The realist perspective rejects the very premise of a regulatory universal human rights framework. The perspective advanced here seeks to overcome this mutual incapability. The proposal articulated in Chapter 7 accepts the self-interested nature of state behaviour in an anarchic environment and articulates a regulatory mechanism derived from an appreciation of what constitutes a viable, if not perfect, constraint on state action, namely positive law. The guiding theoretical framework thus acknowledges the impulses driving state behaviour but not the immutability of current state practice.

Structure of the book

Chapter 2 demonstrates, firstly, the nature of humanitarian intervention's illegality and, secondly, the rationale behind the creation of both sovereign inviolability and sovereign equality in order to highlight the often-overlooked progressive nature of these developments. If, as is often the case, sovereignty is presented narrowly as a means by which tyrants can abuse their domestic population, then clearly one will conclude that there is little merit to such a provision. This chapter, however, will counter this position by demonstrating that sovereignty, normatively, is actually a means by which the weak are protected from the strong. This chapter additionally identifies the legal status of humanitarian intervention, demonstrating that prevailing opinion deems such action as illegal but acknowledging that the legal framework as currently constituted is unacceptable. This 'legal penumbra'[52] has led many who support the morality-orientated approach to humanitarian crises to conclude that existing international law cannot be respected in this area and has led to the determination that illegal action may be permissible. Human rights advocacy has thus increasingly come to champion the determination of non-binding criteria, based on the tenets of the Just War tradition, rather than legal doctrine, by which the actions of states may be judged.

While the normative position is not rigidly homogeneous, a set of core principles can be discerned, and Chapter 3 outlines these basic tenets, highlighting the key advocates and the rationale behind their approach. The normative position is explicitly orientated towards advocacy and prescription and manifests in the solidarist and cosmopolitan frameworks. Though these outlooks differ over the essential validity of states, with cosmopolitanism more revolutionary in its anti-statist orientation, both espouse a framework which prioritizes moral law over positive law and the articulation of constraining criteria. NATO's intervention in Kosovo in 1999, though not without controversy, was greeted with widespread support by normative advocates and commended as an example of the power of human rights advocacy to influence the behaviour of states. The prescriptions advanced by the normative thesis at this time are outlined, thus serving as a foundation for the subsequent post-Kosovo analysis.

Chapter 4 draws on the outline of the normative thesis presented in Chapter 3 and, through the use of case studies on East Timor, Iraq, Darfur and the 2005 World Summit, outlines how state practice since Operation Allied Force has demonstrated the limitations of the approach in terms of both the capacity of moral advocacy to convince states to intervene and the ability of states to utilize the normative rhetorical to legitimize non-humanitarian interventions.

Chapter 5 argues that the tenets of the Just War tradition and the mobilization of global civil society cannot serve as plausible restrictions upon the actions of states in the present international system. The Christian origins of the tradition highlight a fundamental component integral to the early purveyors of the tradition – namely, the presence of a powerful independent judge, that is, God. While the normative perspective seeks to elevate global civil society to the role of benevolent arbitrator, the nebulous nature of global civil society, its inability to proscribe definitive binding prescriptions and its manifest punitive incapacity negate its assumption of this regulatory role. The normative thesis therefore presents a series of prescriptions and restrictions devoid of any mechanism by which these commandments might be assessed or implemented. The criteria routinely proffered have not acted as restrictions or compulsions to intervene. The normative thesis, despite its anti-state pretensions, has in fact strengthened the power of certain states by removing the modest restrictions previously acting upon them.

Chapter 6 outlines the negative consequences of the normative thesis's strategy. The UN has been damaged by the currency of 'illegal but legitimate' interventionism. Its position of authority has been undermined, and this must be acknowledged by proponents of the normative thesis as a tragedy, particularly in the wake of the invasion of Iraq. The idealization of the West has created a two-tiered system – 'the formal rehierarchisation of international society'[53] – with echoes of the eighteenth and nineteenth centuries, to the dismay of the developing world. Additionally, the elevation of the West to a position of global human rights protector has potentially increased the scale of intra-state conflicts. The logic, at the heart of the normative thesis, suggests that atrocities will generate domestic outrage within Western society, which will translate into Western military intervention. Groups engaged in conflict with their host state may well conclude that it is in their interests to provoke their host state into committing acts of violence so egregious that the West will intervene, as happened in Kosovo.

Chapter 8 argues that humanitarian intervention must be independently regulated and based on principles developed through international consensus and the maintenance of sovereign equality if it is to become a legitimate and internationally accepted practice. The most viable means by which this can be achieved is through enabling the UN to incorporate codified guidelines governing the use of force for humanitarian purposes and instituting a judicial evaluative mechanism that is not dependent on the whims of the most powerful states. The purpose of this study is not to detail the minutiae of the legal codification and institutional reform necessary but to suggest that those who seek to enable states to intervene to halt humanitarian catastrophes must accept that this codified and regulatory path is preferable to the 'illegal but legitimate' route advocated by the normative thesis. While this prescription is hypothetical, and arguably normative, it is argued that it has some potential to be both actualized and functional, unlike the cosmopolitan normative framework, which, this study argues, has been shown to have failed.

2
International Law, Sovereignty and Humanitarian Intervention

Introduction

This chapter outlines what have come to be seen as the main obstacles to the realization of the normative thesis regarding humanitarian intervention. The nature of the normative prescriptions are outlined in Chapter 3 and, as will be demonstrated, they explicitly challenge existing legal doctrine. Sovereignty, as enshrined in positive international law, is regularly identified as the clearest barrier to the realization of the normative vision of proactive interventionism constituted on the primacy of 'human security'.

The contemporary tenets of international law are the result of an evolutionary process, the trajectory of which has been to clarify the rights afforded to states and the remit of the international institutions established to regulate state behaviour. Demonstrating the illegality of humanitarian intervention, though not without contention, is relatively unproblematic and many pro-intervention advocates would readily acknowledge this legal proscription. The major contention surrounding humanitarian intervention does not, however, focus on its legal status. Pro-intervention perspectives argue that the existing legal proscription cannot be the final word on the subject and proffer an alternative framework for guiding and constraining state action. This normative prescription seeks to transcend the legal rights afforded to sovereign states and positive law's proscriptions on intervention.

The purpose of this chapter is to demonstrate, firstly, the nature of humanitarian intervention's illegality and, secondly, the rationale behind the creation of both sovereign inviolability and sovereign equality in order to highlight the often-overlooked progressive nature of these developments and thus provide a counter to the contemporary reaction against specifically sovereignty and, more generally, international law.

The legal status of humanitarian intervention

At its core the term intervention refers to the involvement of one state in the internal affairs of another. The legal status of solicited intervention, when state X appeals to state Y to intervene in its internal affairs, is not a contentious issue. The legal status of unsolicited intervention for reasons of self-interest, when state X intervenes in state Y to acquire territory or resources, is explicitly prohibited under international law as a crime of aggression. The status of unsolicited humanitarian intervention occupies a different position in legal terms and its status is conditioned by ethics as well as legal doctrine.

In the post-Cold War era international politics has witnessed an escalation in the tension between respect for state sovereignty and the growing recognition of the inviolability of inalienable human rights. Intra-state conflicts have become a greater source of violence and instability than interstate wars and have challenged the international community's ability to maintain peace and protect human rights within sovereign states.[1] The cycle of violence between separatists and state forces necessarily results in loss of civilian life and attendant violations of human rights.[2] Thus, humanitarian intervention has become an increasingly important issue in international political discourse. NATO's intervention in Kosovo in 1999 'brought the controversy to its most intense head' and highlighted the gulf between contemporary legal doctrine and evolving conceptions of human rights and ethical state behaviour.[3] The conclusion reached by the IICK – 'the NATO military intervention was illegal but legitimate'[4] – is succinctly illustrative of the central problem.

For the purposes of this examination I use Adam Roberts' definition of a humanitarian intervention, namely, 'coercive action by one or more states involving the use of armed force in another state without the consent of its authorities, and with the purpose of preventing widespread suffering or death among the inhabitants'.[5] Thus, this intervention is opposed by the state incurring the intervention though not necessarily by all factions within this state.

Westphalia to San Francisco

International law enshrines the sovereign inviolability of the state. The legal status of sovereignty has evolved from the principle '*cuius regio, eius religio*' first enunciated at the Peace of Augsburg (1555) and later clarified by the Treaty of Westphalia (1648) to the explicit provisions relating to sovereignty in the UN Charter. The concept of sovereignty manifest under the 'Wesphalian System' following 1648 was a conspicuously contingent norm. Though the eighteenth and nineteenth centuries were characterized by the rise of nation states asserting the '*cuius regio, eius religio*' principle, the more powerful European states systematically ignored the notion of self-determination and sovereign inviolability in their colonial quests through *terra nullius* both in and outside Europe. As noted by Christopher Clapham, 'Westphalian sovereignty provided the formula under which territories which did not "count" as states, according to the criteria adopted by the European state system, could be freely appropriated – subject only to their capacity to conquer the incumbent power holders – by those which did count.'[6] The Charter's codification of the sovereign equality of all its members, as detailed in Article 2.1, served as a clarification of this previously selective adherence to sovereignty and, as Chandler notes, the Charter, 'marked, it seemed, the end of the Westphalian system of legitimating great power domination through the use of force'.[7]

The breadth and depth of the prohibition on military intervention is evident from an examination of legal doctrine. The 1929 Kellog-Briand Pact outlawed war as an instrument of state policy except when fought in self-defence or sanctioned by the League of Nations. This principle was incorporated into the UN Charter and finds its clearest expression in Article 2.4: 'All members shall refrain in their international relations from the threat or use of force against the territorial integrity or political independence of any state, or in any other manner inconsistent with the Purposes of the United Nations.' Articles 53 and 64 of the 1969 Vienna Convention on the Law of Treaties states that this particular provision is part of *jus cogens*, and is therefore accepted by the international community of states as a principle from which no derogation is permitted. Additionally, Article 2.7 of the Charter reads, 'Nothing in the present Charter shall authorize the United Nations to intervene in matters which are essentially within the domestic jurisdiction of any state.' The 1970 General Assembly Resolution *Declaration on Principles of International Law Concerning Friendly Relations and Co-Operation Among States* (2625-XXV) asserted, 'Every state has the duty to refrain in its international relations from the threat or use of force against the territorial integrity or political independence of any State ... Such a threat or use of force constitutes a violation of international law and the Charter of the United Nations and shall never be employed as a means of settling international issues.' Clause IV of the *Declaration of Principles Guiding Relations between Participating States of the Helsinki Accords Final Act* of 1975 notes,

'The participating states will respect the territorial integrity of each of the participating states. Accordingly they will refrain from any action ... against the territorial integrity, political independence, or the unity of any participating state.' The Charter, and supplementary international law, therefore, explicitly codifies the sovereignty of the state, enshrining it as the unit of currency in international relations.

The use of force by states, regardless of the motivation, is explicitly proscribed except under certain clearly defined circumstances. Article 51 of the UN Charter reads, 'Nothing in the present Charter shall impair the inherent right of individual or collective self defense if an armed attack occurs against a member of the United Nations.' This is premised, however, by the declaration that this situation – the use of force in self-defence – is only permissible 'until the Security Council has taken measures necessary to maintain international peace and security' and that this right of self-defence 'shall not in any way affect the authority and responsibility of the Security Council'. The International Court of Justice (ICJ) ruled in the 1986 case of *Nicaragua v the United States* that the notion of self-defence should be understood restrictively.[8]

The provisions of Chapter VII of the Charter outline the other circumstance under which the use of force is permissible. Article 39 reads, 'The Security Council shall determine the existence of any threat to the peace, breach of the peace, or act of aggression and shall make recommendations, or decide what measures shall be taken in accordance with Articles 41 and 42, to maintain or restore international peace and security.' Article 41 gives the Security Council the power to determine non-military responses to a perceived threat. Article 42 comes into effect if measures taken under Article 41 prove inadequate and allows the Security Council to sanction more robust measures 'as may be necessary to maintain or restore international peace and security'. The provisions of Chapter VII enable the UN to empower regional actors and organizations to carry out military activity to restore international peace, but as Article 53 asserts, 'no enforcement action shall be taken under regional arrangements or by regional agencies without the authorization of the Security Council'.

Under Article 24 of the Charter, member states acknowledge that the Security Council has 'primary responsibility for the maintenance of international peace and security'. The one possible derogation from this rule is the 1950 General Assembly Resolution 377, *Uniting for Peace*. This resolution enables the General Assembly to act when the Security Council is unable to unanimously sanction action, or demand a cessation to ongoing military action when there is a threat to international peace and stability. The Resolution has been used on ten occasions and was first used during the Suez Canal crises in 1956. However, the lack of effectiveness of this principle was evidenced later that year when the General Assembly used this provision to demand that the Soviet Union cease its intervention in Hungary, to no effect. A two-thirds vote in favour of action would, according to the International Commission on Intervention and State Sovereignty (ICISS), 'provide a high degree of legitimacy for an intervention which subsequently took place, and encourage the Security Council to rethink its position'.[9] A 'high degree of legitimacy' clearly does not constitute an explicit legal endorsement and the Danish Institute of International Affairs (DIIA) found that the *Uniting for Peace* resolution 'Has lost much of its importance [and] is no legal basis for the authorization of humanitarian intervention'.[10]

The UN Charter is clear as to its relationship with regional security organization; Article 103 states: 'In the event of a conflict between the Members of the United Nations under the present Charter and their obligations under any other international agreement, their obligations under the present Charter shall prevail.' The provisions of Chapter VII enable the UN to sanction action by regional security organizations, but this action is subordinate to the UN. NATO's Charter reflects this legal proscription: Article 1 pledges that NATO members will, 'refrain in their international relations from the threat or use of force in any manner inconsistent with the purposes of the United Nations'. Similarly, Article 7 asserts, 'This Treaty does not affect, and shall not be interpreted as affecting in any way, the rights and obligations under the Charter of the Parties which are members of the United Nations, or the primary responsibility of the Security Council for the maintenance of international peace and security.' There is no legal provision that enables a regional security organization to undertake a humanitarian intervention not sanctioned by the Security Council.

The use of force is thus prohibited except under certain clearly defined circumstances and is permissible only in accordance with Security Council authorization. Under existing codified international law, therefore, there is no law sanctioning humanitarian intervention. In its seminal ruling in the *Corfu Channel* Case the ICJ declared that it could

> only regard the alleged right of intervention as the manifestation of a policy of force, such as has, in the past, given rise to most serious abuses and as such cannot, whatever be the present defect in international organization, find a place in international law. Intervention ... would be reserved for the most powerful states and might easily lead to perverting the administration of international justice itself.[11]

In its ruling in the case of *Nicaragua v the United States*, the ICJ further declared, 'While the US might form its own appraisal of the situation as to respect for human rights in Nicaragua, the use of force could not be the appropriate method to monitor or ensure such respect.'[12] In 1986 the UK Foreign Office gave its opinion as to the legal status of humanitarian interventions, stating,

> the overwhelming majority of contemporary legal opinion comes down against the existence of a right of humanitarian intervention for three main reasons: first, the UN Charter and the corpus of modern international law do not seem specifically to incorporate such a rights; secondly, state practice in the past two centuries, and especially since 1945, at best provides only a handful of genuine cases of humanitarian intervention, and on most assessments, none at all; and finally on prudential grounds, that the scope of abusing such a right argues strongly against its creation.[13]

Similarly, in the US, the 1987 *Restatement of Foreign Relations Law* noted, 'Whether a state may intervene with military force in the territory of another state without its consent not to rescue the victims but to prevent or terminate human rights violations, is not agreed or authoritatively determined.'[14]

The provisions of Chapter VII of the UN Charter relating to a threat to international peace and security have been cited as a possible source of legal justification for acting. Security Council practice in the 1990s reflected the emergence of the view that economic, social, ecological and humanitarian instability in a state could be considered a threat under Chapter VII. In his thorough assessment of the 'remarkable transformation' during the 1990s whereby the Security Council authorized an unprecedented number of actions under Chapter VII, Simon Chesterman notes that the application of this provision was haphazard leading to 'ambiguous resolutions and conflicting interpretations [of the new definition]'.[15] Security Council authorization became politicized and was not based on an adherence to legal provisions contained in the Charter.[16] The sanctioning of action under Chapter VII, according to Chesterman, 'depended more upon a coincidence of national interest than on procedural legality'.[17] There is little evidence to suggest that the Security Council has applied the 1992 ruling consistently or that external interference in the affairs of sovereign states on the basis of an economic, social, ecological and humanitarian crisis has widespread acceptance.[18] Additionally, as the DIIA notes,

> It was hardly the intention of the framers of the Charter that internal conflicts and human rights violations should be regarded as a threat to international peace. There is no evidence that they might have envisaged a competence for the Security Council under Chapter VII to take action to cope with situations of humanitarian emergency within a state resulting from civil war or systematic repression.[19]

The IICK similarly states, 'Charter provisions relating to human rights were left deliberately vague, and were clearly not intended when written to provide a legal rationale for any kind of enforcement, much less a free-standing mandate for military intervention without UN Security Council approval.'[20] The IICK concluded, 'At present the Charter does not explicitly give the UN Security Council the power to take measures in cases of violations of human rights.'[21] Indeed, in 1946, the Security Council refused to describe Franco's Spain as a threat under Chapter VII, noting that this Charter provision constituted 'a very sharp instrument' and that care should be taken so that 'this instrument is not blunted or used in any way which would strain the intentions of the Charter or which would not be applicable in all similar cases'.[22]

Nonetheless, during the 1990s the definition of Chapter VII was stretched to facilitate interventions in situations where the threat to international peace and security was minimal. The UN-approved intervention in Haiti in 1994 was premised on the situation constituting a threat of such a magnitude. Following a military coup in 1991, the democratically elected President, Aristide, was ousted from power. The UN imposed economic sanctions, though by 1994 these sanctions were said to have had no effect. Then, in Resolution 940, the Security Council determined that the situation constituted a threat to international peace and stability and ordered, 'Member States to form a multinational force under unified command and control ... [to] ... use all necessary means to facilitate the departure from Haiti of the military leadership ... [and] the prompt return of the legitimately elected President.' This declaration stretched the definition of a threat to international peace and stability to incorporate non-democratic regimes. In practice, as the ongoing situation in many other states attested, the existence of non-democratic regimes and benefactors of military coups was not considered in every instance to present this grave threat. In addition, in keeping with other declarations of a threat to international peace and stability during the 1990s, this Security Council ruling was officially considered an exception. Resolution 940 recognized 'the unique character' of the situation and stated that Haiti's 'deteriorating, complex and extraordinary nature... [required] an exceptional response'. Similarly the sanctioning of action in Somalia in 1992 on the grounds that there existed a threat to international peace was premised on it being 'an exceptional response' and the sanctioning of action in Rwanda through Resolution 929 in 1994 was 'a unique case'. As the DIIA notes, 'This approach reveals unwillingness on the part of the Security Council to set precedents for humanitarian intervention in internal conflicts.'[23] With respects to the process by which practice becomes a customary law, Richard Caplan notes, 'States may choose to support a practice for all manner of reasons... unless that support is accompanied by an expression of belief on the part of states that the practice reflects a new rule of law – in this case a right of humanitarian intervention – it cannot be said that a customary legal basis for such a right exists.'[24] Thus the Security Council's continued prefacing of all Chapter VII declarations during the 1990s with the proviso that each case was unique or extraordinary militates against the evolution of a customary norm.

The provisions of Chapter VII of the Charter do enable the Security Council to sanction military intervention in intra-state conflicts, but not explicitly for humanitarian reasons. While the term 'threat to international peace and stability' may be malleable, and has been questionably broadened to accommodate certain situations, most particularly Haiti, the inconsistency of application, the lack of explicit legal authorization and the reluctance to set a precedent when used militates against the provisions of Chapter VII constituting legal legitimacy for humanitarian intervention, but certainly does not prevent such designations. The provisions of Chapter VII can be, and have been, used to sanction ostensibly humanitarian interventions, but these instances have necessarily stretched existing legal principals and this potentially facilitates the misuse of UN law. Those occasions when interventions have been legitimized on this basis, according to Chesterman, are indicative less of the emergence of a legal capacity to act then of 'more traditional motives'.[25]

Despite the legal proscriptions outlined above, certain figures within NATO did assert a legal justification for the intervention in Kosovo in 1999 though, as Catherine Guicherd notes, 'The argument was obviously more political then legal'.[26] UK Defence Minister George Robertson stated, 'We are in no doubt that NATO is acting within international law. Our legal justification rests upon the accepted principle that force may be used in extreme circumstances to avert a humanitarian catastrophe.'[27] While suggesting that a principle permitting the use of force in extreme circumstances to prevent a humanitarian crisis is 'accepted' is clearly a political statement and certainly not without contention, there is some basis for the assertion that humanitarian intervention is not considered illegal by everyone. In October 1998, the UK Foreign and Commonwealth Office outlined its opinion as to the permissibility of military intervention in Kosovo; they stated that the interventions in Bosnia and Somalia indicated that 'Security Council authorisation to use force for humanitarian purposes is now widely accepted' and that 'force can also be justified on the grounds of overwhelming humanitarian necessity without a UN Security Council Resolution'.[28] The criteria for such action were threefold. First, if 'there is convincing evidence, generally accepted by the international community...of extreme humanitarian distress on a large scale requiring immediate and urgent relief'. Second, if 'it is objectively clear that there is no practicable alternative to the use of force if lives are to be saved' and finally, providing 'the proposed use of force is necessary and proportionate to the aim and is strictly limited in time and scope to this aim'. The document concludes, 'as matters now stand and if action through the Security Council is not possible, military intervention by NATO is lawful on grounds of overwhelming humanitarian necessity'. This argument is essentially based on the fact that since 1945 various international treaties and resolutions have outlawed certain violations of human rights and, therefore, as Roberts paraphrases, 'it cannot be right to tolerate acts which violate widely supported legal norms just because the Charter does not explicitly provide for military action in such circumstances'.[29] The legal defence offered by the UK at this juncture, which contradicts its findings in 1986, lacks any thorough legal justification and, according to Roberts, 'eschewed detail...made little reference to the long tradition of legal writing about humanitarian intervention...[and] said little or nothing about arguably relevant state practice.'[30] The body of laws that have developed since World War II, though comprehensive, constitute the commitments states have given to uphold their own citizen's rights and do not refer to what states should do to uphold the rights of citizens resident outside their own state. Therefore, it is precisely the lack of supporting legal codification of what to do in the event that certain signatories to human rights legislation do not fulfil their commitments, and the lack of consistent and accepted state practice in this regard, which has created the legal vacuum relating to enforcement that is at the heart of the debate regarding humanitarian intervention.

Following the intervention in Kosovo, the UK House of Commons Foreign Affairs Select Committee concluded that NATO's military action was 'of dubious legality in the current state of international law'.[31] In their analysis of the justifications offered Nicholas Wheeler and Tim Dunne acknowledge, 'The [UK] governments legal advisors privately knew that there was no uncontested right of humanitarian intervention in international law, but at the same time they needed a credible legal defence to present to domestic and international audiences'.[32] This tallies with Chesterman's view that the legal arguments articulated in defence of these attacks 'stretched international law to breaking point'.[33]

In contrast to the UK approach the German perspective on the illegality of the intervention was clear: the Bundestag acknowledged that the action was not legal but nonetheless a moral necessity. Bruno Simma notes that this perspective, more so then the strained interpretations of international law proffered by certain NATO members, was the most accurate legal analysis.[34] In fact, the German view expressly highlighted the unique nature of the intervention and explicitly advised against viewing Operation Allied Force as a precedent. In his view the German foreign Minister Klaus Kinkel stated, 'The decision of NATO must not become a precedent. As far as the Security Council monopoly on force is concerned, we must avoid getting on a slippery slope.'[35]

Legal justifications

Essentially three justifications have been articulated defending the legality of humanitarian intervention.[36] The first such justification relates to a particular interpretation of Article 2(4) of the Charter. The argument is that a true humanitarian intervention would not be directed against 'the territorial integrity or political independence' of the targeted state and would thus not be 'inconsistent with the Purposes of the United Nations'.[37] Weiss argues, 'By ratifying the Charter, a national government under scrutiny can no longer claim that such matters [as human rights] are *exclusively* domestic'.[38] Chesterman's analysis of the merits of this argument, drawing on the preliminary meetings held to discuss the composition of the UN Charter in 1945, determines that the 'dominant' legal opinion as to the meaning of Article 2(4) holds that it does not provide any scope for humanitarian intervention and that 'To interpret this [Article] as in any way justifying a right of unilateral humanitarian intervention would stretch even the Orwellian school of interpretation'.[39]

Secondly, there is the 'link theory' justification as proffered by Richard Lillich.[40] Lillich argues that, under Article 1.1 of the Charter, UN member states have a responsibility to maintain international peace and security and when the Security Council is unable to carry out its duties in this respect, the onus is on member states to act and, therefore, the prohibition on the use of force as outlined in Article 2.4 is suspended. Geoffrey Robertson similarly argues that Article 2.4 'really means to prohibit any armed attacks which are inconsistent with Charter purposes, and does not necessarily exclude those which are directed to uphold those purposes'.[41] In its assessment of the merits of the link theory, the DIIA identified three flaws. Firstly, there is no explicit basis for this rationale outlined in the Charter. Although Article 24 states that the Security Council has primary rather than exclusive responsibility for the maintenance of international peace and security, according to the DIIA, '[This] refers to a subsidiary responsibility of other organs of the UN, notably the General Assembly, but not of the Members states'.[42] Secondly, it is not legally sound to assert that the Charter must be suspended when the Security Council fails to act as there is simply no legal basis for this assertion. Thirdly, the prohibition on the use of force between states is a tenet of customary international law and has evolved independently of the UN Charter and therefore 'can hardly be conditioned upon the effectiveness of collective security under Chapter VII'.[43]

The third justification relates to the customary nature of certain aspects of international law. The *Paquete Habana Case* (1900) established that in addition to codified doctrines, treaties and court judgements international law is based on established customary behaviour of states and this is codified in Article 38 of the Statute of the ICJ.[44] As noted by the ICJ, 'Reliance by a State on a novel right or an unprecedented exception to the principle might, if shared in principle by other States, tend towards a modification of customary international law'.[45] In this sense, there may be a legal basis to a principle that has no explicit codification. As noted by Jack Goldsmith, 'If you read the letter of international law, it does not expressly provide an exception for a humanitarian intervention. But many people think such an exception does exist as a matter of custom and practice.'[46] An analysis of customary international law prior to and since the inception of the Charter, however, suggests that humanitarian intervention does not have a place in customary international law. In relation to the pre-Charter era Chesterman's exhaustive analysis concludes, 'pre-Charter state practice illustrates the paucity of evidence of a general right of humanitarian intervention in customary international law'.[47] Chesterman further notes that the examples provided by those authors seeking to prove the existence of such a right have had motives retrospectively attributed to them that were not articulated at the time.[48] Thus, as the DIIA argues, given the lack of any evident norm pre 1945, 'the only possible legal justification for humanitarian intervention without Security Council mandate is the assumption that the practice of states after 1945 has established a right of humanitarian intervention as part of customary international law'.[49] However, Anthony Arend and Robert

Beck's analysis of interventions during the Cold War period concludes, 'between 1945 and 1990 there were no examples of a genuinely humanitarian intervention' and in addition, during this period there was, 'no unambiguous case of state reliance on the right of humanitarian intervention'.[50] In those cases during this period where the greatest case for a 'humanitarian' justification could have been made, such as Vietnam's 1978 intervention in Cambodia and Tanzania's intervention in Uganda in 1979, neither intervening state articulated a humanitarian justification. 'Thus', according to Philip Hilpold,

> it can be inferred from these events and reactions that the necessary elements for the formation of a customary rule allowing measures of humanitarian intervention were not only not present but relevant state practice was a thorough confirmation of the rule which excludes the permissibility of such interventions.[51]

As noted earlier, in 1986 the UK Foreign Office found that no customary norm of humanitarian intervention had evolved. The ICISS similarly reported, 'the many examples of intervention in actual state practice throughout the 20th century did not lead to an abandonment of the norm of non-intervention'.[52] Kai Ambos noted that a customary rule of humanitarian intervention 'did not exist at the beginning of the NATO air strikes against the Federal Republic of Yugoslavia and it can hardly be said that it exists at the moment'[53] a conclusion endorsed by Chesterman who also found that no customary law had evolved by the time of NATO's intervention.[54]

Additionally, Jon Holbrook highlights that customary international law must be a product of a general acceptance of a certain legal principle. While North American and European states may assert that such a principle should be taken as having entered customary international law, the fact that this is opposed by China and Russia, to look only within the Security Council, suggests that, far from there being agreement as to the evolution of a principle, there is active hostility to the development of such a legal norm. Holbrook writes, 'Those who argue that international law has evolved over the last decade to establish or revive a right of humanitarian intervention are reneging on the principle that international legal norms can only be formed where there is a consensus',[55] a perspective echoed by the DIIA.[56] In the aftermath of NATO's intervention in Kosovo the 133 states comprising the G-77 declared, 'We reject the so-called "right" of humanitarian intervention, which has no legal basis in the United Nations charter or in the general principles of international law'.[57]

The debate surrounding the intervention in Kosovo highlights an underlying tension between the rights of states and the rights of individuals and, as Ambos states, 'The Kosovo crisis dramatically shows the limits of international law.'[58] As noted in this chapter's introduction, the crux of the debate, within international relations and popular political discourse, relates less to questions of legality than to ethics. The illegality of humanitarian intervention is accepted by many of its most vociferous proponents who believe that the legal barriers to intervention, particularly sovereignty, must be repealed or simply ignored. The following section highlights the rationale behind these much-maligned restrictions so as to demonstrate the progressive aspect of sovereignty.

The role of law and sovereignty

The idea of a state evolving independently of the international system in sole control over its development is obviously a myth. While certain states have greater capacity than others to resist external influence, few can reasonably claim to be absolutely sovereign in the sense of being completely isolated from international events and fully autonomous, particularly in the contemporary era of globalization. Sovereignty, however, is less a rigid amalgam of specific tenets but rather, as Weiss and Chopra describe it, 'a quality of a fact'.[59] Hence 'sovereign states' may evidence significant dependence upon, or susceptibility to, external forces. However, the significant aspect of juridical sovereignty is the fact that it derives from a recognition by the international community of a state's right to exist and thus the prohibition on *unsolicited* external interference. This at least imbues the state with an international identity which brings with it the right, though not the guarantee, of inviolability.

It is also incorrect to conceptualize sovereignty as imbuing the state with the power to do whatever it wants internally. While sovereign inviolability does clearly prohibit external interference it does not necessarily separate the individual state from the international system which it inhabits. In this sense sovereignty is relative – dependent on certain external factors. 'It is relative', according to Gerry Simpson, 'in that this form of sovereignty must constantly treat with the sovereignty of other states'. Simpson quotes de Visscher who states, 'the theory of relative sovereignty acknowledges the fact that individual states are included in a pattern of relationships which necessarily impose limitations upon their will to be autonomous'. It is also relative, he, notes, in so far as it is 'constrained by the existence of international law itself'.[60] The idea of international law creating and legitimizing the atomization of the international system into self-regulating and wholly independent sovereign states – 'a quagmire of infighting among nations and groups wholly unable to settle pressing collective issues'[61] – is therefore an exaggeration.

Sovereignty as a bulwark against external interference

'Throughout history', John Hertz wrote, 'that unit which affords protection and security to human beings has tended to become the basic political unit'.[62] In this sense the evolution of sovereignty has much to do with the capacity of the state to protect groups from external aggression. While the notion of the state as an organic expression of national consciousness inflates its genesis,[63] the capacity of the tenets of sovereignty, as defined by the UN Charter, to prohibit external interference constituted a major attraction for those determined to extricate themselves from colonialism, as evidenced by the seminal ten-point *Declaration on World Peace and Cooperation* agreed at the Bandung Conference of 1955. The codification of sovereign equality and inviolability in the UN Charter can thus be conceived as a progressive development insofar as it constituted a means by which entitlements, previously almost exclusively enjoyed by Western powers, were universalized. Indicatively, in an address to the General Assembly, Abdelaziz Bouteflika, President of the African Union, described sovereignty as 'our final defense against the rules of an unjust world'.[64]

The prohibition on external interference was a reaction against the historical trend whereby powerful states used military aggression against weaker states, or 'barbarians' devoid of political community languishing in '*terra nullius*'. Frequently this aggression was presented as emancipatory and progressive – the so-called white man's burden – rather than purely self-interested, hence the latter-day suspicion evident in the developing world to the 'humanitarian imperative' cited by Western states.[65] Hedley Bull noted that the fear of external interference and the determination to maintain the principle of sovereign inviolability was championed by many of the states that emerged during the decolonization process in the 1960s and 1970s. This view, he maintained, was understandable given these peoples histories: 'It is by gaining control of states and asserting their rights of sovereignty against other states and the claims of the international community that they have been able effectively to combat the foreign domination to which they were subjected when they lacked these rights.'[66]

The prohibition on external interference thus derives from the normative notion that citizens within states should be free to determine their own political system. In this sense 'restraints to intervention', as noted by Anthony Lang, '[should not] be seen as evil attempts to block the efforts of good humanitarians. Rather, the restraints of sovereignty and the structures of international law that support those restraints serve a moral purpose: the promotion of a community inside clearly defined borders.'[67]

Equality under the law

In discussing the 'fundamental changes in the character of international law' in the twentieth century, Andrew Hurrell argues that the evolutionary trajectory has been orientated:

> away from a system in which international law was made by the strong for the strong, and in which law was designed to fulfill a narrow set of specific purposes and towards a system in which norm creation becomes an increasingly complex and pluralist process, in which ideas of equality become more powerful and pervasive, and in which specific rules come to be understood and interpreted in the light of general legal principles and shared foundational values and as part of an increasingly integrated normative order.[68]

Thus the framework of international law established by the UN Charter can be seen as an 'equalitarian regime'[69] comprising legal doctrine designed to militate the capacity of powerful states to influence weaker states. States are clearly not equal in many respects but international law has sought to emulate pluralist, democratic ideals by fashioning a regime based on the internationalization of 'one man one vote' akin to the Lockean understanding of natural equality.[70] A state's international legal rights are thus not dependent on its economic or military capacity, political composition or culture as L.F.L. Oppenheim's authoritative 1948 description attests:

> The equality before International Law of all member States of the Family of Nations is an invariable equality derived from their international personality. Whatever inequality may exist between states as regards their size, power, degree of civilization, wealth and other qualities, they are nevertheless equals as international persons.[71]

The advance of positive law and sovereign equality derived from a rejection of the 'natural law' approach to international relations prevalent in the eighteenth and early nineteenth century. The conflation of power – be it economic, military or cultural – and legal rights was characteristic of this era of colonialism when states legitimized their actions as benevolent.

A state's recourse to, and invocation of, natural law as legitimizing particular action derived from a sense of cultural superiority and moral rectitude. As Alex Bellamy notes, 'Positive international law... derived as a response to the endemic abuse of natural law'. A system based on natural law is, he states, 'often a more disorderly international society with a much higher incidence of war'.[72] The contemporary move towards the rejection of sovereign equality constitutes the manifestation of what William Bain describes as 'proportionate equality' whereby 'the enjoyment of rights, duties or privileges must be subject to some test of merit' akin to this nineteenth-century approach.[73]

The consequences of the UN Charter and many subsequent Security Council and General Assembly resolutions – in particular, General Assembly Resolution 1514, *The Declaration on the Granting on Independence to Colonial Countries and Peoples* – were that 'it no longer made any sense to speak of a hierarchical society of states in which rights and membership and participation were granted in proportion to a society's development and capability'.[74] The contemporary shift towards proportionate equality, described by Christian Reus-Smit as 'the formal rehierarcitisation of international society',[75] thus contradicts both the doctrine and direction of positive international law. The consequences of this challenge are grave. According to Chandler, the shift

> replaces an enforceable equal standard of state sovereignty with an abstract universality that can never be realised within the confines of contemporary society [which at worst will lead to] the legitimisation of a new more divisive international framework based on economic and military power.[76]

Contemporary moves towards recognizing a hierarchy of states, especially manifest in the renewed interest in trusteeship, will be, according to Bain, 'grounded in practices of alien rule that are fundamentally irreconcilable with a universal society of sovereign states ordered according to the principle of universal equality'.[77] Thus the pluralist ideal of interstate relations and rule formation is fundamentally threatened by the regression from sovereign equality.

Stability and pluralism

According to Gene Lyons and Michael Mastanduno, the creation of the principle of sovereignty and its widespread acceptance led to the development of four major political institutions that enabled international order to be preserved.[78] First, a balance of power developed in Europe that prevented the rise of an overly dominant individual state. Second, over time rules of behaviour became codified in international law and while a distinct and accepted set of laws for international relations did not immediately emerge, certain state practices were generally accepted as either unlawful or standard custom. Third, the acceptance of sovereignty led to the frequent convening of international conferences to settle major disputes that might otherwise have descended into interstate conflict. Finally, as a result of the greater acceptance of the right of other independent states to exist there emerged the growth of accepted diplomatic practices and procedures for state-level contact. These consequences in themselves are certainly not negative.

As discussed in this chapter's earlier sections the recognition of sovereignty up to the signing of the UN Charter was contingent on the whims of the powerful and thus less a legal right than a function of power and/or patronage. Aggressive states have historically proved unwilling to adhere to the notion of sovereign equality and inviolability even after the UN Charter. The occasional breach of the Charter's rules on sovereignty need not, however, be taken as evidence of the wholesale ineffectiveness and impotence of international law and the institutions established to regulate it. In defence of international law and the UN, Simon Chesterman and Michael Byers assert,

> Buffeted by the Cold War, [the UN's] fragile normative edifice stood the test of time, helping – through the modest constraints of international law – to prevent major wars while providing peacekeeping forces for a multitude of smaller conflicts. Its very existence offered the promise of a world in which the short-term goals of self-interested states and leaders would be constrained by generally agreed rules and procedures, allowing the long term common interests of peace and co-operation to prevail.[79]

The capacity of the UN framework to contribute to the prevention of a major international conflagration and also operate as an international forum for debate must therefore be seen as a positive derived from the rejection of subjective natural law and great power diplomacy in favour of positive international law. Undermining this 'fragile normative edifice' through evoking claims of 'conditional sovereignty' and 'illegal but legitimate' interventionism therefore risks compromising the achievement of the goods which have accrued from its establishment and proliferation. Given that the Cold War period was, despite the absence of major conflict, hardly a period of prolonged peace, one may reasonably speculate that in the absence of the UN framework instances of warfare would have been far greater and the development of international norms and practices more arbitrary. Certainly the historical evidence suggests that in the absence of positive law warfare increases, particularly when certain states believe themselves to be acting in the interests of humanity. Here the realist perspective on national interest versus moral responsibility is particularly pertinent.

The realist perspective rejects allocating a primacy to morality in international relations on the basis that 'Theories of morality are ... the product of dominant nations or groups of nations'.[80] Far from advocating that states adopt an immoral, singularly selfish *modus operandi*, the realist tradition stresses the importance of respecting diversity and the equitable interaction of states. The logic of sovereign states progressing along self-defined paths free from external interference, regardless of the ostensibly 'moral' imperatives behind this interference, has been ignored in many of the post-Cold War critiques of realist thinking. As Chandler notes, 'rather than highlight the historical links between realism, the rejection of universal ethics and the advocacy of peaceful co-existence, today traditional international relations theorists are portrayed as if they were advocates of power, injustice and war'.[81] Bellamy, a critic of realism, acknowledges that realism accepts the fluidity of international relations and the contribution made by morality and ethics to this process and hence the 'need to engage in constant conversation with political realities'.[82] Morality and ethics thus inform norm creation but do not determine it.

The realist concern with order therefore attributes great utility to the principles of sovereign equality and inviolability as, in addition to enabling self-determination, they minimize the extent to which states behave according to subjective considerations of justice and rights. This is evident in Bull's perspective; he argues, 'when demands for justice are put forward in the absence of a consensus within international society as to what justice involves, the prospect is opened up that the consensus which does exist about order or minimum co-existence will be undone'.[83] This view was later expressed in more explicit terms: 'Particular states or groups of states that set themselves up as the authoritative judges of the world common good, in disregard of the views of others, are in fact a menace to international order, and thus to effective action in that field.'[84]

This examination, therefore, of the rationale for the creation of the modern sovereign state evidences those progressive and emancipatory aspects of the codification of sovereignty in positive international law. The creation of the UN framework and the legal rights granted to states should not be seen, however, as a bottom-up process whereby major powers bowed to pressure exercised by smaller states demanding equality. Simpson has pointed to those elements of the UN framework which enshrine inequality between states, notably the Security Council, which he terms 'legalised hegemony'.[85] Additionally, Anne Orford sees the international legal order as fundamentally biased towards those militarily and economically powerful states and constructed as a means by which domination by the powerful can be facilitated.[86] The UN framework was of course constructed by the victories Allies who did reserve significant competencies for themselves, some of which still remain. However, the purpose here was not to argue that the international legal system was a perfectly egalitarian order but rather to highlight the extent to which the codification of sovereign equality constituted more than a means to facilitate internal state oppression. Additionally, with respect to the primacy of the Security Council, all UN member states acquiesce to this institution upon becoming members of the UN and this form of 'legalized hegemony', unlike the push towards conditional sovereignty, is thus based on consent, albeit often grudging.

Conclusion

It is difficult to reconcile humanitarian intervention with international law. Whether it should be thus is a different, arguably more salient, issue. The dispute regarding legality stems from the rights afforded to sovereign states under the UN Charter, specifically the notions of inviolability and equality and the powers vested in the Security Council under Chapter VII. The latter part of this chapter has sought to highlight the progressive aspect of the codification of sovereignty, an aspect which has been largely ignored in contemporary critiques of this aspect of international law.

The proscription on external interference has become a key feature of the international system, yet one that has been almost routinely ignored. As Roberts notes,

> Legal prohibitions on forcible military intervention in the territory of sovereign states have a long history and are one of the key foundations of the system of sovereign states. The undoubted fact that their effect was limited does not negate their fundamental importance. They helped to establish the principle that non-intervention was the norm; and when interventions did occur, those responsible generally felt it necessary to produce detailed justifications based on the special and pressing circumstances of the case at hand.[87]

Thus, despite being habitually flouted, the restrictions imposed by international law have had an effect on international relations and at least, as Chesterman and Byers note, hold out the hope that a more egalitarian and peaceful international system will manifest.[88] It is necessarily counterfactual to speculate as to what the international system would be like without the UN legal framework, but it is clear that during the periods when the rights afforded to states were arbitrarily allotted and respected, oppression and great power domination were more prevalent.

It is not the intention of this chapter to reify international law to the extent that its prescriptions are seen as immutable and just. Rather, the perspective here endorses David Armstrong and Theo Farrell's assertion that international law '[is not] a self-contained normative system, capable of existing in splendid isolation from political and social factors. In particular, individuals do not obey the law simply because they are compelled to do so but because they are persuaded of its necessity, utility or moral value.'[89] They further argue,

> Instead of seeing the UN Charter and humanitarian law as laying down the law on when and how states may use force, it might be more useful to view them as political spaces where states engage in normatively bounded deliberation about legitimate action. These sites are normatively bounded in the sense that state reasoning, deliberation and action is constituted and constrained by pre-existing norms that shape social identities and situations.[90]

In this sense international law is normatively conceived as having two important characteristics. First, it constitutes the legal expression of existing moral consensus. Second, it functions as a forum for the equitable interaction and deliberation of internationally recognized representative entities. Clearly these ideals have not been consistently realized and political factors have influenced the evolution and functioning of international laws. Yet the evident inadequacies of the international legal system in practice do not necessarily warrant the radical changes advocated by the normative thesis on humanitarian intervention. The normative thesis is explored in Chapter 3, and following a critique of its prescriptions, Chapter 7 outlines a potential solution to the 'legal penumbra'[91] that is humanitarian intervention which does not necessarily undermine the very basis of the international legal system.

3
The Normative Thesis and Operation Allied Force

Introduction

The end of the Cold War precipitated significant changes in the structure and agenda of international politics. Early speculations as to how the dissolution of the bipolar order would affect post-Cold War peace and stability varied considerably; in light of increased intra-state conflict, Robert Kaplan predicted 'the coming anarchy'[1] while John Mearsheimer warned 'the prospects for major crises and war in Europe are likely to increase markedly [in the post-Cold War era]'.[2]

A more optimistic perspective also emerged, however, which held that the new era presented significant opportunities for the creation of a more equitable order where the rights of the individual would trump those of the state and interstate relations would move beyond military confrontation and economic competition. Martin Shaw encouraged people to 'reject these scaremongering reactions to current instability' and embrace the opportunities presented by the disappearance of the global nuclear stand-off; 'Here is a remarkable opportunity', he stated, 'to replace the politics of military defence and deterrence with a politics of security based on international cooperation and addressing global inequalities.'[3]

The logical consequence of the calls for greater respect for human rights and punitive action against rights violators was the development of significant pressure to revise the tenets of sovereignty. In the early 1990s violence in the Balkans and wars in sub-Saharan Africa contributed to the re-emergence of the tension between the rights of the individual and those of the state. The desire to alleviate suffering clashed with existing principles of international law, particularly those pertaining to the prohibition of the use of force against sovereign states. The question posed by the Wall Street Journal, 'At what point do so-called sovereign governments forfeit their sovereignty through their own despicable acts?' came to encapsulate much of the political debates that took place during the 1990s.[4]

This chapter will focus on the rise of human rights as a key issue in international relations and specifically chart the attendant emergence of advocacy for increased humanitarian intervention. The chapter is divided into three sections: the first section outlines the growth in normative thinking and the precipitous rise of human rights as an international issue and the nature of its relationship with existing state behaviour; the second analyses the nature of global civil society, highlighting the movement's articulation of an international 'human-security' agenda. NATO's intervention in Kosovo in 1999 is the focus of the final section, which will outline the nature of the optimistic prescriptions advanced following this seminal and much-heralded intervention.

The rise of human rights

Following the dissolution of the bipolar order, intra-state conflict emerged as a major challenge to the international community. The implosion of the Soviet Union and the broader diffusion of the previously dominant superpower stand-off precipitated an increase in intra-state crises due to the removal of the domestic and international constraints that had marginalized or suppressed many internal disputes. 'The end of the Cold War', according to Francis Fukuyama, 'left a band of weak or failed states stretching from North Africa through the Balkans and the Middle East to South Asia.'[5] These 'failed' and 'weak' states, newly independent from Moscow or suddenly strategically unimportant, were characterized by internal conflict, mass displacement and human rights violations. Mary Kaldor identified the emergence of 'new wars' which 'involve[d] a blurring of the distinctions between war, organised crime and large scale violations of human rights'.[6]

The 'explosion'[7] of human rights violations caused by these intra-state conflicts posed clear dangers to citizens within the affected states, but this trend was also increasingly cited as a threat to international peace and stability due to the potential for these conflicts to spread. The increased economic interdependence caused by globalization meant that intra-state conflicts, with their potential to provoke regional crises, impacted on Western foreign investment and domestic markets and risked causing 'epidemics of regional disorders', thereby generating international economic instability in addition to political and social disruption.[8] Thus intra-state conflicts came to be seen as the greatest threat to international stability. In 1994 the UN Commission on Global Governance noted, '[While] war between states is not extinct, in the years ahead the world is likely to be troubled primarily by eruptions of violence within countries.'[9] Western states therefore had both humanitarian and self-interested motivations for increasing the focus on intra-state affairs internationally.[10]

The disintegration of the bipolar system, though initially a cause for increased instability, was seen as constituting the potential emancipation of human rights; the diminution of the threat of nuclear annihilation ostensibly enabled Western states to assume greater international responsibility and increase proactive humanitarian internationalism. Thus there was a marked increase in calls from human rights advocates, the so-called new humanitarians,[11] for greater Western involvement in the wider world.

The perspective of these humanitarian activists was informed by a cosmopolitan framework. Kaldor described this 'alternative forward-looking cosmopolitan political project' as one which 'would cross the global/local divide and reconstruct legitimacy around an inclusive, democratic set of values…counter posed against the politics of exclusivism'.[12] The basis of the global civil society project was an explicit rejection of the statist and national outlook in favour of a political cosmopolitanism predicated on a universal ethics and international perspective. Cosmopolitanism, Kaldor notes, 'implies the existence of a human community with certain shared rights and obligations' and 'A break with the assumption of territorially-based political entities'.[13]

This 'political cosmopolitanism' is described by Kim Hutchings as the 'position which prescribes types of political practice and institutions that operate over, above or across the boundaries of the nation-state and which are at least potentially global in their reach'.[14] She suggests that the origin of this perspective can be traced to four phenomena: the end of the Cold War, globalization, the project of European integration and the increased visibility of Transnational actors.[15] Thus the confluence of these factors provided the movement with both the catalysts and also the sense of possibility which spurred on their humanitarian activism. Chandler defined the basis of this position:

> Cosmopolitan international relations theorists envisage a process of expanding cosmopolitan democracy and global governance in which for the first time there is the possibility of global issues being addressed on the basis of new forms of democracy derived from the universal rights of global citizens. They suggest that rather than focus on the territorially limited rights of the citizen at the level of the nation state,

> more emphasis should be placed on extending democracy and human rights to the global sphere.[16]

Human rights advocacy is not, however, a post-1991 phenomenon; concern about human suffering and action to minimize its extent had certainly been evident during the Cold War and expansive human rights legislation was codified in international law during this period, such as the *Convention for the Prevention and Punishment of the Crime of Genocide* (1948), the *Convention on the Elimination of All Forms of Racial Discrimination* (1965), the *Convention on the Elimination of all Forms of Discrimination against Women* (1979) and the *Convention against Torture* (1984). The increased number of legal conventions related to human rights, their expanded scope and heightened prominence suggested to some that the international system was becoming more regulated and the behaviour of states increasingly checked.[17]

However, the manifest violation of these treaties and the inconsistent record of Western states and international institutions – the UN in particular – in enforcing and upholding these laws led to pronounced frustration among many human rights activists. According to Kaldor, 'the new human rights groups can be viewed as progeny of [the Helsinki Accord of 1975]'[18] and constituted those who embraced the codification of human rights detailed by the Accord but later dismayed at the lack of action taken to uphold these laws. Human rights campaigners thus saw the evolution of human rights in international law as constituting a series of declarations and treaties rendered impotent due to their widespread violation and the lack of any effective enforcement.[19]

The end of the Cold War, however, constituted an opportunity to invoke and act upon the various human rights treaties as consensus at the Security Council now seemed more achievable given the removal of the Soviet veto. As argued by the DIIA,

> After the Cold War, more permissive global circumstances have allowed a closer correspondence between universal humanitarian regimes and the enforcement of such regimes in cases of genocide and massive breaches of humanitarian law. The discrepancy between words and deed has been reduced.[20]

Advocates thus hailed 'the age of enforcement'.[21]

Human rights protection is conceptually altruistic and a goal which most actors wish to be associated with, or at the very least not seen as opposed to. Given that, according to the prevailing rhetoric, 'The scale of human suffering in the 1990s is like a tidal wave';[22] the perceived magnitude of the problem facilitated its ascendancy. Human rights discourse permeated to the centre of international political agenda and became an essential component in the manifestos of political parties, the foreign policy agendas of states and the expressed goals of international organizations, both political and financial.[23]

The remarkable surge in rhetorical support for human rights and the issue's new centrality in international politics led unsurprisingly to increased optimism as to the coming era. The union of both the endorsement of the humanitarian cause and the more favourable international systemic conditions suggested that the 'New World Order' predicated by President George Bush in 1991 – involving a new role for the United Nations in enforcing human rights – was within reach.[24]

Yet the optimism was not confined to action carried out through the UN; despite the Soviet collapse it was clear that while both China and Russia retained veto powers, consensus at the Security Council would be difficult to achieve. While a 'period of euphoria overtook UN headquarters'[25] after the success of Operation Desert Storm, the failure of UN peace operations in Bosnia and Somalia, plus the more damaging inaction in the face of Rwanda, led to a sharp decline in the number of 'Blue Helmets' deployed with the UN preferring instead to mandate coalitions of member states to enforce its decisions. In July 1993 there were 78,444 'Blue Helmets' deployed globally, by November 1998 the number was 14,374.[26] Thus support grew for unilateral human rights enforcement by those acting out of a concern for 'human security' on behalf of the oppressed whose plight was highlighted by global civil society. The following section will highlight the nature of this advocacy, its practical manifestation and the prescriptions outlined by its advocates in relation to humanitarian intervention.

Global civil society and the creation of ethical foreign policies

Kaldor, one of the most vocal and active proponents of global civil society, notes that the end of the Cold War enabled humanitarian groups from across the globe to link up and coordinate agendas as never before.[27] The changed international environment thus liberated civil society groups around the world and enabled a greater coordination between these organizations. Given that the project was based on cultivating a sense of common humanity and an attendant willingness to support all those enduring repression and hardship regardless of their ethnicity, religion or location, it inevitably led to the vocal endorsement of pro-active rights enforcement and military humanitarian intervention.

The pro-intervention perspective rejected, and rejects, the positivist approach championed by realism in favour of normative theorizing and the articulation of prescriptions. According to this view, state behaviour, at least Western democratic state behaviour, is malleable and can, through the pressure exercised by global civil society, be reoriented towards a more ethical and altruistic dispensation. The capacity of global civil society to influence the evolution of the debate regarding humanitarian intervention is cited by global civil society's proponents as one of its most manifest and worthy achievements.[28]

It must be noted, however, that this perspective is not rigidly homogeneous. What constitutes 'global civil society' is itself nebulous; as Chandler notes, '[Global civil society] is an actor whose precise shape and contours may be indeterminate and disputed, but whose presence is not.'[29] According to Kaldor, however, this ambiguity is one of the attractions of this movement.[30] The project of global civil society is intimately linked to the process of globalization which is seen as enabling the realization of the projects' universal agenda and described by Jean Grugel as 'an overt attempt to blend normative theory with international relations'.[31] While globalization is thus seen as integral, the capacity for globalization to accentuate economic disparity is acknowledged, hence 'Global civil society for the activists ... is about "civilizing" or democratizing globalization'.[32] The following sub-sections will highlight the major tenets of this movement.

Morality has a role in international relations

Advocacy which stresses the importance of human rights and the need to develop mechanisms for the alleviation of human suffering and the punishment of rights violators, at its core, seeks to integrate morality into international politics and develop normative thinking about the behaviour of states and the structure of the international system.[33] The re-emergence of normative theorizing, described by Chris Brown as 'that body of work which addresses the moral dimension of international relations and the wider questions of meaning and interpretation generated by the discipline',[34] thus challenged the positivist approach avowed by realism in favour of proffering prescriptions as to how states, institutions and individuals *ought* to act. This 'normative turn' constituted a fundamental challenge to existing norms of state behaviour and an explicit rejection of the realist perspective.[35] In addition to the mobilization of civil society the academic discipline of International Relations was itself assigned a role. In his criticism of academic enquiry Ken Booth wrote,

> we [academic students of international relations] are engaged in recording, in some sense passively (and certainly not emoting). Like the supposedly neutral instrument of the camera, we are supposed to represent and transmit the facts before us.[36]

In place of this passivity academic took it upon themselves to support the radical change by embracing normative theorizing and activism.

The normative turn enabled this shift in focus to human security defined by Kaldor as, 'about the security of individuals and communities rather than the security of states...it combines both human rights and human development, freedom from fear and freedom from want'.[37] Where realism stressed the importance of sovereignty, adherence to the national interest and the principle of non-intervention, normative human rights advocacy articulated a vision of international relations where the individual's rights trump those of the state and a concern for 'human-security' constitutes legitimate grounds for intervention. Supporters (accurately) pointed to the various human rights treaties signed since 1945 as evidence of the capacity of states to agree to certain limitations on their behaviour derived from moral concerns thus refuting the, ostensibly, amoral analysis proffered by realists. Thus '[The human-security] approach imposes constraints on state sovereignty through the mobilization of international civil society to safeguard international norms and the sharing of power between state and non-state actors in a globalizing world'.[38]

Disdain for the tenets of realism is evident in much of the humanitarian advocacy.[39] 'The world of the realist's making', according to Patrick Hayden,

> is marked by the instability of power struggles, the casual resort to armed conflict, the pursuit of narrow self-interests, the hyper-production of weaponry, and the callous indifference towards the interests of persons beyond (and perhaps even within) the borders of each state.[40]

Chief among the criticisms is the amorality espoused by realism which is seen as an affront to humanity and a source of artificial boundaries that legitimize the worst human rights abuses.[41] To advocate respect for sovereign inviolability and the privileging of state interests over human rights was 'to be complicit in human rights violations'.[42] Predicated on a universalism that conceptualized a global constituency of individual rights-bearers, the human rights advocates necessarily rejected the comparatively parochial concern with national interests and the principle of sovereign inviolability. Jessica Tuchman Mattews argued, 'our accepted definition of the limits of national security as coinciding with national borders is obsolete', while Inge Kaul advised, 'What is needed today... is not so much territorial security – the security of the state – but human security, the security of the people in their everyday lives.'[43] Accordingly, individual's human rights should replace the rights of states as the central inviolable concern of international relations.

The universality of morality is axiomatic in this perspective. The moral discourse advanced a cosmopolitan ethic which sought to generate a universal ethical ethos among both individuals and states and reject the realist privileging of national interests and relativist notions of moral pluralism. The universality of morality and ethics became a core maxim of the human rights movement which was predicated on a conception of commonality rather than diversity. Hans Kung wrote,

> The one world in which we live has a chance of survival only if there is no longer any room in it for spheres of differing, contradictory, and even antagonistic ethics. This one world needs one basic ethic... If ethics is to function for the wellbeing of all, it must be indivisible. The undivided world increasingly needs an undivided ethic.[44]

Terry Nardin similarly argues that what he calls 'common morality' is binding on all human beings.[45] In his explanation of common morality he writes,

> although the principles of common morality may be 'common' in the sense that they are recognised in different communities, their validity does not depend on such recognition. They are required by a conception of the person and what is owed to persons, not by convention. Common morality is a critical morality possessing wider authority than the moral practices of particular communities, and for this reason it provides a standard by which to criticise these practices. Like the idea of human rights, the idea of common morality is opposed to communitarian ethical theories that ground moral duties on custom and consent.[46]

He further argues that the ethics of humanitarian intervention should be based on common morality rather than religion or international law because only common morality rests on moral reasoning.[47] Thus, moral reasoning is vaunted as preferable to positive law as it is based on a truly universal, and implicitly inclusive, 'common morality' as opposed to the temporal, contrived rules fashioned by states. This conception contrasts sharply with the totemic realist view, as expressed by Hans Morgenthau, that 'Universal moral principles cannot be applied to the actions of states'.[48] The introduction of morality to international relations and the explicit normative turn thus complemented the idealism of the human rights movement, itself based on a 'moral' concern with the plight of others. This concern, it was felt, could be translated from civil society to receptive states who would act on these moral compulsions.

Global civil society is a catalyst for state behaviour

In his analysis of the post-Cold War era Tom Farer notes,

> What has distinguished the new era ... is both the relative absence of those constraints on intervention action previously immanent in the polarised environment of intense superpower competition and the maturation of a global human rights network with unprecedented influence over public and elite opinion, particularly in Western nations.[49]

This 'global human rights network' manifests most obviously in the exponential growth in humanitarian NGOs.[50] These groups sought, and seek, to highlight the suffering of peoples abroad and view their role as catalysts in shaping Western foreign policy; as noted by Margaret Keck and Kathyrn Sikkink, they aim to 'transform state understandings of their national interests, and alter their calculations of the costs and benefits of particular policies'.[51] Kaldor suggests that the end of Cold War

> opened up new possibilities for political emancipation ... what has changed are the opportunities for linking up with other like-minded groups in different parts of the world, and for addressing demands not just to the state but to global institutions and to other states.[52]

While global civil society itself is not seen as wielding actual power, through its capacity to influence states it will ensure that 'policy makers are more likely to act as a Hegelian universal class, in the interests of the human community'.[53]

Global civil society, through the mobilization of non-state groups and the creation of an international forum, was therefore seen to constitute the means by which morality and the normative turn could be realized in international relations. Richard Falk described the 1990s as a period characterized by a 'global justice movement' which 'provided grounds for hopes that normative constraints would impinge on the practice of realist geopolitics'.[54] Shaw argued, 'Global civil society thus constitutes a source of constant pressures on the state system',[55] while 'Normative standards', according to Howard Hensel,

> serve to help delineate and clarify the parameters of the international system and its component parts; provide guidelines for the various actors within the system concerning appropriate behaviour, obligations and expectations; and influence the development of the international system along desired lines. In this way, constitute a pervasive, significant, positive influence on the policies of the states and the other actors in the international system.[56]

This process of pressurizing states to act on behalf of others was seen to be supplemented by increased media coverage of international affairs; as noted by Edward Moxon-Browne, '[In the post-Cold War era]...public opinion is better informed (the CNN effect) about geographically remote conflicts, and less tolerant therefore of inactivity on the part of their own governments.'[57] Thus changes in the scope and capacity of the media facilitated and shaped by globalization, and peoples increased access to news via the Internet and 24-hour broadcasting, heightened the awareness among domestic publics, especially in the West, of the myriad crises occurring around the world. People's innate altruism, it was argued, thus caused a bottom-up dynamic in foreign policymaking as domestic outrage translated into state action.

The receptiveness of states to the pressure exercised by humanitarian organizations was, and is, seen as dependent on the nature of the regime with democracies evidencing a clearer relationship between normative pressure and foreign policy. The susceptibility of democratic states to these influences therefore manifested in the explicit privileging of democratic states as the agents of humanitarian change and the preferred targets of global civil society's advocacy. According to Wheeler,

> Domestic publics and the media have the potential to hold Western state leaders accountable for greater humanitarian responsibility...it is only through the mobilisation of intense pressures on the part of domestic publics that governments will be prepared to embark upon humanitarian policies which they would normally regard as electorally disastrous. Thus, the political project of common humanity depends upon bringing citizens in constitutional states to a level of moral consciousness where their feelings of sympathy for the suffering of

> others lead them to make a sustained moral and practical commitment to the deepening of human solidarity.[58]

In a similar vein, Shaw argued that the power of global civil society could only be manifest through Western states, 'This perspective can only be centered on a new unity of purpose among Western peoples and governments, since only the West has the economic, political and military resources and democratic and multinational institutions and culture necessary to undertake it. The West has a historic responsibility to take on this global leadership.'[59] The consequences of this orientation will be dealt with in greater detail in Chapter 6, but in the context of this chapter the targets of humanitarian advocacy can be seen to be overwhelmingly Western democratic states.

By the latter half of the 1990s there was some evidence to suggest that the capacity of humanitarians to effect change had been realized; President Clinton and Prime Minister Blair inspired a wave of 'third way' social democracy which articulated a commitment to human rights and universalism. The UK Labour government's commitment to an ethical dimension to its foreign policy and its pledge 'to act as a force for good in the world'[60] were lauded as manifestly good and indicative of the capacity of humanitarian advocacy.[61] The evolving perception therefore was of the Western state as highly receptive to the blandishments of global civil society. The realist notion of national interest was therefore considered old fashioned and inaccurate and accused of offering 'no convincing explanation for why relatively weak non-state actors could have an impact on state policy or why states would concern themselves with the internal human rights practices of other states'.[62]

Sovereignty must be redefined

The centrality of the state in international relations is not a modern phenomenon and, as has been oft repeated, derives its eminence from the 1555 Peace of Augsburg and the 1648 Treaty of Westphalia and many subsequent legal declarations. The UN Charter firmly entrenched the state's position and significantly added to its universality by virtue of enshrining the principle of sovereign equality and inviolability in Articles 2.1, 2.4 and 2.7.[63] The notion of both equality and inviolability were challenged by the emergence of human rights advocacy and the 'normative turn'. Sovereignty was increasingly portrayed negatively and charged with enabling states to oppress, torture and murder their citizens.[64] Indeed, according to Booth, 'sovereignty and statism constructed from the seventeenth to the twentieth century led inexorably to the Holocaust and atomic warfare.'[65] Sovereignty construed as such created artificial barriers to integration which would become sources of dissonance and contestation leading eventually to 'a quagmire of infighting among nations and groups wholly unable to settle pressing collective issues'.[66]

The universality of human rights and the primacy of human security thus combined to challenge the basis of the existing system and specifically the rights enjoyed by states. In a typical expression of the growth in international awareness of human rights and the movement against sovereignty, Antonio Cassese wrote,

> today human rights are no longer of exclusive concern to the particular state where they may be infringed. Human rights are increasingly becoming the main concern of the world community as a whole. There is a widespread sense that they cannot, and should not, be trampled upon with impunity in any part of the world.[67]

The rights afforded to states were thus challenged; as Weiss notes, 'As a result of the normative efforts, the four characteristics of a sovereign state spelled out in the 1933 Montevideo Convention – territory, authority, population and independence – have been complemented by another, a modicum of respect for human rights.'[68] Thus, states deemed to have failed to adhere to human rights forfeited their sovereign inviolability, and external intervention to redress this failing was deemed legitimate. Andrew Linklater identified the aim of the humanitarian project as, 'Transcending state sovereignty' which he considered 'essential to promoting narratives of increasing cosmopolitanism'.[69]

The notion of sovereign equality was thus challenged with a state's sovereign rights increasingly considered to be dependent on their human rights record. The principle of equality thus gave way to a conception of a sovereignty hierarchy: 'The reality is', wrote Geoffrey Robertson, 'that states are not equal.'[70] While this perspective found no ready manifestation in positive law, the 'revolution against unfettered sovereignty'[71] swept aside these restrictive concerns. As Deen Chatterjee and Don Scheid note, in light of the violence in the Balkans and particularly the genocide in Rwanda, 'something of a consensus developed, namely that a state's sovereignty should not shield it from outside military intervention when it brutalises its own people'.[72]

The UN is not the only legitimate authority

The emergence of the perspective which explicitly sought to alter state behaviour and re-orientate the focus of international relations inevitably clashed with existing international norms. The response to crises in Africa and the Balkans suggested that states on the Security Council were unwilling to endorse the universalism espoused by humanitarian advocacy thus rendering the UN impotent. Adherents to the normative primacy of human rights over state sovereignty, in many cases, concluded that the state-based, and Security Council dominated, UN was not capable of acting on the humanitarian prescriptions being advanced. As Michael Barnett stated with respect to the genocide in Rwanda, 'Only an indifferent UN comprising self absorbed states could have ignored such an unambiguous moral imperative.'[73] Similarly, due to its record and state-based composition, Robertson argued that 'humanitarian intervention cannot be the prerogative of the UN'.[74]

The UN's composition and the Charter's privileging of sovereign inviolability led to the emergence of an, albeit often heavy-hearted, endorsement of action outside the UN framework. If a group of states, supporters argued, sought to intervene to stop genocide but were prevented from doing so through the UN by a Chinese or Russian veto, surely they could operate outside of this restrictive framework and 'do the rights thing'. While strained interpretations of existing international law sought to demonstrate that action undertaken without explicit Security Council authorization was legal, the concern with legality was essentially deemed secondary to the moral imperative. The greatest manifestation of this position, NATO's intervention in Kosovo, will be addressed in the later section of this chapter.

The creation of criteria will govern intervention

In light of the failings inherent in the international legal system as governed by the UN Charter, it was argued that unilateral, and hence illegal, action could, under certain circumstances, be legitimate. Thus the blanket prohibition on the use of force outside of UN authorization needed to be revised. Given the UN's incapacity it was, according to some, inevitable that states would have to act outside of the framework of positive law.[75] In its assessment the DIIA found that humanitarian intervention was illegal but determined 'it is hardly realistic in the foreseeable future that states should altogether refrain from such intervention if it is deemed imperative on moral and political grounds'.[76] While the promotion of human rights clearly sought to remove the restrictions on intervention imposed by positive international law and the centrality of the UN in international politics, advocates cautioned against a limitless right to intervene.

To guard against the abuse of this humanitarian exception many, described by Michael Burton as 'conditionalists',[77] compiled lists of criteria that states *should* adhere to for their interventions to be deemed legitimate.[78] This effort at constraining intervention was predicated on the assumption that states were mindful of the power wielded by global civil society and their domestic populace and would undertake interventions only if they could be endorsed by this community. Advocates of this perspective clearly believed in the power of global civil society to constrain state behaviour and the criteria proffered were seen as a substitute for the evaluative and legitimizing powers previously centred in the UN.

In many cases the theoretical basis for the criteria proffered were the tenets of the Just War tradition, described by Bryan Hehir as the 'moral normative tradition'.[79] Accordingly, intervention was deemed legitimate if criteria, akin to the *jus ad bellum* and *jus in bello* categories, were met. The many sets of criteria proffered, though different in some minor respects, generally evidenced a strong degree of commonality, owing no doubt to their shared origins in the Just War tradition.

Supporters of criteria maintained that they comprised a means by which state action could be assessed and shaped. In defence of his criteria, Nicholas Wheeler argued, 'the number of cases that could plausibly be defended in terms of these norms is limited, it is wrong to think that permitting a right of humanitarian intervention will open the floodgates to interventions'.[80] In a similar vein, Jane Stromseth rejects moves towards legal codification in favour of 'identifying patterns and common elements in recent practice as guidance for the future'.[81] Having outlined her criteria she asserts that the creation of criteria 'puts a very high burden of justification on those who would intervene without UN authorisation'. In the longer term criteria are seen as shaping the UN's approach, and Stromseth states, 'the recent proliferation of efforts to articulate criteria for interventions even without Security Council authorisation may put some useful pressure on the Security Council to step up to the plate if and when situations like Kosovo arise again.'[82] The DIIA, specifically drawing on the Just War tradition for the foundational principles, proffered a list of criteria noting, 'Such a list could be used to justify one's own interventions and to criticise those of others.'[83] They suggest that equipped with this criteria 'the international community... may choose on a case by case basis not to condemn if the intervention is truly humanitarian and morally justifiable'.[84]

Thus the creation of criteria was considered to constitute the means by which legitimate humanitarian action could be realized. This, coupled with the belief in the capacity of global civil society to exercise leverage on Western governments in their foreign affairs, led to a belief in the emergence of a solution to the problem of alleviating humanitarian crises in uncooperative sovereign states. As the following section demonstrates, this perspective was ostensibly realized through NATO's intervention in 1999.

Operation Allied Force

NATO's intervention in Kosovo constituted a major vindication for supporters of pro-active humanitarianism who believed in the capacity of global civil society to pressurize states, and specifically Western states, into acting ethically. Operation Allied Force seemingly constituted the most manifest illustration of the shift away from a realist foreign policy towards universal moral action. President Clinton spoke of the 'moral imperative' to intervene and Prime Minister Blair lauded this 'just war in a just cause ... for the values of civilisation'.[85] It was seen to 'represent the wave of the future'[86] and many heralded the dawn of a new age of human rights. Robertson described Operation Allied Force as 'the first war waged for ethical principles alone' and but one of many 'hopeful signs that we are indeed entering the third age of the human rights revolution: the era of enforcement'.[87]

The intervention highlighted the gulf between permissible action under international law and the new dispensation to act morally.[88] Here, supporters claimed, was an archetypal case where the restrictions imposed by positive law, and the Security Council veto in particular, clashed with a moral duty to intervene. The case for illegal but legitimate intervention was readily manifest. Stromseth argued that the intervention showed that deviation from the Charter and international law could be legitimate in this and other 'exceptional circumstances'.[89] Supporters of the intervention did not necessarily rejoice in NATO's bypassing of the UN but rather looked to natural or moral law in preference to positive law. Václav Havel, then President of the Czech Republic, succinctly articulated this sentiment,

> This war places human rights above the rights of the state ... although it has no direct mandate from the UN, it did not happen as an act of aggression or out of disrespect for international law. It happened, on the contrary, out of respect for a law that ranks higher than the law which protects the sovereignty of states.[90]

Following the intervention the Independent International Commission on Kosovo (IICK) undertook an extensive appraisal of the intervention and the origins of the conflict. Though critical of the pre-intervention diplomacy and the manner in which the intervention was prosecuted, the Commission endorsed NATO's decision to intervene. It declared that the intervention contravened international law but concluded that the intervention was 'illegal but legitimate' and argued, 'The Charter as originally written is not satisfactory for a world order that is increasingly called upon to respond to humanitarian challenges.'[91] This finding was a clear boost to the humanitarian cause.

The intervention, supporters argued, highlighted the changed attitudes of Western states and specifically their new moral concern. Constituting 'the first war of humanitarian intervention ever carried out by the Western military powers',[92] the extensive humanitarian rationale espoused by the intervening states suggested that the pressure exerted by proponents of human-security had effected change. Bellamy argued that Operation Allied Force highlighted 'the extent to which international values and interests have begun to come together during the 1990s'.[93] Ivo Daalder and Michael O'Hanlon stated that it showed NATO would 'not allow itself to be prevented from stopping mass murder in its own backyard by unreasonable demands from foreign capitals'.[94] Wheeler and Dunne highlighted the UK's particularly important role in pushing for the intervention and hailed the Blair government as a 'norm entrepreneur'.[95] Operation Allied Force thus was held to illustrate the capacity of the human rights movement and global civil society to compel Western states to alter their priorities from narrow national interests towards a universal concern with human security.

The crisis in Kosovo, albeit somewhat fleetingly, dominated the international political agenda becoming a major source of contestation and debate. The situation highlighted in dramatic fashion the tension between existing international law, UN procedures and the increasingly vociferous and powerful human rights movement demanding radical, pro-active humanitarianism. To address this tension Kofi Annan called for new thinking on the issue. His call was heeded by the Canadian Government which established the International Commission on Intervention and State Sovereignty (ICISS) to investigate the issue and the Commission released its report – *The Responsibility to Protect* – in December 2001. The Report constitutes a significant juncture in the evolution of the humanitarian intervention debate and has come to be emblematic of the underlying controversy and considered 'an essential framework' for debate since.[96] The Report rejected the term 'humanitarian intervention' because of its association with aid provision and the fact that 'an inherently approving word like "humanitarian" tends to prejudge the very question at issue'.[97] In place of humanitarian intervention or the notion of a right to intervene the phrase 'Responsibility to Protect' was employed.

The Responsibility to Protect, in many respects, constituted an endorsement of the pro-intervention perspective that had achieved prominence during the 1990s. The ICISS notes that the starting point for considerations of intervention should be the norm of non-intervention stating, 'All members of the UN have an interest in maintaining an order of sovereign, self-reliant, responsible, yet interdependent states. In most situations this interest is best served if all states, large and small, abstain from intervening in the domestic affairs of other states.'[98] The ICISS, however, qualified this position,

> Yet there are exceptional circumstances in which the very interest that all states have in maintaining a stable international order requires them to react when all order within a state has broken down or when civil conflict and repression are so violent that civilians are threatened with massacre, genocide or ethnic cleansing on a large scale.[99]

The Commission proffers a list of criteria an intervention must meet to be deemed legitimate. The list is not unusual or significantly different to the many similar lists previously proffered.[100] Of most significance within the list, however, is the Report's consideration of right authority.

The Report notes, 'the authority of the UN is underpinned not by coercive power, but by its role as the applicator of legitimacy... Attempts to enforce authority can only be made by the legitimate agents of that authority.'[101] Though critical of the composition and record of the Security Council the Report advises, 'The task is not to find alternatives to the Security Council as a source of authority, but to make [it] work much better than it has.'[102] The Commission warns, however, that unless the Security Council takes a more proactive role with respect to humanitarian intervention it runs the risk of discrediting the organization and encouraging other states, or regional organizations, to take unilateral action. To overcome the issue of the sectional use of the veto the Commission suggests a 'code of conduct' whereby 'a permanent member, in matters where its vital national interests were not claimed to be involved, would not use its veto to obstruct the passage of what would otherwise be a majority resolution.'[103]

While the Commission advised that all prospective intervening states should seek Security Council authorization[104] it also asserted,

> if the Security Council expressly rejects a proposal for intervention where humanitarian or human rights issues are significantly at stake, or the Council fails to deal with such a proposal for intervention within

> a reasonable time, it is difficult to argue that alternative means of discharging the responsibility to protect can be entirely discounted.[105]

Thus action taken outside of UN approval could be legitimate despite its illegality, provided it was undertaken on moral grounds.

The Report's views on sovereignty endorsed the perspectives advanced by pro-interventionists prior to Operation Allied Force. Wheeler, indicative of the increasingly dominant conception of sovereignty, had previously written, 'states should satisfy certain basic requirements of decency before they qualify for the protection which the principle of non-intervention provides.'[106] The basis of *The Responsibility to Protect* was the duties that states had to their own citizens but also to citizens in other states. In its opening paragraph the Report notes,

> State sovereignty implies responsibility, and the primary responsibility for the protection of its people lies with the state itself. Where a population is suffering serious harm ... and the state in question is unwilling or unable to halt or avert it, the principle of non-intervention yields to the international responsibility to protect.[107]

The Commission explicitly calls on states to act as 'moral agents' internally *and* externally noting that states which fail to exercise their moral duties internally can be subject to legitimate intervention by other states 'capable of acting as agents of common humanity'.[108] The Report further asserts,

> Rather than accept the view that all states are legitimate ... states should only qualify as legitimate if they meet certain basic standards of common humanity ... if by its actions and indeed, crimes a state destroys the lives and rights of its citizens, it forfeits temporarily its moral claim to be treated as legitimate.[109]

Sovereignty, therefore, is contingent on the promotion and protection of human rights and can be suspended.[110]

Conclusion

In the decade after the end of the Cold War optimism regarding human rights enforcement was so prevalent, and the capacity of ethical actors to affect change so firmly held, that this period was described by Manella Castells as the 'happy nineties'.[111] The rise of human rights and the mobilization of global civil society into an actor of nebulous form but definite presence constituted seminal developments in this period. Roberts described the decade as one when 'humanitarian issues have played a historically unprecedented role in international politics'.[112] The rise of the human rights agenda was most emblematically manifest in the increased calls for humanitarian interventions; as noted by Leslie Gelb, 'The notion that states could invade the sovereign territory of other states to stop massive bloodshed... was inconceivable until the 1990s.'[113]

The prominence afforded to the 'human-security' agenda was credited to the activities of humanitarian organizations and NGOs working as part of global civil society. According to Kaldor, 'By the end of the 1990s, it could be said that pressure from global civil society had given rise to widespread acceptance of humanitarian norms',[114] while Bellamy and Wheeler wrote, 'What emerges from a study of state practice in the 1990s is that it is not states but an emergent global civil society that is the principal agent promoting humanitarian values in global politics.'[115] Robertson identified the impetus for radical change as stemming from the 'millions of ordinary men and women, and of the non-governmental organisations which many of them support'.[116]

The rise, both numerically and influentially, of global civil society was lauded by its supporters as a radical departure from the previously statist nature of the international system with its allegedly inherent disregard for human rights. In their radical normative prescriptions the new humanitarians rejected not just the realist conception of state behaviour and the duties incumbent upon states, but also disavowed positive international law in favour of 'moral laws' which, supporters argued, were orientated towards the individual rather than the state and hence natural rather than contrived. Thus existing notions of sovereign inviolability and equality were discounted as out of step with reality and, fundamentally, immoral. The question of intervening to halt atrocities was seen as axiomatically a good thing and an expression of the emergence of normative and humanitarian impulses. According to Wheeler, 'Humanitarian intervention serves to highlight the normative limitations of a system of international law that encourages law-abiding states to break the law when this is demanded by the requirements of common humanity.'[117] The dangers inherent in creating significant scope for abusing this new right to intervene was mitigated by the power of global civil society to restrain states. Whereas in past eras the scope for abuse was real, the changed environment of the post-Cold War era removed this risk.[118]

NATO's war against Milosevic's Yugoslavia in 1999 was thus greeted enthusiastically by the vast majority of human rights advocates and supported by most Western states. The IICK analysis of the intervention as 'illegal but legitimate' and the adoption by the ICISS of the key aspects of the humanitarian project's agenda constituted significant objective endorsements of the broader project of normative cosmopolitanism and global civil society's capacity. The ICISS's conception of sovereignty as responsibility and its (qualified) blessing of unilateral humanitarian intervention heralded, it seemed, a new era. The Western state, owing to its receptiveness to global civil society and domestic advocacy, thus assumed a privileged position where it had the right, if not in fact a duty, to intervene to uphold human rights. Evidence from the 1990s, and Operation Allied Force in particular, suggested that the Western state was becoming the 'moral agent' proponents of humanitarianism sought.

Having established the tenets of the normative thesis and the impact of the intervention in Kosovo on this perspective, the following chapter outlines the record of intervention and human rights advocacy post Kosovo so as to determine whether the pronounced optimism prevalent at the turn of the millennium came to fruition.

4
Humanitarian Intervention after Kosovo

Introduction

As discussed in Chapter 2, following the intervention in Kosovo and the subsequent publication of *The Responsibility to Protect* optimism abounded regarding the capacity of human rights advocates, and global civil society in particular, to influence the behaviour of Western states and, more ambitiously, alter the norms governing international relations. The prescriptions advanced by the ICISS tallied significantly with the goals expressed by global civil society and those generally concerned with promulgating the human security agenda. The intervention in Kosovo and the publication of *The Responsibility to Protect* thus appeared to respectively constitute a precedent and a blueprint for the new interventionism.

This chapter assesses international relations in the period since the intervention in Kosovo, with a view to determining whether the optimistic predictions manifested. This chapter has four sections, each dealing with seminal events in the post-Kosovo period; the first section analyses the interventions in East Timor (1999) and Afghanistan (2001), the second section examines the invasion of Iraq (2003) and its impact on the debate, the third section analyses international engagement with the crisis in Darfur (2003–), and the final section looks at the 2005 World Summit. It is argued that these events highlight the extent to which the prescriptions advanced after Operation Allied Force have clearly failed to materialize.

East Timor and Afghanistan

East Timor 1999

Within two months of the conclusion of Operation Allied Force, the international community faced a new intra-state humanitarian crisis in

East Timor. The origins of the conflict were derived from the Indonesian army's invasion and occupation of the former Portuguese colony in 1975. The East Timorese rejected Indonesian authority and continued to seek independence from Jakarta. By the end of the 1990s the status of East Timor was a major domestic issue within Indonesia and the issue had attracted international attention. Following the resignation of President Suharto in May 1998, B. J. Habibie became President of Indonesia and in January 1999 agreed to hold a plebiscite, or 'popular consultation', on whether the East Timorese would accept autonomy rather than independence. The plebiscite was scheduled for August, and on 11 June, following the 5 May agreement with Indonesia, the Security Council established the UN Mission in East Timor (UNAMET) to oversee the plebiscite.

During the referendum campaign Indonesian militias issued threats to the East Timorese should they choose independence, and between 40,000 and 85,000 people were displaced by militia intimidation.[1] The militia's tactics were indicative of their concern as to the likely outcome of the referendum, and the outspoken desire for independence voiced by the East Timorese certainly supported the militia's fears. The Habbi government, however, appears to have convinced itself that the result was not a foregone conclusion. The government became convinced, it seems, by the assurances of the pro-integration parties in East Timor, such as the East Timor People's Front, that autonomy would be accepted or at least rejected by such a slim majority that independence would be untenable.[2] The ballot was held on 30 August and the results announced on 5 September; following a 98 per cent turnout, 78.5 per cent of voters chose independence over autonomy within Indonesia.

What followed was described by UNAMET as 'nothing less than a systematic implementation of a "scorched earth" policy in East Timor, under the direction of the Indonesian military'.[3] The campaign – Operation Clean Sweep – was characterized by extreme brutality, the large-scale loss of life, displacement and extensive infrastructural damage.[4] The Indonesian Armed Forces (TNI) was identified as leading and participating in the attacks, despite Jakarta's insistence that independent militias were solely responsible. It was clear, however, that the planning, logistics and resources required to prosecute the violence could only have been provided by the TNI.[5]

The outbreak of violence, though shocking in its scale, was 'widely predicted'.[6] In what came to be a clear understatement, the Secretary General had warned the Security Council in early August that 'the situation in East Timor will be *rather delicate* as the Territory prepares for the implementation of the result of the popular consultation'.[7] Human Rights

Watch asserted that the violence was 'predictable and preventable' and described the carnage as 'a betrayal of the East Timorese who braved everything to vote'.[8] Indeed, Australian intelligence sources based in East Timor had alerted John Howard's government to the TNI's involvement in, and planning of, intimidation against the pro-independence Timorese.[9]

International reaction to the crisis was influenced by the extensive media coverage of the unfolding violence especially in nearby Australia where public outrage was greatest.[10] The international political response was almost universally condemnatory, though significantly less robust than the statements made months earlier regarding Kosovo. Participating states at a special Security Council meeting convened to discuss the situation 'accepted as a given ... that unilateral action on the model of NATO's intervention in Kosovo was unacceptable'.[11] While both Indonesia's complicity in the violence and the need for a peacekeeping force were acknowledged, it was clear that no intervention would take place without Indonesia's consent. President Clinton declared '[Indonesia] must invite – it must invite – the international community to assist in restoring security'.[12] This desire for an 'invitation' was echoed by Kofi Annan, who declared, 'The time has clearly come for [Indonesia] to seek help from the international community.'[13] On 5 September the Australian government issued a statement declaring its willingness to lead a multinational force if four criteria were met: if there was a Security Council mandate, if the Indonesian government consented, if the mission was a short-term one with the aim of restoring security prior to the deployment of a UN force and if the force had a strong regional component.[14] Australia, therefore, did respond to popular outrage, but there were clear limits to its commitment. According to Alex Bellamy, 'The delays this [insistence on the fulfillment of certain criteria] caused meant that although Australia did intervene, intervention came only after the worst of the violence was over.'[15] World Bank and IMF loans to Indonesia were withdrawn and this appears to have been a key factor in Habbi's decision to agree to UN-sanctioned intervention force. Australia led an intervening force onto the island on 20 September and was successful in bringing order.

The East Timor case can be read in two ways: according to Nicholas Wheeler and Tim Dunne, 'East Timor is a barometer for how far the normative structure of international society has been transformed' and they contrast the West's collusion in the annexation of East Timor in 1975 with Western support for independence in 1999.[16] They further state, 'the new normative context of humanitarianism constrained the exercise of Indonesian sovereignty and enabled the deployment of a multinational force.'[17] Australia's interests were not served by intervening, they argue, thereby adding further credence to the normative perspective's notion of ethical state behaviour.[18]

Simon Chesterman, however, criticizes the 'chorus of self-congratulatory rhetoric to the effect that East Timor proved that the international community had made good the promise of Kosovo'.[19] He in fact charges the West with hypocrisy by contrasting its bellicose rhetoric regarding Kosovo with its 'great reluctance to intervene [in East Timor]'.[20] Given that Indonesia's jurisdiction over East Timor was not recognized by the international community (apart from Australia), there was, Chesterman notes, 'no legal basis for requiring Indonesia's consent', yet despite this 'it was clear that no enforcement action was possible unless Indonesia consented to it'.[21] Security Council Resolution 1264, which authorized the deployment of the Australian-led multi-national force acknowledged 'the readiness of Indonesia to accept an international peacekeeping force', reaffirmed 'respect for the sovereignty and territorial integrity of Indonesia' and established the force 'pursuant to the request of the Government of Indonesia'. '[I]t is clear', Chesterman argues, 'that nothing would have happened had Indonesian President B. J. Habibie not given the go-ahead.'[22]

Additionally, the intervention was so dependent on Australia that Chesterman suggests that no action would have occurred without Australia's offer to lead the multinational force.[23] The US was clearly unwilling to countenance any military action; Sandy Berger, President Clinton's National Security Advisor, stated at the time, 'Because we bombed in Kosovo doesn't mean we should bomb in Dili.'[24] Chesterman further argues that Australia's motives for intervening were not as benevolent as Wheeler and Dunne suggest, given the Howard government's fear of refugee flows if the violence continued and Australia's 'measure of contrition for its previous policies on East Timor'.[25] Echoing these sentiments, Gil Gonzalez-Foerster, highlighting the international ambivalence to Indonesian oppression in East Timor for the previous 24 years which caused the deaths of some 35–43 per cent of the islands' population, suggests that the intervention 'did not symbolize a general "revolution of moral concern" in international relations but was rather the result of a unique set of circumstances'.[26]

The crisis in East Timor in 1999 thus highlighted the contingent nature of the West's humanitarian inclinations. While intervention did occur, and Wheeler and Dunne are right to favourably contrast this with the West's behaviour in 1975, it is clear that the consent of Indonesia was essential. In this sense the intervention cannot in fact be considered a humanitarian intervention according to most definitions, such as Robert's 'the use of armed force in another state *without* the consent of its authorities'.[27] The fact that the consent of the Indonesian government – so obviously complicit in the carnage and not even the legal authority in East Timor – was an essential prerequisite for the eventual intervention stands in sharp contrast to the rhetoric advanced only months earlier by the West regarding Kosovo.

Afghanistan 2001

Following the terrorist attacks of September 11, 2001, the US received unprecedented international support and sympathy. The attacks were soon attributed to al-Qaeda and attention thus turned to the Taliban regime in Afghanistan which had cultivated clear links with Osama bin Laden and provided his groups with extensive logistical support and resources.[28] When the Taliban rejected US demands to hand over bin Laden, Operation Enduring Freedom was launched on 10 October.

From the outset the intervention was legitimized as more than just an act of self-defence. In tandem with the security rationale, extensive effort was expended in highlighting the humanitarian benefits that would derive from the US-led intervention. President Bush declared, 'The oppressed people of Afghanistan will know the generosity of America and its allies. As we strike military targets, we'll also drop food, medicine and supplies to the starving and suffering men and women and children of Afghanistan.'[29] The mantra of dropping of 'bombs *and* aid' was oft repeated, as was the oppressive nature of the Taliban regime, with the treatment of women particularly stressed. Indicatively, US General Tommy Franks, in discussing the humanitarian effort undertaken during the 'liberation' of Afghanistan, highlighted the extensive provision of food aid, the opening of hospitals, the reopening of schools, the employment of women and a new UN-led demining programme.[30] The intervention was thus presented as both an act of self-defence and liberation. When the Taliban were defeated Secretary of Defense Donald Rumsfeld stated, in response to a question on what the war had achieved,

> number one is the fact that the Taliban no longer are the governing factor in that country. And in that sense, the people of Afghanistan have, in a significant way, been liberated from the policies and the repressive actions of the Taliban government.[31]

Focus immediately turned to state-building and democracy promotion considered to be the logical successor to the initial humanitarian intervention.

The conflation between humanitarianism and military objectives was most pronounced with respects to the nature of the aid provided by the intervening coalition and the rhetoric which accompanied it. Médecins Sans Frontières (MSF) found that despite the generosity implied by the coalition's rhetoric the impact of the aid provision was 'extremely marginal', highlighting the fact that one month of air drops only provided enough food for a million people for one day. The aid was also the same colour and shape as cluster bombs, leading to 'a number of lethal mistakes'.[32] The coalition explicitly sought to subvert the neutrality of humanitarian organizations based in Afghanistan; Prime Minister Blair called on these organizations to join the intervening force in forming a grand 'military–humanitarian coalition' while US Secretary of State Colin Powell asked these groups to convey a positive message about US values and become a 'force multiplier for us' and 'an important part of our combat team'.[33] Furthermore, MSF assert that US troops on the ground dressed in civilian clothes and introduced themselves as 'humanitarian volunteers'. 'The aim', according to MSF, 'was to justify the international military presence by endowing it with a friendlier image'.[34]

The humanitarian aspect of the intervention is therefore contentious for two primary reasons. First, it appears that the actual humanitarian practices had far less impact than the rhetoric proffered by the interveners suggested. Second, and of greater pertinence for this study, the articulation of the humanitarian motivations and intentions appears to have been prompted by a desire to reap positive media coverage. As Wheeler notes, '[President Bush] felt it was necessary to publicly defend the action in humanitarian terms, an implicit admission that this justification was a necessary enabling condition of the action.' The US-led intervening coalition 'recognized the importance of being seen to address the humanitarian crisis in bolstering international support for US action'.[35] Undoubtedly the pervasive anti-Taliban propaganda promulgated after September 11 stands in stark contrast to the mild condemnation articulated prior to the terrorist attacks. As MSF note, while prior to September 11, 2001, the international community condemned certain acts of cultural oppression executed by the Taliban, such as the destruction of the Buddhas of Bamyan and the obligatory wearing of the *burqa*, by contrast, 'it accepted the mass violence perpetrated, without distinction of gender, against some ethnic communities, the *refoulment* of refugees, and the closure of the country's Western borders to Afghan's fleeing hunger, war and oppression'.[36] The reason for the sudden outrage at the humanitarian abuses perpetrated by the Taliban thus appears to have derived from a need to sweeten the intervention for domestic and international consumption. Unlike Operation Allied Force, the invasion of Afghanistan *did* have a strong claim to be legal; Yoram Dinstein's authoritative analysis of the legality of Operation Enduring Freedom concludes, 'the military operations in Afghanistan were a classical State versus State exercise in self-defense',[37] and through Security Resolutions 1378 and 1383 the UN had provided the US with near explicit legitimacy for the invasion. Yet the humanitarian rationale was clearly considered to be a necessary supplementary component to the legal authorization.

Operation Enduring Freedom thus illustrated the importance of humanitarian justifications to Western states undertaking an intervention. Despite the rationale behind the intervention being so obviously security orientated, it was evidently felt that a humanitarian angle had to be contrived to facilitate both international and domestic support. As David Chandler notes, 'Far from stressing US national interests in responding to an attack on its major symbols of economic and military dominance, the US establishment and the coalition of supporting states stressed the ethical and humanitarian nature of the military response.'[38] This aspect of the intervention was thus troubling for proponents of the new humanitarianism as it highlighted the capacity of humanitarian rhetoric to be abused. Indicatively, while Wheeler is quite sympathetic to the intervention as a limited act of self-defence and counter-terrorism, he criticizes the intervention because it failed to achieve the moral objectives initially outlined by its proponents.[39] The seemingly cynical invocation of humanitarian justifications during Operation Enduring Freedom thus signalled a trend towards the misuse of 'humanitarian imperatives' to intervene. According to MSF, 'the American military campaign against the Taliban regime provides a particularly interesting example of the way "just" wars are engineered, and the consequences of this illusory concept.'[40] Following the conclusion of Operation Enduring Freedom, Wheeler noted, with significant prescience for the subsequent invasion of Iraq, 'the danger is that US policy makers will come to believe that they can use force without legal or moral censure as long as they couple force with token humanitarianism that will nullify dissent.'[41]

Operation Iraqi Freedom

The path that led the United States and its 'coalition of the willing' to war against Iraq in 2003 is well documented elsewhere and is not the subject of this enquiry.[42] The importance of the invasion for this enquiry relates to the justifications offered before and after the military action occurred. The following sections look at two aspects of Operation Iraqi

Freedom: first, the humanitarian rationale espoused by the architects of the invasion; second, the extent to which the intervening coalition manipulated information prior to the invasion to garner popular and international support. The final section explores the implications these two aspects of the invasion have for the normative thesis.

The humanitarian dimension

The primary rationale proffered for invading Iraq centred on the arsenal of weapons of mass destruction Iraq was said to possess, the regime's purported links with al-Qaeda and its attempt to import nuclear material from Niger. However, while greatest emphasis was placed on the security-orientated rationale, the extent to which a humanitarian rationale was additionally proffered cannot be ignored. Indeed, in clarifying the United States' goals shortly after the invasion had begun, President Bush stated, 'our mission is clear, to disarm Iraq of weapons of mass destruction, to end Saddam Hussein's support for terrorism, *and to free the Iraqi people*'.[43] Of course, the very name of the military operation – Iraqi Freedom – attests to the emphasis sought for this aspect of the proffered rationale.

While the most vociferous statesmen supportive of the invasion issued many apocalyptic warnings about the threat posed by Hussein's regime, they each additionally emphasized, in often graphic detail, the human rights abuses perpetrated by Hussein and the overwhelming moral case for overthrowing him. In a speech to the UN in late 2002 President Bush stated,

> Tens of thousands of political opponents and ordinary citizens have been subjected to arbitrary arrest and imprisonment, summary execution and torture by beating and burning, electric shock, starvation, mutilation and rape. Wives are tortured in front of their husbands, children in the presence of their parents – and all of these horrors concealed from the world by the apparatus of a totalitarian state.[44]

Tony Blair similarly declared, 'Riding the world of Saddam will be an act of humanity. It is leaving him there that is in truth inhumane.'[45] Wheeler and Morris in fact suggest that Blair's moral instincts, more than his security concerns, pushed him towards the decision to invade. They note, with respect to his interventionist outlook, 'there is ample evidence that Blair saw himself as acting pursuant to this world view… [the security concerns only] served to reinforce his powerful humanitarian instincts'.[46] They in fact suggest that the security concerns were articulated because Blair knew the humanitarian argument was illegal.[47]

John Howard, Prime Minister of Australia, adopted a similar mixture of security and humanitarianism in his justifications for the invasion. Prior to the invasion he stated, 'the end of Saddam Hussein's regime would provide an opportunity to lessen the suffering of the Iraqi people' and he warned of 'the enormous humanitarian cost...to the people of Iraq, of Saddam Hussein remaining in charge.' Howard described in explicit detail the abuses carried out by Iraq, such as the mutilation of children and the systematic amputation of tongues, and noted, '...is undeniable that if all the humanitarian considerations are put into the balance there is a very powerful case to the effect that the removal of Saddam Hussein's regime would produce a better life and less suffering for the people of Iraq than its continuation'.[48]

Bush had similarly stated, in an address directed at Iraqi citizens, 'the day [Saddam Hussein] and his regime are removed from your country will be the day of your liberation.'[49] On 17 March 2003, Bush, in a televised address, gave Hussein and his sons 48 hours to leave Iraq or be bombed. Bush, in addition to highlighting the threat Iraq's (non-existent) arsenal of weapons of mass destruction (WMD) posed to the US and Iraq's neighbours, emphasized the humanitarian aspect of the looming intervention:

> Many Iraqis can hear me tonight in a translated radio broadcast, and I have a message for them. If we must begin a military campaign, it will be directed against the lawless men who rule your country and not against you. As our coalition takes away their power, we will deliver the food and medicine you need. We will tear down the apparatus of terror and we will help you to build a new Iraq that is prosperous and free. In a free Iraq, there will be no more wars of aggression against your neighbors, no more poison factories, no more executions of dissidents, no more torture chambers and rape rooms. The tyrant will soon be gone. The day of your liberation is near.[50]

As Bellamy observes, when it became clear that the Security Council was not going to sanction the invasion the emphasis shifted markedly from the security-orientated rationale to the humanitarian justifications. Blair, in particular, advanced this redirection focusing on the negatives that would accrue from pursuing either of the two alternatives to invasion: first, the continuation of the sanctions regime, which he argued 'leads to thousands of people dying needlessly in Iraq every year' and, second, inaction, which he deemed morally unacceptable given Saddam's personal record of human rights abuse as documented in a 2002 report by the UK's Foreign and Commonwealth Office. This report stated, 'Saddam Hussein has been ruthless in his treatment of any opposition to him... A cruel and callous disregard for suffering remain the hallmarks of his regime.'[51] Bellamy thus concludes, 'it appears that humanitarian justifications were abused to justify a war that could not be justified by either positive international law or reasons of the state (the defense of the state and its allies).'[52]

In a move similar to the policies previously carried out during Operation Enduring Freedom, the use of humanitarian aid provision became intertwined with the intervention itself. The US made its funding of humanitarian aid agencies conditional on their agreement to display the US flag.[53] Throughout the five-week conflict with the Iraqi army the US-led coalition emphasized the humanitarian dimension to their operations, describing various operations as 'humanitarian'. The discrepancy between the actions of the coalition and the rhetoric surrounding them led Rony Brauman and Pierre Salignon of MSF to warn, 'It is high time we realized that the term "humanitarian", when employed in such conditions, is purely propaganda.'[54]

The actual military campaign against the Iraqi army was relatively short and hugely successful. While Bush's 'mission accomplished' declaration aboard the USS Lincoln on May 1 2003 now appears embarrassingly premature, at the time the intervening coalition had grounds for such self-congratulation. The scale of the ensuing insurgency and the exposé of the enormous intelligence failure regarding the non-existent WMDs and the lack of any link between Hussein and al-Qaeda soon undermined support for the invasion. At this point, great emphasis was again placed on the moral aspect of the intervention which, it was claimed, meant that even though the security-orientated rationale proved largely false, the invasion was still justifiable on humanitarian grounds. As Blair stated,

> I can apologise for the information that turned out to be wrong, but I can't, sincerely at least, apologise for removing Saddam. The world is a better place with Saddam in prison not in power... success for us in Iraq is not success for America or Britain or even Iraq itself but for the values and way of life that democracy represents.[55]

In an earlier speech to his constituency party, as the credibility of the security rationale was slipping away, Blair declared, 'we surely have a responsibility to act when a nation's people are subjected to a regime such as Saddam's.'[56] This particular speech explicitly drew parallels between Kosovo and Operation Iraqi Freedom, and Blair emphatically reiterated his belief in the 'Doctrine of the International Community' speech he made during the intervention in Kosovo.

President Bush similarly focused more on the humanitarian side of the invasion as the reality of Saddam's military capability came to light. In an April 2004 address, Bush spoke of 'America's commitment to freedom in Iraq' and outlined why his administration was so committed:

> A free Iraq is vital because 25 million Iraqis have as much right to live in freedom as we do. A free Iraq will stand as an example to reformers across the Middle East. A free Iraq will show that America is on the side of Muslims who wish to live in peace, as we have already shown in Kuwait and Kosovo, Bosnia and Afghanistan. A free Iraq will confirm to a watching world that America's word, once given, can be relied upon, even in the toughest times.[57]

On 10 April 2006 Bush declared the day 'marked the third anniversary of a great moment in the history of freedom – it was the liberation of Iraq'.[58]

The post-invasion inflation of the humanitarian aspect of the intervention did initially work according to Richard Melanson, who notes that the American public seemed willing to forgive the Bush administration's mistakes, or lies, about WMD because the invasion seemed to have brought such rich humanitarian benefits.[59] This popular endorsement of the invasion as a worthy humanitarian intervention was short-lived, of course. The combination of the revelations of extensive atrocities perpetrated by coalition forces in Iraq, most particularly at Abu-Ghraib, the rising death toll and the obvious resistance among the citizens of Iraq to the 'liberators' clearly undermined the purported 'humanitarian' inclinations and effects.

Selling the invasion

That the intervening coalition, and the Bush administration in particular, manipulated intelligence to support their determination to go to war with Iraq today appears largely incontrovertible. Richard Clark, chief counter-terrorism adviser on the US National Security Council, has written of Bush's determination, immediately after 9/11, to blame Hussein's regime and find some evidence that 'Iraq did this'.[60] Certainly by July 2002 the UK government were convinced that the US was committed to invading Iraq regardless of what the weapons inspectors found. Jack Straw, the then UK Foreign Secretary, following a meeting with US officials, stated: 'It seemed clear that Bush had made up his mind to take military action, even if the timing was not yet decided.'[61] According to Paul Wolfowitz, the then US Deputy Secretary of Defense, the Bush administration chose to focus primarily on WMD because it offered the greatest potential for garnering support, rather than because it was an accurate assessment of Iraq's military capability. He stated, 'The truth is that for reasons that have a lot to do with US government bureaucracy we settled on the one issue that everyone could agree on, which was weapons of mass destruction as the core reason.'[62] David Malone thus concludes that the US had decided to go to war in by at least July 2002 and subsequently determined to 'fix' intelligence to that end.[63] The Project for a New American Century (PNAC), established in 1997, had called for regime change in Iraq long before 9/11[64] and many of the PNAC's members – such as Donald Rumsfeld, Paul Wolfowitz, Richard Perle and John Bolton – went on to hold key positions in the Bush administration. Their determination, as they saw it, to 'finish the job' begun in 1991 with Operation Desert Storm appears to have led them to utilize the fear of international terrorism, rife following 9/11, to sell the invasion. Within months of 9/11 the Bush administration began to contradict many earlier declarations which suggested that Saddam's military capability had been crippled by the sanctions regime in favour of issuing dire warnings about the threat his regime ostensibly posed, such as Condoleezza Rice's now infamous statement 'we don't want the smoking gun to be a mushroom cloud'.[65]

As is now abundantly clear, Hussein's Iraq did not constitute the threat alleged prior to the invasion. As stated by Hans Blix, Iraq was 'not an imminent or even a remote threat to the United States or to Iraq's neighbors'.[66] Few could dispute Hussein's hostility towards the US and its allies or his resistance to weapons inspections, yet his ability to attack the US, Europe or even Israel was clearly exaggerated. The 'intelligence failure' argument has been regularly offered as an excuse for the reality uncovered in Iraq, yet it is difficult to accept that the WMD debacle was merely a function of faulty intelligence given the manner in which the intelligence supportive of intervention so suddenly appeared in ever-increasing volume and scale immediately after 9/11 when previously Iraq had not been considered a major threat. The obvious determination among the so-called 'neo-cons' to attack Iraq was long-held, and according to Malone, 'In retrospect the fear of WMD seems to have been instrumentalized to sell a decision to go to war that had already been made in Washington.'[67]

Lessons?

The invasion of Iraq has three major implications for this particular study, which will be elaborated on in Chapter 5. First, while the security rationale was the primary justification offered, the centrality of the humanitarian justifications cannot be overlooked particularly since they have come to dominate in the period since the WMD's failed to materialize.

As Mary Kaldor notes, since the invasion Bush and Blair have stressed 'that their concern in Iraq is humanitarian rather than national'.[68] Whether the intervention was prompted by genuine humanitarian concerns[69] or nefarious capitalistic impulses[70] does not alter the implication this episode has for the normative thesis; the intervention is and was presented by its proponents as, to some significant degree, a humanitarian intervention. The fact that this humanitarianism is rejected by arguably the majority of analysts, and certainly most proponents of the normative thesis, demonstrates that the creation of a 'humanitarian exception' and the endorsement of 'illegal but legitimate' interventionism is not an objectively observable phenomena and is open to abuse.

Second, it is clear that in this case states felt that the humanitarian discourse ascendant in the 1990s, reaching its zenith with Operation Allied Force, was sufficiently convincing and malleable that its inclusion in a general body of legitimization was deemed essential to bolster international and domestic support. It was, as such, considered to be a necessary aspect of interventionist propaganda rather than a genuine impulse motivating action.

Third, the extent to which the intervening coalition were at best creative with the truth, at worst complicit in a massive international deception, must undermine any notions of Western democracies being necessarily open, honest and ethical and thus somehow to be trusted with an exceptional interventionist capacity.

Darfur: 'The collective yawn'

The current crisis in Sudan began in February 2003 when the Sudanese Liberation Army (SLA) launched attacks against government military installations. Soon after, the Justice and Equality Movement (JEM) joined the SLA in attacking the national army. While the rebel forces achieved some initial success, the Khartoum-based government soon launched a fierce counter-attack. The Sudanese Air Force was deployed to devastating effect but it was the mobilization of the Janjaweed militia which proved most destructive. Armed by the government in Khartoum the militias undertook a campaign of terror designed to kill and displace all those suspected of rebel sympathies. According to Human Rights Watch,

> As part of its operations against the rebels, government forces waged a systematic campaign of 'ethnic cleansing' against the civilian population who are members of the same ethnic groups as the rebels. Sudanese government forces and the Janjaweed militias burned and

> destroyed hundreds of villages, caused tens of thousands of civilian deaths, displaced millions of people, and raped and assaulted thousands of women and girls.[71]

The scale of the violence and the barbarity of the militia soon generated international attention. A series of negotiations and ceasefires followed, but all failed to effect tangible results. By April 2004 the counter-insurgency is estimated to have killed 30,000 people, most of whom were civilians; this figure rose to 70,000 by September by which time some 1.2 million people had fled their homes, with 200,000 entering Chad.[72] By mid-2004 the World Health Organization estimated that between 240 and 440 people were dying every day.[73] Darfur was by this stage, 'commonly described within the UN system and Western states as "the most serious humanitarian emergency in the world today"'.[74]

The first Security Council resolution to mention the situation in Darfur was passed on 11 June 2004, 16 months after the conflict had begun. Resolution 1547 devotes one sentence to Darfur, stating, '[The Security Council] calls upon the parties to use their influence to bring an immediate halt to the fighting in the Darfur region.' The resolution did not blame any one of the 'parties' for the humanitarian crisis and issued no threats of further action. Resolution 1556, adopted on 30 July 2004, did go further though again lacked real substance. In a similar tone to the resolutions regarding East Timor in 1999, Resolution 1556 recognized the territorial integrity of Sudan and called on the Sudanese government to protect its civilians from the Janjaweed – imploring the government to 'establish credible security conditions for the protection of the civilian population'. The Resolution calls on the government to disarm, apprehend and bring to justice the Janjaweed responsible for the humanitarian crisis. These calls for the government to protect the vulnerable and stop the Janjaweed appeared particularly curious given that the Khartoum regime had been instrumental in orchestrating the crisis and were not, as the Resolution essentially implies, a third party to the conflict. In April 2004 the UN High Commissioner for Refugees found, 'It is the manner of the response to this rebellion by the Government of Sudan which has led to the current crisis in Darfur.' The Report further stated, 'It is clear there is a reign of terror in Darfur' and declared unequivocally, 'the mission identified disturbing patterns of massive human rights violations in Darfur perpetrated by the Government of the Sudan and its proxy militia'.[75]

When the Security Council passed Resolution 1556, the United States issued a statement extolling the virtues of the Resolution and condemning in forceful language the government of Sudan for its actions. It threatened, however, only to impose further sanctions if the government did not cooperate.[76] None of the states who voted in favour of the Resolution mentioned that the Security Council had a right or duty to intervene to protect the people of Darfur; in fact the onus was placed on the Sudanese government and failing that, the African Union (AU).

As endorsed by Resolution 1556, the AU did deploy a small force – the African Union Mission in Sudan (AMIS) – in Darfur in August 2004. However, AMIS was understaffed and under-resourced and it soon became clear that the AU was unable to muster the resources necessary to deploy the 3000 troops envisaged. By December Kofi Annan reported that AMIS was 'not working'.[77]

On 18 September 2004 the Security Council passed Resolution 1564 which recognized that the government in Khartoum had failed to adhere to the stipulations contained in Resolution 1556. The resolution did not implement any punitive measures, however, stating instead that the council 'shall consider taking additional measures' should Sudan's non-compliance continue. Human rights groups had been hoping for a stronger resolution; Adotei Akwei, a spokesman for Amnesty International, said the organization was 'extremely disappointed' describing the Resolution as 'represent[ing] the abandonment of the people of Darfur and an abdication of the Security Council's role as a human rights enforcing agent'.[78]

Seven further Resolutions in 2005 did little to effect real change and constituted various strongly worded condemnations but little punitive action beyond the extension of AMIS's mandate and the creation of a 'Panel of Experts' to oversee and report on the crisis. By April 2006 the Security Council had agreed only to impose targeted sanctions against four individuals; according to Thomas Weiss, 'the chasm between the magnitude of the suffering and the international response could hardly have been greater'.[79]

On 31 August 2006 the Security Council passed Resolution 1706 which did finally authorize the deployment of 17,300 troops and 3300 civilian police to replace the 7000 strong AU force. However, the Resolution 'invites the consent of the Government of National Unity' and requests their involvement in the decision regarding the deployment of the new force. This therefore constituted a regression from the proposals put forward by *The Responsibility to Protect* which explicitly state that consent is not required.[80] The expressed desire for an invitation, according to Weiss, 'mocks the values of the emerging R2P norm'.[81]

The situation remains bleak; according to a recent Human Rights Watch report,

> As of September 2007, approximately 2.2 million displaced people live in camps in Darfur and more than 200,000 people have fled to neighboring Chad, where they live in refugee camps. In addition to the people displaced by the conflict, at least 2 million additional people are considered 'conflict-affected' by the UN and many need some form of food assistance because the conflict has damaged the local economy, markets, and trade in Darfur.[82]

Estimates as to the number of deaths range from 73,700 to 172,154.[83] The violence has continued, and has continued to be reported. The UN, international media, NGO's and regional organizations have all sought to highlight the suffering in Darfur. Throughout 2006 high-profile international figures led mass marches calling for greater action on Darfur. The history of the conflict in Darfur since 2003 thus evidences a striking contrast between massive international publicity of the 'genocide' and the hesitant, timid and equivocal action on the part of the UN Security Council and Western states.

The spectre of Rwanda

The scale of the humanitarian disaster in Darfur has evoked memories of the genocide in Rwanda. The international community's wilful paralysis in the face of the genocide in 1994 has become one of the most frequently decried episodes in contemporary international politics. 'Never again' became a frequent refrain of political leaders following the genocide, and the optimistic pronouncements made after the intervention in Kosovo suggested that this determination was being realized. The crisis in Darfur, however, had stronger parallels with Rwanda than Kosovo did, not least because the conflict took place in Africa as opposed to Europe. Hugo Slim thus described Darfur as '[The] test case by which to judge whether the international community has got any better at responding to genocide and crimes against humanity [since Rwanda]'.[84]

The spectre of Rwanda loomed over Darfur from an early stage and by March 2004 the UN's Humanitarian Coordinator in Khartoum Mukesh Kapila publicly drew parallels between the crisis in Darfur and the early stages of the genocide in Rwanda.[85] The coverage of the unfolding disaster in Darfur, in fact, received more attention than the initial stage of the Rwandan genocide, and there is no basis for excusing the inaction on the grounds of ignorance. Roméo Dallaire, who served as Force Commander for the United Nations Assistance Mission in Rwanda and watched first hand as the genocide in 1994 unfolded, wrote,

> Although the early stages of the Darfur situation received more news coverage than the Rwanda genocide did, at some level the Western governments are still approaching it with the same lack of priority. In the end, it receives the same intuitive reaction: 'What's in it for us? Is it in our "national" interest?'

Dallaire described the reaction to Darfur bluntly as 'not nearly enough'.[86] More damningly, there is evidence that an early intervention would have achieved significant results; a Report by the US National Defense University found 'an intervening coalition would have had little trouble stopping killings by the Janjaweed'.[87] Yet no intervention occurred, instead, as John Mueller notes, 'the international community, after ten years of mea culpa breast beating over its failure to intervene in Rwanda, responded with little more than huffing and puffing'.[88]

In some respects the response to Darfur was more shameful than the response to Rwanda. As Slim notes, unlike Rwanda, there was no attempt to deny what was happening in Darfur.[89] Indeed, in his testimony before the United States Senate Foreign Relations Committee, Secretary of State Colin Powell announced, 'genocide has been committed in Darfur and… the Government of Sudan and the Jingaweit [*sic*] bear responsibility'. Yet he subsequently added,

> no new action is dictated by this determination. We have been doing everything we can to get the Sudanese Government to act responsibly. So let us not be too preoccupied with this designation. These people are in desperate need and we must help them. Call it civil war; call it ethnic cleansing; call it genocide; call it 'none of the above'. The reality is the same. There are people in Darfur who desperately need the help of the international community.[90]

This plea to 'not be too preoccupied with this designation' is quite disingenuous suggesting, as it does, that the determination of genocide is merely a semantic exercise. From a strict legal perspective, Powell and the US administration were correct to state that the determination that genocide was occurring compelled them only to refer the matter to the Security Council – which they did – rather than to take action. As Dinstein notes, 'no state acting alone (or even jointly with like-minded allies) has a legal option of resorting to force against another State, with a view to averting genocide or bringing it to an end.'[91] Yet, while from a dispassionate legal perspective this is correct, to acknowledge that genocide is occurring and then articulate a legal justification as to why despite this no action needed to be taken certainly undermines the 'never again' declarations and the prescriptions advanced by the normative perspective. Bellamy noted that the 'just cause threshold' had clearly been passed and thus, from the normative perspective, 'regional organizations, coalitions of the willing and individual states are entitled to intervene to protect Darfur's civilians without either Security Council authorization or the Sudanese government's consent'.[92] Similarly Weiss laments,

> At least in 1994 there was an attempt to maintain the fiction that no such horror was under way... If we recognize the existence of genocide and do nothing besides ask the ICC to split genocidal hairs, the 1948 Convention on the Prevention and Punishment of the Crime of Genocide is literally not worth the paper on which it is reproduced.

In these respects Weiss argues, 'The collective yawn in the face of Darfur's disaster could be even more destructive of the fabric of international law than the 800,000 deaths in Rwanda.'[93]

The details of the reaction of the international community to the crisis in Darfur constitute an unedifying portrait of the capacity of existing international political and legal structures to halt humanitarian disasters. The Security Council's legal wrangling and habitual calls for more information in the face of evident tragedy cannot but be seen as a black mark on its record. As Slim states, 'Whatever the right legal label, such extreme policies operated by the Sudanese government demanded a concerted, immediate and assertive international political and humanitarian response. No such response emerged.'[94] The parallels with the Rwandan genocide, itself evocative of the holocaust, were clear both in terms of the massacres on the ground and in terms of the international inaction. According to Kofi Annan, 'We were slow, hesitant, uncaring and we had learnt nothing from Rwanda.'[95]

2005 World Summit

The 2005 World Summit, held in New York on 14–16 September, marked the 60th anniversary of the UN and was billed as 'A once in a generation opportunity to reform and revive the United Nations' and the forum where 'the UN must undergo the most sweeping overhaul in its 60-year history'.[96] Representatives from all of the world's states attended and engaged in negotiations in an atmosphere of mistrust and anger caused, to a large extent, by the US-led invasion of Iraq.

Two paragraphs – 138 and 139 – were included in the final *Outcome Document* explicitly endorsing the notion of a responsibility to protect.[97] The fact that this agreement was reached suggests on one level a success on the part of the advocates of *The Responsibility to Protect*. However, the compromises which secured the inclusion of these paragraphs undermined the essence of the original proposal.

In terms of explaining how the *Responsibility to Protect* came to be included, Bellamy suggests that three major concessions were made. First, regarding the question of authority, the idea of the Security Council members agreeing not to use their veto powers was jettisoned early on in the negotiations. The original ICISS document stated, 'The idea essentially is that a permanent member, in matters where its vital national interests were not claimed to be involved, would not use its veto to obstruct the passage of what would otherwise be a majority resolution.'[98] How this was to actually work in practice, in particular how one might usefully define 'vital national interests' was left unclear in the original document. In the course of the negotiations at the World Summit this aspect of the Report was dropped. Additionally, the notion of legitimate intervention without Security Council approval – integral to the original ICISS proposal – was 'sidestepped in favor of a concept wedded to Security Council authorization'.[99] Secondly, the just cause threshold included in the *Outcome Document* actually restricted the instances when the Security Council could legitimately intervene. Security Council practice in the 1990s had broadened the Security Council's remit to act, including, in the case of Haiti in 1994, the right to intervene if a democratically elected government was overthrown. With authority being once again clearly vested in the Security Council, and the criteria for intervention limited to 'genocide, war crimes, ethnic cleansing and crimes against humanity', as stated in paragraph 138, the scope for intervention was thus restricted. Thirdly, while the ICISS originally stated that the responsibility to protect transferred from the state to the international community when the host state was deemed 'unable or unwilling' to exercise its responsibilities, in the *Outcome Document* this was amended to cases where the host state was guilty of a 'manifest failure' – a semantic change but one which raised the threshold, thereby further restricting the scope for violating a state's sovereignty.

The reluctance of Western powers to be obliged to intervene was an evident factor in the World Summit negotiations. In a letter to the President of the General Assembly prior to the World Summit, John Bolton suggested amending the section in the draft document regarding the responsibility to protect because 'we note that the Charter has never been interpreted as creating a legal obligation for Security Council members to support enforcement action in various cases involving serious breaches of international peace'.[100] The draft *Outcome Document* originally read, 'The international community, through the United Nations, also has the obligation to use diplomatic, humanitarian and other peaceful means, including under Chapter VI and VIII of the Charter to help protect populations from genocide, war crimes, ethnic cleansing and crimes against humanity.' Bolton suggested changing this to read 'The international community, through the United Nations, also has moral responsibility to use appropriate diplomatic, economic, humanitarian and other peaceful means, including under Chapter VI and VIII of the Charter to help protect populations from such atrocities.' 'Moral responsibility' and 'obligation' are clearly two very different duties. Additionally, instead of the sentence 'In this context, we recognize our shared responsibility to take collective action…', Bolton suggested 'In this context, we stand ready to take collective action…'. The final version, which appears in paragraph 139 of the *Outcome Document*, corresponds more closely to that suggested by Bolton; the wording states the international community, acting through the UN has a 'responsibility' rather than an obligation to act and states that the Security Council is 'prepared' to act rather than noting a 'shared responsibility to take collective action', as stated in the draft document.

These changes, therefore, amounted to enabling the Security Council to determine what, if indeed any, action to take in the event of a humanitarian tragedy occurring, thereby removing any obligation to act in all situations where the threshold was breached. From a political perspective it is clearly preferable to choose when and where to deploy ones forces rather than be compelled to do so by an external trigger, yet, from a moral point of view it is difficult, if not impossible, to justify equivocation in the face of humanitarian atrocities which are internationally agreed to be unacceptable violations of human rights. Yet, it is precisely to enable what could accurately be termed '*a la carte* interventionism' that the wording regarding the responsibility to protect in the *Outcome Document* appeared as it did.

Supporters of *The Responsibility to Protect* sought to achieve two things at the World Summit: first, they wanted the General Assembly to make a commitment to the tenets of the original ICISS document; second, they sought to persuade the Security Council to do three things. First, to adopt a resolution committing it to act whenever the just cause thresholds were crossed; second, to submit its decisions to public deliberation about the use of force based on the precautionary principles; and third, to agree not to use the veto in cases of humanitarian emergencies where they did not have some clear national interests at stake.[101] The two major initiatives proffered by adherents to the original R2P – that of securing the P5 endorsement of an obligation to act and the agreement to remove the veto – were not accepted into the *Outcome Document*. Additionally, the goal of further strengthening the capacity of states to legitimately act outside of the Security Council was unsuccessful, as the endorsement of the basic tenets of *The Responsibility to Protect* was made conditional on the re-statement of the Security Council's primacy. This reversion to Security Council primacy for some constituted a 'step-backward… R2P lite'.[102] According to Bellamy, 'the responsibility to protect statement in the outcome document has done little to increase the likelihood of preventing future Rwandas and Kosovos… in order to secure consensus, the concept's advocates have abandoned many of its central tenets, significantly reducing the likelihood of progress in the near future'.[103] The consensus reached was, he states, 'produced not by the power of humanitarian argument but by bargaining away key tenets of the ICISS's recommendations'.[104]

The shift back towards the Security Council as the only legitimate authority capable of authorizing intervention means the conditional endorsement of unilateral interventions outside of the Security Council advocated in *The Responsibility to Protect* has been rejected. As Wheeler notes, the *Outcome Document* 'fails to address the fundamental question of what should happen if the Security Council is unable or unwilling to authorize the use of force to prevent or end a humanitarian tragedy, and secondly, it fails to address the question of how this norm could be better implemented to save strangers in the future'.[105] Paragraph 139, as Wheeler notes, does nothing to address the question of political will which has been the greatest barrier to the alleviation of suffering.[106]

When the *Outcome Document* was agreed, Jack Straw, the then UK Foreign Secretary, stated, 'If this new responsibility had been in place a decade ago, thousands in Srebrenica and Rwanda would have been saved.'[107] To the hundreds of thousands suffering genocide and ethnic cleansing in Darfur this bold statement will doubtless have seemed dubious at the very least. Clearly, the inclusion of paragraphs 138 and 139 in the *Outcome Document* signified some kind of consensus regarding the responsibility to protect. These paragraphs do, it seems, confirm the impermissibility of complete sovereign inviolability. Yet, while the idea that sovereignty cannot afford a state unlimited capacity domestically has now achieved clear expression through the *Outcome Document*, it is debatable whether any substantive change that would insure the 'Never again' refrain will be applied in practice has really occurred. According to Weiss, 'there is still appallingly sparse responsibility to protect those suffering from atrocities that shock the human conscience'.[108] Certainly the *Outcome Document* is far less than many advocates of *The Responsibility to Protect* wanted and in certain key respects actually constitutes a regression. It is clear also that the idea of the West as constituting norm entrepreneurs spearheading progressive change does not correspond to their negotiating style at the World Summit where a pronounced reluctance to protect was a very evident concern.

Conclusion: Assessing the record

Few reasonable analysts of international relations, even in the heady atmosphere after the success of Operation Allied Force, suggested that all would now be well internationally and that suffering would thereafter be immediately alleviated. It would be wrong to ascribe extreme idealism to the normative position and then confront this perspective with the harsh reality of international politics and the ongoing suffering of thousands across the globe. This has certainly not been the intention of this chapter; the aim has not been to simply highlight that suffering has continued to occur, but rather to challenge key normative assumptions and prescriptions by examining seminal moments in international relations since Kosovo. The events examined here in this clearly (and necessarily) selective history of the 1999–2007 period have been chosen because they constitute cases where different aspects of the normative thesis's flaws are readily evident, as will be explored in greater depth in the following chapter.

The dominance of humanitarian intervention as an issue in international relations, both among academics and in international politics, has waned and the initiation of the war on terror has certainly overshadowed all other international issues. However, while some have concluded the issue is in terminal decline,[109] there is evidence that not only has it remained salient post Kosovo but that the new security-orientated discourse borrows heavily from its humanitarian predecessor. While the cases examined above highlight the fact that the promise and prescriptions articulated after Operation Allied Force have failed to manifest, in each case the rhetoric of humanitarianism is readily evident. In cases of both action, such as Iraq, and inaction, such as Darfur, the discourse of humanitarianism, and *The Responsibility to Protect* in particular, has been employed. The history of humanitarianism post Kosovo thus evidences not the disappearance of humanitarianism but its alternate manifestation derived from a clearly inherent malleability. The issue is not, therefore, the vitality of humanitarianism but the direction which it has taken. The adoption of the humanitarian discourse by Western states, so evident during Operation Allied Force, has not manifest as the proactive propagation of benevolent Western humanitarianism, but rather as a rhetorical rationale for invading Iraq and ignoring Darfur, clearly not what the normative thesis anticipated. It is not, however, true that the blame for this record since Kosovo derives solely from the nefarious impulses of certain states or leaders within states, but rather that the normative thesis itself was, and is, fundamentally flawed and thus a key contributing factor in the evolution of international relations post-Kosovo. Chapter 5 analyses the events detailed in this chapter and demonstrates how these cases individually and collectively undermine the normative thesis.

5
The Normative Flaws

Introduction

This Chapter identifies the aspects of the normative thesis which contrived to produce the record of intervention and non-intervention identified in the previous chapter. Clearly, the optimism prevalent in the aftermath of NATO's intervention in Kosovo in 1999 was not realized. Explaining why this has been the case is the aim of this Chapter.

The simplest answer relates to the character of Western states. One could argue that these states never intended to act on the commitments made in 1999 and hence lied to their domestic publics and the international community. Similarly, one could argue that the election of the 'neo-cons' in 2000 in the US altered the strategy of the West's leading power. Certainly there is evidence to support these claims, each of which are explored in this chapter. This explanation, suggesting as it does that the normative perspective overestimated the humanitarian commitment of the West, essentially exonerates the prescriptions articulated by proponents of global civil society and the normative thesis, putting the blame instead on the duplicity of Western states. While it is acknowledged that the behaviour of Western states has been hypocritical and inconsistent, this chapter argues that the normative thesis itself has proven flawed in a number of key respects and thus the failure of its prescriptions to manifest in the post-Kosovo period is not solely the fault of nefarious state behaviour.

It is argued that the normative thesis has three inherent flaws: first, it has overestimated the capacity of global civil society to influence the behaviour of Western states; second, the presumption that articulating criteria, which must be met for an intervention to be 'illegal but legitimate', would constrain state behaviour has proved mistaken; and third, the strategy advocated by the normative thesis, rather than constituting a challenge to the dominance of the state, actually increases the power of states in crucial respects.

The idealization of the West

The optimistic prescriptions advanced after Operation Allied Force by proponents of the normative thesis and global civil society were predicated on the assumption that Western states had transcended narrow national interests. In this vein, Chris Brown, writing about the Blair government, noted,

> The present government clearly believes in the importance of international law and international cooperation.... It is in terms of this kind of international civility as an expression of a willingness to reconcile the national interest with the norms of international society that the true ethical dimension of foreign policy is to be found – and on its record in this area the new government passes, if not with flying colours, then at least with some merit.[1]

The optimism within the human rights movement as to the evolving trajectory of international politics was sustained by the conviction that the world's most powerful group of states were committed to acting beyond their borders for the cause of humanity. This was certainly the view consistently articulated by NATO members in 1999 during and after the 'just war in a just cause... [fought] for the values of civilization'.[2] This belief obviously contrasts sharply with the realist perspective on international relations which holds that national interest and the quest for power are the primary, if not only, motivations determining a state's foreign policy. Denying the validity of realism was, however, a popular exercise and the nature of the West's new disposition led many to wonder if realism, predicated as it supposedly was on outdated assumptions about the primacy of national interest, was in fact dead.[3]

While many suggested that an ethical foreign policy was not necessarily contrary to a state's national interest and that certain beneficial consequences would accrue from a concern for morality,[4] the basic assumption about the changed priorities went beyond the conviction that national interests went hand-in-hand with ethical internationalism. The normative thesis, however, did not go so far as to suggest that Western states no longer cared about their respective national interests. Rather, the basic belief was that the West now stood ready to act when suffering required external intervention and that in calculating whether to intervene morality would be a paramount consideration. Thus, a humanitarian tragedy would compel Western states to act because the humanitarian situation in itself was sufficiently powerful to induce action. Western states thus came to be conceived as the means by which the normative agenda could be realized due to their new propensity to look beyond narrow national interest.

According to Wheeler, 'a new norm has developed that supports the use of force to protect civilians from genocide, mass murder, and ethnic cleansing. This norm is strongest in Western states, which were the key players throughout the 1990s in establishing this new principle in international society.'[5] In explaining why Western states came to adopt this disposition, when previously it was lacking, Mervyn Frost suggested that the meeting of ethical convictions held by global civil society and those held by 'the society of democratic and democratising states' had created the scope for this new disposition.[6] Frost argued that the new right to intervention extended to all democracies while the traditional right of sovereign inviolability could now only be enjoyed by democratic states.[7] This perspective is indicative of a characteristic feature of normative discourse post-Operation Allied Force, namely the privileging of democratic governance and specifically the Western system.

Democracy thus became increasingly portrayed as a prerequisite for sovereignty and essential for the realization of human rights and the broader normative agenda. Mary Kaldor argued that democracy is 'the necessary condition for political emancipation',[8] while according to Thomas Weiss, 'Human rights can only be defended by democratic states with the authority and the monopoly of force to sustain such norms'.[9] Allen Buchanan and Robert Keohane suggested that a coalition of democratic states should be created as an institutional arbitrator on human rights issues.[10] Existing democratic states thus, unsurprisingly, were portrayed as more legitimate actors than states with different system and inherently more receptive to humanitarian advocacy. Western states should be afforded unique rights of intervention, it was argued, so that operations such as Operation Allied Force could be facilitated but reserved for a privileged few.[11]

The record since Operation Allied Force, however, does not readily support this view. A number of the cases explored in Chapter 3 highlight the extent to which calculations of national interest have clearly impacted on the West's foreign policy since Operation Allied Force. The West's insistence on receiving an 'invitation' from Indonesia before intervening in East Timor constituted an indication of the West's adherence to geopolitical concerns regardless of the scale of the suffering taking place. As is clear, no intervention would have occurred without Indonesia's consent, despite Indonesia's complicity in the massacres and the illegality of Jakarta's jurisdiction over the region. Indonesia has long been a key strategically both of the United States and Australia while the UK has cultivated a profitable business exporting military machinery to the country.[12] It would, therefore, seem logical to conclude that the unwillingness to intervene without Indonesia's consent derived from a desire to avoid a total breakdown in relations with a strategic ally.

The scale of the tragedy in Darfur was, as others have suggested, of sufficient magnitude to legitimately warrant external intervention. As is clear, the response of the international community, including the West, has been condemnatory but ultimately muted and weak. It is difficult not to conclude that, as with Rwanda in 1994, the scale of the 'genocide' in Darfur was not sufficient to compel Western states to overcome their reluctance to become embroiled in the internal affairs of an African state for fear of the costs involved. The so-called Somalia syndrome, derived from the US's experiences in Somalia in 1993, appears to have been a key influence on the decision not to intervene in Rwanda in 1994 and again in Darfur in 2004.[13] This syndrome suggests that interventions in Africa are doomed to fail, given the endemic ethnic hatreds and violent opposition towards external interference prevalent in the region. Additionally, as Weiss notes, the US has been engaged in two major combat operations (Afghanistan and Iraq) almost since the crisis in Darfur began and were in this sense 'disinclined to commit significant political and military resources to human protection'.[14] The decision not to intervene appears to be the result of an, arguably quite rational if amoral, appraisal of the likely consequences of such action. This appraisal clearly privileged national interest over the alleviation of human suffering. If, as many have suggested, Darfur constitutes the worst humanitarian crisis in the post-Kosovo period, and if the Sudanese government have been directly responsible, as many UN reports explicitly state, then the response to Darfur clearly stands in stark contrast to the commitments made and action taken regarding Kosovo in 1999.

The 2005 World Summit additionally highlighted the unwillingness of Western states, the US in particular, to rescind their capacity to independently decide when and where to deploy their troops. Their refusal to do so suggests that deciding when to intervene remains influenced by strategic interests more than by the scale of any suffering taking place. Clearly, as evidenced from John Bolton's letter to President of the General Assembly prior to the summit, the US was unwilling to commit to a proposal that would make it impossible *not* to deploy troops when a humanitarian disaster was definitely occurring.[15] This is perhaps not an unreasonable preference but it certainly highlights the secondary place afforded to moral imperatives in foreign policy decision-making.

John Mueller provides a comprehensive explanation as to why Western states will not undertake humanitarian interventions with any reliability or consistency:

> because they often have little interest in humanitarian problems in distant areas of the globe, because they sometimes subscribe to a misguided impression about ancient ethnic hatreds that provides them with a convenient excuse for neglect, because they have a low tolerance for casualties in such ventures, because they have an aversion to the costs and problems that attend long-term policing, because there seems to be little domestic political gain from success in policing ventures, because there seems to be little domestic political gain from success in policing ventures, and because they harbour something of a bias against undertakings that could be construed as aggression.[16]

Mueller's analysis highlights that inaction is not derived exclusively from disinterest or amorality but from a complex combination of factors that contrive to determine the response to any given situation. Western states will intervene, he argues, 'only when their interests seem importantly engaged or where they manage to become self-entrapped'.[17]

It is additionally clear that Western states have no compunction about cultivating alliances with states with poor human rights records. The United States' ongoing alliances with, for example, Pakistan, Saudi Arabia and Israel – each noted as systematic violators of human rights[18] – implies that key strategic considerations are given preference over humanitarian concerns. Evidence certainly suggests that the relationship a state has with the West will determine the extent to which its record on human rights becomes an issue.[19]

Western states have themselves systematically violated human rights domestically, and humanitarian law internationally. The detention centre at Guantanamo Bay and the many violations of the laws of war which occurred during the invasion of Iraq certainly undermine notions of the Western state as inherently concerned with human rights and morality. This record also clearly contrasts with the West's own opinion of itself; according to the 2006 *US National Strategy for Combating Terrorism*, '[Democratic states] ... exercise effective sovereignty and maintain order within their own borders, address causes of conflict peacefully, protect independent and impartial systems of justice, punish crime, embrace the rule of law, and resist corruption.'[20] This assessment of how democracies behave is clearly an exaggeration.

It is clear that the (mis)behaviour of Western states since Operation Allied Force has undermined the credibility of the normative thesis. Yet, while this may be the case, those sympathetic to the normative perspective could reasonably argue that this constitutes a critique of the normative prescriptions derived from factors beyond the control of normative proponents rather than from any flaws intrinsic to the normative thesis. Western states certainly stated their intention to behave altruistically and act beyond the national interests; the fact that they haven't tarnishes their reputation but can only, at worst, highlight gullibility or naivety among proponents of the normative perspective who, in this sense, were guilty only of believing the West's commitments. The following section, however, goes beyond this critique by highlighting that the failure of the normative prescriptions advanced at the time of Kosovo to materialize in the period since is a function not only of Western hypocrisy but also flaws inherent in the normative thesis.

The normative flaws

The effect of moral pressure

Central to the normative thesis is the assumption that global civil society is a powerful force for good capable of shaping the foreign policy of Western democratic states through the application of moral pressure. The Western state is conceived as receptive to moral pressure by virtue of its inherent humanitarian concerns, its transparency and accountability, and the strong links between civil society and the democratically elected government.[21] The normative project is, therefore, predicated on a belief in the capacity of global civil society to encourage Western states to increase their (already relatively more advanced) propensity towards moral action. Western foreign policy since Operation Allied Force, however, does not support this theory.

The international media, NGOs and the UN have consistently highlighted the suffering occurring in Darfur since 2003. Additionally, many states have acknowledged the extent of the violence, with the US going so far as to describe the crisis as genocide. While, as Chapter 4 attests, Western states have been vociferous in their condemnation of the Sudanese government's actions in Darfur, the practical steps taken to stop the killings have been, from the perspective of respected international observers, half-hearted and weak.[22] NGOs, such as Human Rights Watch, the International Crisis Group and Amnesty International, have regularly decried the response of the international community and called for more direct international engagement. In certain quarters the inaction is portrayed as a function of the UN leading some humanitarian activists to call on Western powers to take unilateral action. Indicatively, John O'Shea, head of the Charity GOAL, decrying the inaction, declared, 'The US as the superpower should take the action on its own ... There is nothing that the UN has done since day one that has saved the life of a single person in Darfur.'[23] The US has in fact maintained a very close adherence to the deliberations and rulings of the Security Council in contrast to its behaviour over Kosovo and Iraq. The UN's capacity to act is, of course, dependent on the Security Council which is itself reliant on its permanent members, including the US.

The NGO umbrella group SaveDarfur has been to the fore in highlighting the issue of Darfur within the United States. The organization comprises 114 different NGOs and some 48 regional groups based in the US. In terms of outlining how it actually helps the people of Darfur, SaveDarfur advances a rationale which endorses the basic assumptions behind global civil society: 'We utilize media outreach, public education, targeted coalition building and grassroots mobilization to pressure policymakers and other decision-makers in the United States and abroad to help the people of Darfur.'[24] In January 2006 the group launched the 'Million Voices for Darfur' campaign with the goal being to get one million people in the United States to sign postcards urging the Bush administration to support the deployment of a large military force to the region. By the end of June the million postcards had been collected and delivered to the President. On 30 April 2006 hundreds of thousands of people attended approximately 20 separate rallies across the United States calling on President Bush to do more to stop the conflict in Darfur, and a second rally was held on 17 September.[25]

Despite these efforts the prognosis is that the US has not demonstrated a willingness to act according to the pressure exerted by SaveDarfur and other similar groups. The campaign to raise awareness has been a success; according to SaveDarfur, 'just about everyone who's heard of Darfur believes that more should be done to help Darfur'. Yet despite the massive public outcry, they describe their campaign to date as 'complex, grinding, and profoundly frustrating'. They credit the African Union with taking a proactive approach contrasting this with 'the rest of the international community [who] stood by and watched'.[26] This analysis clearly does complement the notion that sustained and widespread pressure will force democratic states to act abroad. Paradoxically, the African Union – the only group singled out for praise by SaveDarfur – comprises states with a poor record on democracy and domestic freedom.[27] In this case, despite the widespread mobilization of domestic and global civil society in favour of robust military intervention, the US, and the West generally, has demonstrably resisted acceding to popular moral outrage.

The case of Iraq also supports the proposition that massive domestic pressure can be resisted by Western states. The scale of the opposition to the invasion was unprecedented; up to one million people marched in each of London, Rome and Madrid on 15 February 2003 in what David Cortright described as 'the largest-scale single day of anti-war protest in human history' when, in classic global civil society rhetoric, 'Demonstrators believed themselves to be part of a truly global struggle'.[28] Patrick Tyler wrote that the demonstrations highlighted that the US now faced a 'rival superpower' – namely world public opinion.

> President Bush appears to be eyeball to eyeball with a tenacious new adversary: millions of people who flooded the streets of New York and dozens of other world cities to say they are against war based on the evidence at hand ... an exceptional phenomenon has appeared on the streets of world cities ... politicians and leaders are unlikely to ignore it.[29]

Of course, the global movement against the war and the massive demonstrations were ignored when a month later the US led the invasion of Iraq. This highlights, at the very least, a breakdown in communication between the government and the public within these democracies. At worst it suggests that governments – even democratic ones – determined to pursue what they believe to be a necessary foreign policy will do so regardless of whether there is support for this policy within their domestic constituency. Cortright, however, rejects this negative diagnosis: 'Although the movement was unable to stop the march to war, and did not prevent the re-election of pro-war administrations a year and a half later in the United States and Australia, it nonetheless exerted considerable international influence.'[30] In terms of identifying where this 'considerable international influence' manifests he suggests, 'the strength of worldwide anti-war sentiment prevented the Bush administration from gaining UN support for its planned invasion and forced the administration to abandon efforts to win UN endorsement'. The suggestion is, therefore, that while global civil society was unable to prevent the US and the UK from going to war, the anti-war movement, an 'unprecedented expression of collective consciousness and action', was able to compel the Security

Council to oppose supporting the war. France, Russia and China's opposition to the invasion was thus it seems a function of the anti-war demonstrations. While it is difficult to determine exactly why these countries refused to support the invasion, a number of potential explanations stand out; the impact of the anti-war movement is not one of them.[31] Indeed, it is difficult to believe that government officials in Moscow and Beijing were influenced in their deliberations over their respective policies on the impending invasion of Iraq by images of anti-war demonstrations in Western cities.

The evidence since Kosovo thus suggests that Western states are prepared to ignore extensive domestic pressure when determining and executing their foreign policy. According to Alex Bellamy, 'there is little evidence to suggest that states intervene in foreign emergencies because they are in some sense morally shamed into doing so by either domestic or global public opinion'.[32] He further argues that those two cases often cited as evidence of the 'public-pressure-leads-to-political-action' thesis, namely Somalia (1992) and East Timor (1999), in fact evidence a number of factors that compromise the accuracy of this perspective. This therefore has profound consequences for the normative thesis which clearly overestimated the capacity of global civil society and underestimated the willingness of Western states to act in defiance of popular sentiment.

The utility of criteria as a constraint on state behaviour

As noted in Chapter 3 many proponents of the normative thesis have argued that positive international law is anachronistic and restrictive. States wishing to intervene in other states for humanitarian purposes, it is argued, have the moral right to do so and should not be constrained by immoral legal obstacles. This conviction was manifest in the justifications proffered by NATO officials before and during the intervention in Kosovo and explicit in the findings of the Independent International Commission on Kosovo.[33] In order to preserve some means by which the actions of states could be evaluated and 'illegal but legitimate' interventions distinguished from 'illegal and illegitimate' interventions, many 'conditionalists'[34] compiled lists of criteria which states had to meet for their actions to be deemed acceptable breaches of positive law. This idea of operating outside of the Security Council was tacitly endorsed by the International Commission on Intervention and State Sovereignty which proffered its own criteria to constrain such action.[35] The proliferation of these criteria would, it was claimed, limit the circumstances under which illegal but legitimate intervention could take place and hence guard against the abuse of the precept.[36] In practice these criteria have proved of little utility for two major reasons, which are dealt with in this section. First, the criteria are inherently subjective and fail to provide the clarity necessary to serve as a useful guide when operating outside of positive law. Second, criteria without legal expression are open to abuse.

The majority of the lists of criteria cite 'supreme humanitarian emergency' or some similar term as a necessary prerequisite for launching a humanitarian intervention, yet establishing if this criterion has been met it is not straightforward. The determination of a crisis's magnitude and the necessity of external intervention can be a source of genuine disagreement. For example, as noted in Chapter 4, while the US determined that the crisis in Darfur constituted genocide, many others, like the African Union and reputable humanitarian organizations such as MSF, disagreed.[37] Indeed, throughout 2004 the African Union continued to assert that the situation in Darfur was improving in contrast to the many UN reports stating precisely the opposite.[38] The intervention in Kosovo in 1999 was similarly characterized by disagreements over the scale of the suffering in the region; indicatively, according to Gordon Bardos, 'there was no humanitarian crisis in Kosovo in 1997, or in 1998, or in 1999 in any conventionally understood sense of the term',[39] whereas Timothy Garton-Ash claims, 'Anyone who was in Kosovo, as I was, in the winter of 1998–1999 could see that there was a humanitarian disaster.'[40] As Philip Hipold states regarding criteria,

> It is interesting to note that these catalogues, which, as noted, only slightly differ in their content, applied to the situation in Kosovo, brought completely different results depending on the personal view taken by the various authors ... we can conclude that the drafting of these catalogues does not really contribute to give an answer to the question why and when humanitarian intervention should be permissible.[41]

Similar legitimate concerns can be raised with respects to the other criteria routinely presented, namely last resort, right authority, proportional means and positive outcome. In the case of last resort, much of the controversy surrounding the interventions in Kosovo and Iraq centred on this aspect of the use of force in both cases.[42] Similarly, regarding the notion of proportionality, during Operation Allied Force NATO consistently asserted that their campaign was proportionate and discriminatory.[43] Yet NATO's tactics were criticized by UN High Commissioner for Human Rights, Mary Robinson,[44] and the campaign was also retrospectively criticized by Amnesty International and Human Rights Watch.[45]

The scope for genuine disagreements over the scale of a crisis, the necessity of intervention and the means employed clearly constitute major problems with utilizing criteria. This question of potential ambiguity is not a problem unique to these criteria, however. The potential for subjective and contrasting interpretation is also identifiable in positive law. The dispute over the invasion of Iraq is indicative; the cause of much of the international dissonance in 2002–3 was the different interpretations of Article 51 and Chapter VII of the UN Charter, while ultimately the dispute in the Security Council centred, to a large extent, on the meaning of the term 'serious consequences' as used in Security Council Resolution 1441.[46] In this sense positive law has suffered from definitional terminological subjectivity similar to that surrounding the criteria proffered.

There is, however, a significant difference between the legal status of certain acts of intervention and war and the criteria articulated by adherents to the normative thesis. Those who proffer criteria have asserted that their criteria are sufficient in themselves to guard against abuse and do not require an independent evaluative structure because, in essence, global civil society fulfils this role. The utility of criteria is therefore predicated on an assumption about the capacity of global civil society to shame states if they misuse or fail to meet the criteria. This is supposedly particularly the case with respect to democratic states which, normatively, must ensure that their foreign policy is acceptable to their domestic public. According to Buchanan and Keohane, when democracies 'violate cosmopolitan principles, they are more likely to be criticized by their citizens for doing so, and will be more likely to rectify their behavior in response'.[47] Hence, if the state articulates an 'illegal but legitimate' rationale for an intervention and expresses adherence to the criteria for such action, global civil society can interrogate the state on their purported adherence to the criteria and therefore there *is* a framework for judging the rightness of state action and publicly condemning illegitimate policies.[48] This normative process breaks down, of course, if states are not receptive to the blandishments of domestic or global civil society. The preceding section makes this very point. Thus, the rejection of the positive legal regulatory framework in favour of global civil society adjudicating on criteria and cajoling states accordingly is flawed. The utility of criteria must be judged in light of its capacity to withstand politicization and willful abuse.

An examination of the 2003 invasion of Iraq (see Chapter 4) highlights that the intervening coalition did make a case to have adhered to the criteria and, perhaps more damningly, were not significantly influenced by the rejection of the veracity of their humanitarian claims by the majority of the proponents of global civil society. There are few objective observers who endorse the US-led coalition's humanitarian claims regarding Operation Iraqi Freedom; if the humanitarian justifications were prompted by a desire to present a sectional intervention as a more palatable act of altruism, then, as evidenced by the now routine rejection of these claims, this strategy has failed.[49] This failure does not, however, mean that the normative perspective has emerged unscathed from the Iraq invasion. The US proffered mixed motives for the intervention comprising both security concerns and humanitarian impulses. This mixture, even if weighted in favour of the security rational, does not preclude the intervention from being deemed humanitarian; key proponents of humanitarian intervention have asserted that motives will almost always be mixed and that this in itself does not undermine the humanitarian nature of a particular action.[50] The attempt, albeit a failed one, to portray the invasion of Iraq as humanitarian and explicitly claim adherence to normative criteria tells us much about how Western states perceive the ascendancy of the normative movement. It suggests that merely token rhetorical commitment to humanitarianism is required as the criteria are malleable and the costs of antagonizing global civil society minimal.

The utility of criteria is thus in some doubt. Criteria can be sources of genuine disagreement and also, more worryingly, are insufficiently robust to resist manipulation and misuse. They therefore do not constitute viable alternatives to positive law. Positive international law gained increased currency in the eighteenth and nineteenth centuries precisely because of the endemic abuse of natural law and the reliance on states adhering to moral norms.[51] To proffer criteria is thus to regress to this pre-positive law system in the hope that contemporary states are more likely to abide by non-binding moral codes than in previous eras; the evidence for this, as noted above, is lacking.

'(Its your) responsibility to protect': The statist aspects of the normative thesis

The rise of global civil society has been portrayed by its proponents as a challenge to the conservative, selfish inclinations often characteristic of states. The capacity of global civil society to pressurize (ostensibly inherently receptive) democratic states to act ethically in their foreign affairs was heralded as constituting a means by which the decision-making autonomy of states was undermined by a new force whose perspective had to be heeded. In fact, far from constituting a challenge to the primacy of the state and its dominance in international affairs, the strategy adopted by global civil society ascribes to the state a position of central importance. Three aspects of the strategy contrive to both consolidate and strengthen the state, namely the utilization of Just War theory, the centrality of state power in the practice of humanitarian intervention and the capacity of the widely vaunted 'responsibility to protect' to enable international inaction and internal oppression. The following sections deal with each in turn.

According to Bellamy, the Just War tradition fulfils two roles: 'It provides a common language that actors can use to legitimize recourse to force and the conduct of war and that others use to evaluate those claims. It can also inhibit actions that cannot be justified.'[52] Those orientated towards determining when it is right and just to intervene to 'save strangers' in the post-Cold War era have sought to establish a framework for such intervention that restricts the capacity of states to intervene in all but a few 'just' cases. As noted above, in so doing many have compiled lists of criteria which states must meet to have their interventions deemed legitimate. In compiling these lists many naturally looked to the Just War tradition as the basis for their prescriptions and its tenets have become central to the normative perspective.[53]

The tenets of the Just War tradition are invariably divided into three sections, *jus ad bellum, jus in bello* and *jus post bellum*, and there is little argument about the criteria within each category.[54] One of the key criterion within the *jus ad bellum* category is 'right authority'. It is precisely the manner in which this criterion has been conceptualized by the Just War theory which leads to its statist inclination. St Augustine (354–430) and St Aquinas (1224–74) are recognized as the founding fathers of the modern Just War tradition and their respective views on right authority imbue the state with considerable power.

Augustine determined that the sin of violence was not the act in itself but the motivations behind the act.[55] Augustine argued that force was justified if the intention was just and if the act was ordered by a just ruler. It therefore followed that a soldier acting on the orders of his ruler to use force was acting justly because it was not he who had decided to kill. The soldier personally took no pleasure in the act but rather served the state. Augustine viewed the state as a source of order that enabled humans to fulfil God's prescriptions. The state was neither moral nor good, but its utility lay in its instrumental value – that of providing the forum for the adherence to, and application of, God's laws.

The role of the authority ordering the use of force is of paramount importance in Augustine's schema. He suggested that soldiers must obey their ruler. Soldiers who carry out the orders of their ruler are exempt from blame as they were fulfilling their duty; it is only the rulers who will face (divine) censure if their actions are immoral. This clearly state-centric conception is understandable, however, when one considers Augustine's religious convictions. His perspective suggested that humans can never achieve true justice or righteousness and that ultimately it was God who rewards and punishes. The temporal abuse of the framework he avows is therefore insignificant given the capacity of God to punish wicked rulers. Robert Holmes' analysis, however, highlights the implications of this perspective: 'The net effect is that it is the interests of the state that are paramount and that it's laws, so long as they do not directly contravene divine law, should be obeyed unquestioningly.'[56] This perspective, Holmes argues, laid the ground for Realism and its privileging of the primacy of the state.

Aquinas viewed the state as a political community, a natural, organic entity identified with its members rather than distinct from them. Like Augustine he viewed the state as a unit of order for the common good rather than an aggregation of individuals.[57] The state's utility lay in its capacity to promote and facilitate the common good rather than collective individual goods. Individual good was essentially subsumed through the state into the collective good. Aquinas favoured a political system which mixed monarchy with limited democracy and like Augustine recommended that citizens obey the state in all but the most extreme circumstances. Regarding revolt against the state he wrote, 'The harms that so often follow from revolution, whether successful or unsuccessful, are such that acquiescence and passive disobedience should be assumed to be the morally better option.'[58]

The nature of just authority, central to Aquinas' schema, is somewhat ambiguous. As John Tooke notes, '[A] common complaint is that Aquinas's doctrine in no way reflects or is adapted to contemporary political, ecclesiastical and social conditions or ideas, such as feudalism and imperialism...who, in the 13th century, such person [deemed to have right authority] might be, was a rather delicate question needing serious discussion'.[59] Aquinas suggests that 'right authority' is one who has no authority above them. Those who served a master must seek authorization from him.

Additionally Tooke notes, 'the "common good" of which Aquinas wrote and which must be the aim of a Just War, was rather a limited good, that of a city or province, and never the international good of all'.[60] Thus in Aquinas' work there is a clear focus on the state, its security and proliferation. Aquinas wrote, 'it is the king's duty to make sure that the community subject to him is made safe against its enemies. There is no point in guarding against internal dangers, when defence from the enemies without is impossible.'[61] As with Augustine the state-centric nature of

Aquinas's prescriptions is ultimately explained by his instrumental conception of the state and belief in divine judgement. Individuals acting out of a duty to the state need not necessarily fear that their own state was commanding an unjust act as the rulers would face divine retribution while the compliant citizens would not be punished for their obedience.

Subsequent writers who added to the Just War tradition's evolution evidence a similar statist disposition. Vittoria's (1492–1546) writings are of paramount importance to the evolution to Just War thinking; according to Bellamy, 'in popular modern renderings of the natural law approach to the Just War tradition, virtually all of Francisco de Vitoria's ideas remain intact in one form or another'.[62] In Vitoria's view on right authority the state is conceived as the locus of this authority. Like Augustine and Aquinas he suggested that citizens should obey the leader, and if in doubt trust their sovereigns.[63] As Bellamy notes, Vitoria's perspective 'paved the way for later realists and legalists to argue that as objective knowledge of just causes was impossible, it should be assumed that war waged by sovereigns was just, placing the normative emphasis on its conduct'.[64] Thus the Just War tradition evidences an inclination towards examining the conduct of war rather than the recourse to war. According to Anthony Coates, 'The criterion of legitimate authority has become the most neglected of all the criteria that have been traditionally employed in the moral assessment of war.'[65] Enquiries into the nature of *jus ad bellum* focus largely on determining what injuries incurred by a state are sufficiently grave to legitimize its recourse to violent self-defense; the authority of the state to wage war is axiomatic.

The Just War tradition does not provide sufficiently detailed criteria to mitigate against differing conceptions of any given intervention, and the decision to employ force is essentially left to the state to make. This abrogation of ultimate authority to the state imbues leaders with significant power and the scope for dissonance regarding each of the criteria is great. The tradition is a self-proclaimed ethical and moral framework and does not comprise a legally binding or objective schema and thus its utility in political terms is contingent on a coincidence between the moral perspectives of both the actor and the judge. Even where there are shared conception of moral norms and ethical behaviour the scope for disagreement over each of the criteria is great. Employing these necessarily subjective, and possibly culturally particular, moral norms outside of a binding and universal legal framework compromises the framework's utility. The tradition is best employed, as Nicholas Rengger suggests, as a means by which the use of force by a state can be evaluated, not facilitated.[66] Charles Reed and David Ryall similarly warn against the use of the Just War criteria as 'a sort of checklist that can be ticked or crossed' and argue that the theory should not be 'seen as an attempt to moralise war with the intention of making it easier to fight'.[67] George Wiegel argues that Just War theory has been misunderstand in the contemporary era and treated 'as essentially a matter of casuistry. Here the tradition is (mis)conceived as a set of hurdles set before statesmen by Just War analysts'.[68]

Many of the key theorists associated with the tradition identified the state or God as having evaluative power. The normative thesis, however, applies the Just War framework in an authoritative vacuum evoking neither the state, a particular international organization nor God. Yet, without an endorsement of a divine entity or the restructuring of the state system to incorporate an overarching entity capable of passing and enforcing humanitarian law, the necessarily subjective criteria are open to misapplication. Therefore the utilization of the Just War tradition in the creation of the criteria presented as an alternative to international law actually results in the concentration of power in states, thus compromising the radical agenda articulated by the normative thesis and global civil society.

Secondly, the normative solution to humanitarian crises – the very act of humanitarian intervention – also undermines the radical agenda proffered by those seeking to diminish the power of the state. According to Mark Evans, 'although the existence of states continues to have some intrinsic value, their sovereignty is ultimately premised upon their support for, and contribution to, the maintenance of global civil society as a moral society'.[69] In this conception the state's value, utility and very existence derives from its support for global civil society. A hierarchy is thus conceived with the state dependent on global civil society. In reality, however, in terms of the means by which humanitarian interventions are to occur, the normative perspective necessarily depends on the opposite relationship.

Mark Evans, building on his conception of the relationship between states and global civil society, argues,

> people have rights which both yield and limit the moral sovereignty of states and, as expressed in the moral possibility of humanitarian intervention, establish moral ties between peoples of different states such that one people could have the moral right, and perhaps the duty, to come to the aid of another against their own state. The moral theory in which we should house this claim is, therefore, going to be trans-statist.[70]

This 'trans-statist' notion can only manifest, however, if the people with the 'moral right, and perhaps the duty, to come to the aid of another against their own state' have an independent capacity to execute a military intervention. No such capacity exists. Those sufficiently outraged to determine that intervention is warranted have no capacity to either order or execute an intervention. The only means by which people outraged at the oppression occurring within another state can actively halt the oppression is through the mobilization of their host state's military. Thus 'peoples of different states' now imbued with this right, if not duty, to intervene cannot undertake an intervention without the support of the state.

The normative perspective holds, of course, that the Western state acts according to the wishes of its citizens and thus domestic outrage *will* lead to state action. The evidence in Chapter 4 refutes this. Yet, even if the evidence did not compromise this notion, the centrality of the state and its military to the normative position would remain. The action demanded by global civil society requires the assent of the state and the utilization of its military. Thus the state becomes an essential conduit for moral opprobrium akin to the controller of a valve who is ultimately capable of stemming or releasing civil society's fury. The radical agenda is thus compromised by the centrality of the state in link between global civil society and those suffering. As Orford notes,

> many human rights activists see humanitarian intervention as unquestionably a good thing precisely because it appears to enact a commitment to the emancipatory ideals of freedom from oppression, respect for human dignity and valuing of human life... While on the one hand the appeal to human rights is used to undermine the legitimacy of 'rogue', 'failed' or target states in the context of intervention, that appeal also serves at the same time to authorize or legitimize the actions of those powerful states who collectively act as the 'international community'. Human rights discourse thus seems to contain forces moving in opposite directions in the debate about intervention.[71]

The ostensibly radical, trans-statist agenda proffered by the normative thesis thus actually delegates to the state a position of central importance through its reliance on the state's consent.

The third aspect of the normative thesis which facilitates the primacy of the state is the very idea of 'the responsibility to protect'. The fear, expressed by a number of authors after Operation Allied Force and the publication of the ICISS's report, that the West was about to undertake myriad spurious 'humanitarian interventions' has proved misplaced.[72] The 'responsibility to protect' has not become a means by which the West has dramatically increased its interventionism. While the interventions in Iraq and, possibly to a lesser extent, Afghanistan highlighted the malleability of humanitarian rhetoric, it is difficult to believe that these interventions occurred exclusively due to the enabling rhetorical schema advanced by *The Responsibility to Protect*. The character of the Bush administration and, most obviously, the events of September 11, 2001, are more plausible catalysts for these interventions. Indeed, the permanent members of the Security Council, especially the US, greeted *The Responsibility to Protect* with little enthusiasm.[73]

In fact, one consequence of the emergence of 'the responsibility to protect doctrine' not widely predicted by its critics was the extent to which the notion actually facilitated Western *inaction*. States can, and have, claimed that, in the spirit of 'the responsibility to protect, host states have the primary responsibility to deal with intra-state crises and should be left alone to do so.[74] This has been especially obvious with respects to the response to the crisis in Darfur as examined in the previous chapter. As Bellamy notes, 'In the Darfur case… "responsibility to protect" language has now enabled anti-interventionists to legitimize arguments against action by claiming the primary responsibility in certain contested cases still lies with the state and not (yet) with an international body'.[75] Indeed, the UK's position appears to reflect this; during deliberations on what to do should Sudan fail to abide by Resolution 1556 a senior Foreign Office official stated, 'the best way to deliver security to the people of Darfur is to get those with the primary responsibility for it to do it… the government of Sudan'.[76] The language used in the majority of Security Council Resolutions on Darfur certainly put the onus on the Sudanese government to resolve the crisis despite the UN's own investigations charging the Khartoum regime with complicity in the crisis.

As noted in the previous chapter, the adoption of aspects of the responsibility to protect in the *Outcome Document* of the 2005 World Summit was conditional on the removal of any reference to a duty incumbent on states to intervene. In his letter to the President of the General Assembly prior to the World Summit John Bolton, the Representative of the US to the UN, outlined his country's position on the responsibility to protect:

> we agree that the host state has a responsibility to protect its populations from such atrocities, and we agree in a more general and moral sense that the international community has a responsibility to act when the host state allows such atrocities. But the responsibility of

> the other countries in the international community is not of the same character as the responsibility of the host, and we thus want to avoid formulations that suggest that the other countries are inheriting the same responsibility that the host state has.[77]

It is therefore clear that the 'responsibility to protect' adopted at the 2005 World Summit was not a means by which intervention could be increased, but rather a delineation of responsibility which put the emphasis on the host state rather than the watching international community. The *Outcome Document* certainly didn't proscribe external intervention but neither did it create a means by which such action could be said to have become a duty. The language of the responsibility to protect can thus be employed by those wishing to avoid intervening and those wishing to block an intervention. There is, as Bellamy notes, 'a real danger that states of all stripes will co-opt the language of the responsibility to protect to legitimate inaction and irresponsibility'.[78] Therefore the rhetorical shift from 'humanitarian intervention' to 'the responsibility to protect', described by some as 'ingenious',[79] creates significant scope for states to utilize the new discourse to legitimize both non-intervention and domestic oppression.

Conclusion

The normative thesis outlines a solution to the perennial problem of what to do when a state is unable or unwilling to halt the suffering of its citizens. Central to the purported solution is a belief in the capacity of global civil society to influence the foreign policy of Western states. Global civil society and the normative thesis are variously portrayed as 'trans-statist', a 'rival superpower' and an international force comprising the 'indignant pity of the civilised world' capable of forging a new era of human rights enforcement.[80] This new international movement has been portrayed as offering a viable and radical alternative to the shameful spectacle of inertia and obfuscation which historically constituted the international response to humanitarian crises. Global civil society would ostensibly act as 'the guarantors of civil behaviour both by official institutions (states and international institutions) and in the wider world at large'.[81] Certain humanitarian organizations endorsed this view; Human Rights Watch described the 1999 interventions in Kosovo and East Timor as indicative of 'a new era for the human rights movement' in which humanitarians can 'count on governments to use their police powers to enforce human rights law'. 'Victims of atrocities', they claimed, in language similar to that used by NATO at the time of Operation Allied Force, will receive 'effective assistance wherever they cry out for help'.[82]

This optimistic assessment of the post-Kosovo era has not materialized. The slaughter in Darfur is perhaps most indicative of this failure. According to MSF, 'The media attention and political involvement means that everyone knows about the conflict here, but in the last four years the situation has not improved. In fact, for most people things have got worse.'[83] As Weiss notes, while 'never again' was the mantra espoused post Rwanda, the crisis in Darfur and the attendant international inaction means '"here we go again" is closer to the truth'.[84] The invasion of Iraq and the inaction over Darfur have respectively suggested that the moral character of Western states and their willingness to act beyond narrow national interest have been exaggerated. Clearly, the progress ostensibly made by the human rights movement and global civil society by the end of 1990s was inflated; use of humanitarian discourse during and after the invasion of Iraq suggests that at best the normative agenda has evolved to the point when it has come to be seen as a necessary rhetorical component in any intervention, so malleable that in the case of Iraq it could be applied to even the most obviously sectional intervention. This status hardly corresponds to the revolutionary impact adherents to the normative approach so emphatically predicted in the late 1990s.

Identifying the source of the normative thesis' failing has been the aim of this Chapter. It is clear that while Western states promised much at the time of Operation Allied Force, they have consciously reneged on these commitments in the period since. Those who articulated optimistic predictions about Western foreign policy can therefore justifiably claim to have been misled. The normative thesis' failure to accurately predict the behaviour of states in the post-Kosovo era cannot, however, be blamed exclusively on the hypocrisy of Western states. This chapter has also identified key flaws with the normative perspective itself which contributed to the failure of its prescriptions to materialize.

First, the normative perspective overestimated the capacity of global civil society to influence and constrain Western state behaviour. Global civil society has demonstrated its capacity to mobilize on a truly massive, global scale, but the effect of this mobilization on Western foreign policy has been relatively minimal. The criteria proffered by many proponents of the normative thesis as a substitute for the constraints imposed by (ostensibly anachronistic) positive international law have failed to constrain state action. Given that, as certain proponents of the normative thesis admit, global civil society is an ideal rather than a reality, this is not altogether surprising.[85] In certain cases, the criteria proffered have merely been co-opted by states as a rhetorical justification for their otherwise self-serving action.

The normative prescriptions have also in certain key respects strengthened the position of the state by affording it a position of central importance in their strategy. The utilization of the Just War theory in the absence of a defined authority figure other than the state, such as God or an international organization, has meant that states are their own judge regarding their adherence to the criteria proffered for just interventionism. The Just War tradition and the normative criteria thus become stripped of any real utility; as Robert Myers notes, 'If everyone's war is just, then those who believe they must go to war, out of necessity, fear or honor, should turn to realism for policy and "Just War" for propaganda and self-service.'[86]

The normative thesis also requires the machinery of the state to halt oppression abroad. The solution to humanitarian crises is portrayed as military intervention; global civil society has no independent military capability and, as there is no expressed desire for an international army or police force, the military apparatus of Western states are required. The idea that domestic public pressure within Western democracies determines how Western militaries are deployed has been disproved by events since Operation Allied Force. Finally, the oft-used phrase 'The Responsibility to Protect', portrayed as an innovative solution to the tension between sovereignty and human rights, has come to be used in ways which have enabled Western states to avoid intervention. The manner in which the notion was treated at the 2005 World Summit particularly highlights this development as the two paragraphs devoted to the responsibility to protect in the *Outcome Document* removed any reference to a duty incumbent on others to intervene.

The flaws identified above have contrived to prevent the realization of the normative vision articulated with such confidence after Operation Allied Force. While Chapter 4 highlighted the evidence of this failure, Chapter 6 outlines the negative consequences the rejection of international law, central to the normative thesis, has had and may continue to have if the strategy continues.

6
The Dangers of Unregulated Humanitarian Intervention

Introduction

Operation Allied Force was a key juncture for the normative thesis and NATO's intervention has been used as a springboard for broader international advocacy and a basis for the normative critique of existing international law. While the invasion of Iraq generated more international debate and public interest, the intervention in Kosovo arguably constituted a more important juncture in post-Cold War international relations. As David Armstrong and Theo Farrell note,

> The Kosovo case illustrated, perhaps even more starkly than the Iraq case, the tension between law and legitimacy in the use of force. It also clearly demonstrated the tensions within international law – in the case between, on the one hand, the non-intervention and non-use of force norms and on the other, norms of human rights. Arguably, Kosovo also revealed the crusading militancy of liberalism.[1]

This tension between law and legitimacy has been a major catalyst for the normative thesis. Expressions of outrage and anger at the existing legal codes and structure of the UN system are common among supporters of humanitarian intervention. The existing system 'rewards tyrants',[2] respect for sovereign inviolability constitutes 'complicity in war crimes'[3] and Western democratic states are urged to 'develop the kind of moral sensitivity that will enable them to recognise what is the right thing to do in such appalling circumstances, and the strength of character to act upon this recognition'.[4] This 'strength of character' was ostensibly evident when NATO launched Operation Allied Force.

The great outpouring of support for NATO's intervention among Western states was echoed by human rights campaigners and sympathetic academics who rejoiced at the subversion of the old system. Bernard Kouchner, writing after NATO's intervention, heralded 'an irresistible shift in public attitudes towards the belief that the defence of the oppressed in the name of morality should prevail over frontiers and legal documents'.[5] Advocates of intervention identified the principles of sovereign inviolability and sovereign equality as particularly anathematic; Fernando Teson wrote, 'Non-intervention is a doctrine of the past. It feeds on illiberal intellectual traditions (relativism, communitarianism, nationalism and statism) that are objectionable for various reasons and that, where implemented, have caused grievous harm to persons.'[6] The progressive aspects of the UN Charter's codification of sovereignty, as identified in Chapter 2, were ignored.

International events since 1999, as detailed in Chapter 4, evidence a clear contrast between the theoretical evolution of international politics as predicted by the normative thesis and actual state practice. Chapter 5 explained the record of the normative thesis' prescriptions since Operation Allied Force by identifying those flaws inherent in the normative thesis which have militated against the achievement of the normative vision. This Chapter examines the negative consequences, both real and potential, of the normative thesis' prescriptions. The basic goal of the normative thesis – that of making the international system better able to halt and prevent suffering – is certainly worthy. It is the contention of this chapter, however, that the prescriptions advanced by the normative thesis are regressive and threaten international peace and stability.

The challenge to international law

Chapter 2 highlighted the extent to which NATO's intervention in Kosovo constituted a breach of international law. The illegality of Operation Allied Force was, however, readily acknowledged by many of its supporters who argued that positive law regarding sovereignty is anachronistic and cannot be allowed to obstruct the alleviation of suffering.[7] While certain NATO officials did offer legal justifications for their actions this constituted a minor aspect of the overall rationale and was, to a large extent, tokenistic.[8] The major justification offered was thus undoubtedly the 'moral imperative'.[9]

Operation Allied Force constituted, according to Walter J. Rockler, a prosecutor at the Nuremberg War Crimes Trials, 'flagrant military aggression [and] a war crime'.[10] Those who highlighted the illegality of the intervention, such as Rockler, were accused, however, of having 'indulged in a form of procedural fetishism by which a discredited veto system was considered more important than the prevention of crimes against humanity'. Arguments decrying the legality of NATO's actions ostensibly 'relied on a static interpretation of international law that ignored its tendency to evolve in accordance with custom and practice'.[11] NATO's breach of international law was portrayed as a petty, procedural issue compared with the magnitude of the moral benefits derived from the intervention. NATO's intervention was considered an instance when 'respect for the rule of law [was] sacrificed on the altar of human compassion'.[12]

The UN's authority and centrality in international relations was fundamentally undermined by NATO's actions. By the time of Operation Allied Force the UN had endured years of criticism for its structure, overly bureaucratic style and adherence to the ostensibly outdated and illiberal tenets of international law. A key aspect of the pro-intervention perspective was, and remains, the need to periodically bypass the organization. Tim Dunne and Nicholas Wheeler heralded the Blair government for its willingness to subvert the Security Council. Supporters of interventionism therefore advocated shifting the locus of power from the UN, and particularly the much-maligned Security Council, to certain states – those cognizant of human rights and altruistic in outlook – identified as 'norm entrepreneurs'.[13]

This retreat from the UN necessarily led to the emergence of a conception of the international system as comprising a core and periphery where the core states, due to their democratic and liberal composition, should be afforded special rights and privileges so as to enable them to both protect themselves and come to the aid of those suffering in the periphery. The existing provisions of international law explicitly outlaw such privileges and this aspect of the normative thesis thus constitutes a fundamental rejection of a key element of the UN system.[14]

This core–periphery dichotomy has become integral to the foreign policy outlook of many Western states, with the US and UK particularly supportive of the idea. As Michael Glennon observes, 'The West's new rules of thumb on intervention accord less deference to the old idea of sovereign equality...The new posture recognises the hollowness of this concept, accepting that all states are not in fact the same in their power, wealth, or commitment to human rights.'[15] In particular, this latter 'commitment to human right' has come to be considered a key determinant of a state's rights. Richard Haas, a foreign policy adviser in the Bush administration, succinctly captured the essence of this perspective:

> Sovereignty entails obligations... If a government fails to meet these obligations, then it forfeits some of the normal advantages of sovereignty, including the right to be left alone inside your own territory. Other governments, including the United States, gain the right to intervene.[16]

This perspective clearly challenges existing international law and the authority of the UN. This is not, however, necessarily a negative development. The character of the international system has changed markedly since 1989 and attendant change in international law and the structures designed to administer it is thus conceivably warranted.[17] International law is also capable of evolution and historically has changed in tandem with great geopolitical shifts.[18] The issue is, therefore, whether the changes proposed, and in certain respects manifest, constitute a progressive development. The following sections outline the adverse consequences such developments have had, and may continue to have, for international peace and stability.

The end of the UN?

The UN is neither dynamic nor fluid and its record on facilitating international peace and stability is decidedly mixed. It has regularly been criticized for failing to prevent and halt humanitarian crises, in particular the genocides in Rwanda in 1994 and more recently in Darfur. The UN's record on human rights promotion is also controversial; the United Nations Commission on Human Rights (UNCHD), which operated from 1946 until 2006, often provoked ridicule when states such as Libya and Saudi Arabia were elected as members. In 2004, in the midst of the crisis in Darfur, Sudan was elected onto the UNCHD, to general dismay. The UN's pronouncements and resolutions are routinely flouted or simply ignored. The composition of the Security Council is decidedly unrepresentative and while the General Assembly *is* representative, the powers vested in this institution are minimal. Scandals, such as those surrounding the Oil-for-Food-Programme and allegations surrounding sex abuse by UN peacekeepers, have further eroded the organization's reputation.

Those sympathetic to the UN can point to the organization's record in dealing with health hazards such smallpox, the SARS virus and AIDS. Additionally, the UN has performed numerous global oversight functions, such as monitoring crime and narcotics statistics and policing nuclear proliferation.[19] The UN High Commission for Refugees also constitutes a UN organ of wide repute. These positives, however, are pale in comparison to those more evident, high-profile failings such as the Rwandan genocide, the crisis in Darfur and the invasion of Iraq when the UN has appeared highly ineffectual.

A momentum in favour of ignoring or even disbanding the UN has thus gained currency in recent years. It is certainly clear that many neoconservatives within the US wish to see the UN – 'an abject failure' – disbanded.[20] Though these arguments are not notable for their subtlety their critique is certainly consistent. The dominant perspective avowed by the normative thesis, however, lacks this consistency and coherence. According to David Clark, during Operation Allied Force, 'the interventionists were at one in maintaining that the values of the UN Charter should be upheld even if it meant bypassing its institutions'.[21] To express support for the UN and then offer prescriptions which transfer vast powers away from the organization to Western states and global civil society is fundamentally contradictory and, as demonstrated by the US invasion of Iraq, untenable. Before examining the consequences of legitimizing the use of force outside of the UN framework, the following section will first examine the nature of the UN's periodic paralysis in the face of humanitarian crises.

The Rwandan genocide and the crisis in Darfur are routinely cited by critics as instances of abject failure for the UN. It is questionable, however, whether the blame for the lack of action during these two crises can be levelled against the UN. Thomas Frank, for example, argues that the UN's legal framework proved to be deeply flawed during the Rwandan genocide. He suggests it would have been worth deviating from the law to have enabled a force to enter Rwanda and stop the violence.[22] The lack of intervention was not caused, however, by the restrictions imposed by international law or the UN's dogged adherence to these restrictions. Rather, the lack of will on the part of the states on the Security Council and the wider international community led to the paralysis. The UN Secretary General's report issued at the end of May 1994 declared that genocide was taking place and by the end of April Boutros Boutros-Ghali appealed to the Security Council to take 'forceful action'.[23] As Simon Chesterman notes, had the Security Council acknowledged the obvious – that genocide was occurring – then it would have been more difficult not to act under international law.[24] It was, therefore, precisely the fear that international law would compel intervention, not block it, which led the states on the Security Council, and the US in particular, to contrive ever more imaginative ways to avoid using the 'G-word' to describe the massacre of 800,000 people.

Likewise, as detailed in Chapter 4, UN officials repeatedly highlighted the scale of the atrocities in Darfur throughout 2004 and didn't flinch from accusing the Sudanese government of complicity in the slaughter. This information was provided to the Security Council by UN officials but did not translate into forceful action. The blame for this can only reasonably be attributed to the members of the Security Council rather than the UN. In many key respects the UN is dependent on the will of those states controlling the Security Council and therefore 'UN inertia' actually derives from the policies of states, not the UN itself. The UN has no independent military capacity and cannot deploy troops abroad without the assent of the Security Council. The view, therefore, that the UN somehow neglected to employ the tools at its disposal does not equate with the facts.

Despite this, the idea that the UN has failed when confronted by humanitarian crises persists. There is no doubt, of course, that the veto powers of the permanent members of the Security Council have been the cause of much of the expressed frustration. China and Russia are regularly cited as obstructionists wedded to conservative notions of sovereignty, and there is some evidence to support these claims. The logic of ignoring or bypassing the UN because its central political organ is often unresponsive and highly politicized has a certain merit if one believes, as neo-conservatives do, that the centrality of the Security Council and its many flaws renders the entire UN defunct. To argue, however, that it is permissible, under certain circumstances, to subvert the power of the Security Council and simultaneously respect the UN's authority is not a feasible proposition, yet this is what the normative thesis attempts.

David Held has argued that the need to address the suffering of people around the world, especially those persecuted by their own states, requires 'the formation of an authoritative assembly of all democratic states and agencies'. Such an assembly would, by virtue of its democratic composition and inherently humanitarian disposition, act decisively to halt humanitarian crises wherever they occurred. The UN, Held argues,

> cannot, almost by definition, be an effective institutional framework to represent the peoples and movements of the world ... The establishment of an independent assembly of democratic peoples, directly elected by them and accountable to them, is an unavoidable institutional requirement.[25]

Yet, despite this prescription, Held suggests such an organization could serve as 'a compliment to the UN' before possibly subsuming it.[26]

The ICISS articulated a similar argument; their report notes, 'the Commission is in absolutely no doubt that there is no better or more appropriate body than the Security Council to deal with military intervention issues for human protection purposes' and states that their aim is 'not to find alternatives to the Security Council as a source of authority, but to make the Security Council work much better than it has'.[27] It is clear, however, that the respect afforded to the Security Council is highly contingent. Rather than being the only source of legitimate authority the Security Council is in fact 'the first port of call' and 'alternative means of discharging the responsibility to protect [cannot] be entirely discounted'.[28] The Report suggests that states or groups of states can legitimately act without a UN mandate, provided they adhere to a set of criteria drawn up by the ICISS. The UN's status as the actor with sole authority to permit the use of force is therefore explicitly challenged. This clearly does not sit comfortably with the ICISS's commitments to respect the competency of the UN, and specifically the Security Council.

The suggestion, made by the ICISS and others, that creating the means by which legitimate action can take place without UN authorization would somehow strengthen the organization, and certainly not undermine it, has proved incorrect. The conclusion reached by the Independent International Commission on Kosovo regarding Operation Allied Force – that it was illegal but legitimate – certainly provided additional support for those eager to identify alternative sources of legitimization other than the UN. While this principal was widely endorsed at the time of Operation Allied Force, and following the publication of *The Responsibility to Protect*, the invasion of Iraq highlighted the scope for abusing the new principle. Before the invasion President Bush stated that the UN was not the only source of legitimacy, noting, 'We don't really need the United Nation's approval to act.'[29] Thus for some the invasion of Iraq was an 'inevitable consequence of the rise and evolution of the new interventionism', rather than an aberration from it.[30] The invasion certainly complements the post-Cold War era trend, particularly evident during Operation Allied Force, whereby self-appointed guardians of the peace have come to reject both international law and specifically the UN. As White notes,

> In many ways the Iraq crisis of 2003 was the culmination of a decade of pressure by the US and UK directed at changing the legal framework governing the use of force contained in the UN Charter, in a concerted effort to widen both exceptions to the ban on the threat or use of force.[31]

The extent to which the rhetoric advanced by the US and the UK prior to the invasion of Iraq echoed that articulated before, during and after Operation Allied Force led many supporters of NATO's intervention to lament the appropriation of their arguments.[32] Richard Falk, a supporter of Operation Allied Force, observed after the invasion of Iraq that the UN had been relegated to the role of 'a debating society, where if the state seeking to engage in controversial behaviour cannot make its case persuasively, it will proceed to act in any event'.[33]

The potential for abusing the 'illegal but legitimate' route and ignoring the UN was certainly acknowledged by certain supporters of Operation Allied Force. The solution to this potential problem, as noted in Chapter 3, was presented as being the articulation of criteria, derived from the Just War tradition, which could be used, by global civil society, to assess the legitimacy of any illegal use of force portrayed as humanitarian. Evans described Operation Iraqi Freedom 'as a laboratory in which the [Just War] theory may be put to the most exacting tests'.[34] Global civil society and the Just War tradition clearly failed, however, to act as robust alternatives to the UN during the invasion of Iraq. While the invasion has ultimately proved unpopular, the massive public opposition to the war failed to stop the invasion. Additionally, when the primary rationale for the invasion – Iraq's arsenal of WMD – proved entirely flawed, public support was initially maintained when the previously secondary rationale – the humanitarian imperative – was more vociferously advanced.[35] Few argue that the US-led coalition acted in accordance with the Just War criteria but, ultimately, the governments of both states, and Blair and Bush in particular, would argue that they did. In the absence of any authoritative judge the question of adherence to non-binding criteria becomes so subjective as to be irresolvable.

It seems clear therefore that the process of lessening the power of the UN and increasing the role of global civil society has weakened the restraints on the use of force and significantly undermined the standing of the UN. The diminution of the UN's status as sole authority constitutes a clear aim of the normative thesis but, as argued in Chapter 5, this is a perspective predicated on an unrealistic view of global civil society's capacity as an alternative. The UN and positive international law more generally *do*, however, have the capacity to influence the behaviour of powerful states. The principle of sovereign equality, according to Simon Chesterman and Michael Byers, 'operates in a multitude of ways to constrain the law-making influence of the powerful'.[36] The tenets of international law have evolved in ways largely designed to constrain the capacity of powerful states to exclusively shape international norms and rules governing the use of force.[37] As Andrew Hurrell argues,

> The degree to which the legal order has grown more complex and harder for even powerful states to control is one of the reasons why US frustration with international law has grown sharper, shifting the balance between law's power-cementing and legitimacy creating advantages and its constraining and ensnaring costs.[38]

Indeed, Vittoria Emmanuel Parsi suggests that the US views the UN as 'a hindrance',[39] and it could be argued that the world's most powerful state *should* feel frustrated and hindered by the UN. Clearly the US is, like many other states, willing to act without authorization from the organization, but there is evidently a clear desire for UN legitimization when undertaking military action. The erosion of the UN's status as the authoritative source of legitimacy, as advocated by the normative thesis, can thus be said to have lessened existing restraints on aggression, increased the scope for the misuse of humanitarian rhetoric and fundamentally undermined the status of the UN.

The return of the crusaders

As noted in Chapter 2, international law has developed a set of rules and norms, described as the 'equalitarian regime', that rest on the principles of sovereign equality, sovereign inviolability and the circumscription of the use of force in international affairs.[40] Since the emergence of this regime in 1945, with the signing of the UN Charter, there has been a fourfold increase in the number of states, but also a decline in the number of interstate wars.[41] The effect of the codification of sovereign equality in the UN Charter and subsequent international legislation, in particular the 1960 General Assembly *Declaration on the Granting of Independence to Colonial Countries and Peoples* (1514), was that 'it no longer made sense to speak of a hierarchical society of states in which rights of membership and participation were granted in proportion to a society's development and capability'.[42]

This 'equalitarian regime' and the tenets of sovereignty in particular are the targets of the normative thesis and the proponents of global civil society. As noted in Chapter 3, the normative thesis advocates the diminution of sovereign inviolability and the creation of a system where there is a correlation between a state's human rights record and the legal rights it enjoys. Gerry Simpson describes the ideology behind this view as 'liberal anti-pluralism', characterizing it as 'endowed with a sort of moralistic fervour, a conviction and, at times, an intolerance of the illiberal'.[43] This 'formal rehierarchisation of international society' has important implications for the evolution of the international system and the conduct of international relations.[44]

Determining the circumstances under which states may legitimately use force in international affairs is of paramount importance. It is questionable whether constructing a hierarchy of states with differing competencies and rights will be beneficial to international peace and stability. International relations in the nineteenth century were characterized by such a hierarchy based on so-called 'standards of civilisation'.[45] This hierarchical system did not lead to peace and stability but rather 'fractured the international system for the best part of a century and the effects can still be felt today'.[46]

In terms of the discourse of intervention it is evident that a perceived schism between civilized and uncivilized states is being proliferated both consciously and unconsciously. Kaldor writes that in the post-Cold War world 'zones of civility and zones of incivility exist side by side'[47] and she has advocated a strategy of intervention whereby external actors identify 'islands of civility' within the zones of incivility with whom alliances can be made.[48] Similarly, Glennon advocates greater rights for 'enlightened states' while Robert Cooper asserts that the West's 'post-modern' consciousness means, 'Imperialism is dead, at least among Western powers' and thus Western intervention in the contemporary era is clearly different to that which took place during the period of colonialism.[49] The methods which must be employed, however, remain remarkably similar; Post-modern states, Cooper argues,

> need to get used to the idea of double standards ... when dealing with more old fashioned kinds of states outside the post-modern limits, Europeans need to revert to the rougher methods of an earlier era – force, pre-emptive attack, deception, whatever is necessary for those who still live in the 19th century world of every state for itself. In the jungle, one must use the laws of the jungle.[50]

The need for intervention is articulated in particularly stark terms by Tom Farer who asserts, 'peoples in a state of ecstatic mutual fear ... [are likely] to go on clawing at each other unless external actors can either club them into submission, break the stalemate ... and/or guarantee the safety of those willing to assume a defensive posture'.[51] The imagery of peoples 'clawing at each other' and external actors clubbing them into submission for their own good obviously resonates with the rationale advanced by those who advocated the 'civilising missions' to Africa in the 18th and 19th centuries. The advocates of the new hierarchical system thus 'ignore a history in which imperial powers announced and celebrated their superiority in similar language, with tragic consequences'.[52] This history is not confined to European colonialism; following the annexation of half the territory of Mexico in 1848 US President Polk stated, '[Had these territories remained part of Mexico they would have been] little value to her or any nation, while as part of our Union they will be productive of vast benefits to the United States, to the commercial world, and the general interests of mankind.' Fifty years later following the invasion of the Philippines US President McKinley stated, 'We intervene not for conquest. We intervene for humanity's sake [and to] earn the praises of every lover of freedom the world over.'[53]

The present discourse, which parallels that of earlier eras, essentially entails, according to Simpson, 'the idea of separating the globe into zones – the democratic-liberal or descent society of states operating in a sphere of cosmopolitan law and the failed state/outlaw state subsisting in the state of nature'.[54] This division of the world, as exemplified by Cooper's advice above, manifests in the creation of parallel legal systems which apply only to certain states. Certain legal codes, such as sovereign inviolability, apply only to the core group of states, while the laws governing the use of force by core states against those in the periphery are significantly relaxed. As Falk notes,

> the extreme version of this kind of politicised approach is to claim an exemption from legal constraint for itself while acting as an enforcer of the very same constraints with respect to those other states seen as challenging the established order of world politics. Such a posture has been adopted by the Bush administration.[55]

While this division is legitimized as a progressive development designed to lessen incidents of humanitarian crises and ultimately portrayed as a precursor to a more peaceful international system, evidence suggests that the incidence of warfare is likely to increase when such a perspective is dominant. Writing in the late seventeenth century Pufendorf argued,

> We are not to imagine that every man, even they who live in the liberty of nature, has a right to correct and punish with war any person

> who has done another an injury ... [for it is] ... contrary to the natural equality of mankind for a man to force himself upon the world for a judge and decider of controversies ... Any man might make war upon any man upon such a pleasure.[56]

The point made by Pufendorf is that when states believe themselves to be guardians of morality and the welfare of others they legitimize moral crusading and, given that moral codes differ and morality is inherently malleable, 'any man may make war upon any man' under such a system. As Bellamy notes, history shows that the rejection of positive law in favour of morality and the more nebulous natural law increases instability and incidences of war for this very reason.[57]

Positive law developed precisely because reliance on moral or natural law had created a situation where sovereigns were the sole judge of their actions and could therefore undertake myriad 'just interventions'. As Tucker observes, 'historically, states interpreted the principles of justice in war in such an elastic way that they have caused them to seem compatible with any act of war'.[58] Indeed, the ICISS found that in the ten cases of intervention they analysed 'the rhetoric of humanitarianism had been used most stridently in cases where the humanitarian motive was weakest'.[59] The danger is, therefore, that as the rights states enjoy become increasingly linked to their adherence to moral norms or human rights, as judged by a core group of self-appointed moral authorities, it is more likely that states will articulate moral justifications for their actions and military interventions. These justifications are inherently less objective and more malleable than legal codes, therefore this significantly increases the scope for self-interested intervention.

The belief in the need for both a proactive humanitarianism and the diminution of sovereign equality is predicated, as Michael Pugh observes, on the belief in the notion of 'soldiers of freedom' being 'dispatched from zones of peace into zones of unruliness and dysfunctional criminality to win conflicts against "rogue" governments'.[60] This perspective, indicative of what Oliver Richmond describes as 'a liberal and cosmopolitan faith on the part of the interveners in the infallibility of their approach', can be seen to have clear parallels with earlier more violent eras when just such rhetoric was used.

Christian Reus-Smit notes that the argument in support of benevolent interventionism is based on two dubious assumptions. First, that because non-democracies do not embody their citizen's will, 'the governments of democracies have a right to interpret that will and to act accordingly. And, second, that it would be the will of such peoples to see democratic states gain special international rights while the rights of their own states were compromised'.[61] Scepticism as to the benefits to be derived from realigning the international system in such a way has been voiced by non-Western state leaders; Hugo Chavez, unsurprisingly a critic of the new agenda, described *The Responsibility to Protect* as part of a movement whereby 'a few countries try to reinterpret the principles of international law in order to impose new doctrines' and he asked rhetorically, 'Who is going to protect us? Are they going to protect us?'.[62] This view echoes the negative response of developing states to NATO's intervention in Kosovo; in April 2000 the 133 states in the G-77 issued a declaration stating: 'We reject the so-called "right" of humanitarian intervention, which has no legal basis in the United Nations Charter or in general principles of international law.'[63] Given these countries' direct experiences of the consequences of an international system based on a presumed moral hierarchy this view is understandable.

Optimistic miscalculation

The proposals proffered by the normative thesis could potentially contribute to the escalation of intra-state conflicts and instances of violent state repression. Many intra-state wars in the post-Cold War era have comprised a conflict between a secessionist group and their host state's central government. In the face of their host state's implacability secessionist groups have often resorted to violence convinced that this strategy constitutes the most viable means of achieving their goals. This decision to resort to armed force will, assuming the rationality of those involved, constitute a calculation based on a cost–benefit analysis of the consequences of using force. If external 'humanitarian intervention' is a possibility then groups may conclude that they can provoke their host state into a retaliatory attack so severe that it will compel external forces to launch a humanitarian intervention on their behalf. Therefore, escalating the severity of their community's repression could be seen as beneficial in the long run. This scenario is worsened by the fact that, according to the normative thesis, the decision to intervene can be made by individual Western states without the approval of the UN which increases the secessionist's incentive to contrive a sufficiently large humanitarian crisis to garner Western media attention.

Studies suggest that in the majority of cases acts of genocide are retributive.[64] Alan Kuperman thus concludes that in most incidents 'rebels provoke their own group's demise by violently challenging the state's authority'.[65] Potential rebels, Kuperman argues, will only violently challenge the state if they believe that the consequences of doing so will ultimately be beneficial. Therefore, aside from instances where there is a misreading of the state's intentions or capabilities, rebels will use force only if they conclude that they have superior military strength, or if they believe the possibility exists that following their attack their host state will launch reprisals so severe that external actors will feel compelled to intervene. An escalation imperative is thus created, predicated on the logic 'the greater the tragedy the more likely the response'. The problem is thus twofold; while the possibility of intervention exists rebel groups that ordinarily would not have used military force may do so. Second, having attacked the state and provoked a retaliatory attack there is no guarantee that intervention will take place, therefore rebels may create and then endure a humanitarian crisis. According to Kuperman,

> [The norm of humanitarian intervention] encourages disgruntled sub-state groups to rebel because they expect intervention to protect them from genocidal retaliation by the state. Actual intervention, however, is often too late or feeble to prevent such retaliation. Thus, the norm causes some genocidal violence that otherwise would not occur.[66]

The possibility of external intervention, therefore, compromises the balance between the state and the secessionists. The state will tend towards the preservation of order and stability and will be reluctant to jeopardize this by launching a major military operation against passive, albeit disgruntled, secessionists. The secessionists, meanwhile, though dissatisfied, will have a similar interest in stability for fear of provoking harsh state retaliation. When the state's retaliation becomes perceived as a step towards external intervention this uneasy stability is jeopardized and violence can erupt.

The evolution of the conflict in Kosovo in the 1990s and the strategy of the Kosovo Liberation Army (KLA) is a compelling example of this theory in practice. While the Kosovo Albanians rejected Belgrade's authority and despised Milosevic's regime, especially after 1989, the violent tactics of the KLA were initially unpopular among the Kosovar Albanians who overwhelmingly supported the pacifism of Ibrahim Rugova and his party, the Democratic League of Kosovo. The rise in support for the KLA, especially after 1995, derived from the growth in frustration within the broader ethnic Albanian population at the lack of tangible results from Rugova's tactics. Despite winning international praise for extolling pacifism while violence raged in other parts of the Balkans, Rugova's strategy had paradoxically led external observers to conclude that the situation in Kosovo was a low priority. This was exemplified by the fact that Kosovo was ignored during the 1991 Carrington process despite Rugova's repeated efforts to achieve some recognition for his community's cause.[67] Similarly, the Dayton Accords, signed in 1995 – heralded as the final solution to Yugoslavia's violent collapse – made no mention of Kosovo. Article 1 of the Accords in fact recognized the territorial integrity of all parties to the agreement, thereby recognizing Yugoslavia's authority over Kosovo. This marked a key turning point for the Kosovo Albanians; according to Tim Judah, '[Dayton] confirmed to them in the most dramatic and humiliating way that Rugova's policy of passive resistance had failed. And not only that, but that his idea that they would be rewarded for their good behaviour by Western countries had been just plain wrong'.[68]

In certain key respects, such as the constitutional arrangements for Bosnia and the recognition afforded to Republic Srbska, the Dayton Accords legitimized ethnic identity as a political force and recognized ethnic territories. Additionally the consolidation of Bosnia's independence and Croatia's authority in Eastern Slavonia suggested that external intervention was a viable means of achieving territorial and political gain. External support in these cases was a consequence, however, of conflicts sufficiently violent to attract international media attention. Passive political struggle lost its appeal in the light of these lessons from Dayton. As Hodge notes, 'In effect Dayton told autonomists in Kosovo that the metal in Kosovo was not hot enough to bring about political change. The KLA decided to make it glow.'[69] Thereafter, according to James Gow, the KLA adopted a strategy of 'armed engagement designed to provoke atrocities'[70] which would generate international attention. Dugi Gorami, a Kosovo Albanian negotiator at the Rambouillet talks in 1999 outlined the logic behind the KLA's strategy: 'there was this foreign diplomat who once told me "Look unless you pass the quota of five thousand deaths you'll never have anybody permanently present in Kosovo from the foreign diplomacy"'.[71] International attention was contingent on mass tragedy and the KLA, not illogically, decided to create one.

Ultimately the KLA's gamble worked and NATO intervened. However, this strategy was clearly responsible for the deaths of many civilians who, it is reasonable to conclude, would not have died had the KLA not wished to provoke a humanitarian intervention. Hashim Thaci, leader of the KLA, admitted: 'We knew full well that any armed action we undertook would trigger a ruthless retaliation by Serbs against our people... We knew we were endangering civilian lives, too, a great number of civilian lives.'[72] Indeed, the initiation of the intervention by NATO caused a counter-action by the Yugoslav military against the KLA and contributed to the refugee flows which became the emotive image of NATO's campaign.

There is no guarantee, however, that external actors will always feel compelled to act. This leads to what Blainey describes as 'optimistic miscalculation'.[73] Kuperman's analysis of this phenomenon finds,

> in the post-Cold War era, a main source of such optimistic miscalculation has been the expectation by subordinate groups that the 'international community' will intervene to protect them on humanitarian grounds if their challenge to authority provokes retaliatory violence.[74]

The fate of the Kurds who rebelled against Saddam Hussein in 1991 is a sad illustration of what can happen when the rebel group's faith in external actors proves mistaken. More recently, the rebellion launched by in Darfur in 2003 would appear to have been an instance where similar logic catalysed a humanitarian crisis.

The problems highlighted above derive from the possibility of humanitarian intervention regardless of the identity of the interveners. If the UN had independent military capacity then similar difficulties could possibly still arise as the principle of escalating a conflict to compel external intervention would still apply.[75] This problem is exasperated, however, by the normative prescriptions which imbue Western states with the authority to determine when an intervention should take place. The logic behind this derives from the power supposedly wielded by global civil society. Domestic publics in Western states are more likely to see and hear about humanitarian crises due to their greater access to media and, through the democratic channels inherent in Western states, outraged citizens can pressurize their leaders to launch interventions to halt the suffering. The role of the domestic population is thus central to this normative cycle but so is that of the media.

Domestic populations are made aware of international issues predominately through domestic and international media and therefore media coverage is the catalyst for public outrage and ultimately state action. The international media is not, however, an objective, dispassionate source of information. Even leaving aside the potential for individual or collective bias in media reportage it is axiomatic that the vast majority of media groups are profit-orientated. In this sense they cover stories they believe will interest the general public who are consumers in this equation. It is highly likely, therefore, that conflicts with the highest death toll or involving barbaric acts of violence will be reported most. Additionally, it is more likely that a crisis which resonates with the Western public's imagination will receive more coverage than that which involves groups with whom empathy is less developed. As Christine Chinkin notes, 'It is better to be a refugee in Europe (where "they look like us") than in Africa.'[76] Additionally, due to financial considerations and political barriers media groups are restricted in their capacity. A crisis in Eastern Europe is thus more likely to be covered than the situation in Chechnya or Tibet. Between 1998 and 2003 some four million people were killed in the Democratic Republic of the Congo (DRC), yet this conflict received scant international attention. This point was noted by Nelson Mandela who highlighted the disparity between the attention Kosovo received and the many arguably worse humanitarian crises occurring in Africa at the time.[77]

The problem is not with the media's reportage as such, however; media groups are entitled to pursue profitable stories. The problem lies with the fact that these profit-orientated organizations are central to the normative evolution of humanitarian intervention. Citizens in Western democracies can, of course, receive information on international crises from NGO's, the UN and other sources, but interest in these reports obviously pales in comparison to popular media outlets. Subordinate groups involved in a dispute with their host state could reasonably conclude, as the KLA did, that they must provoke greater levels of violence and killing to attract the media's attention. If intervention by Western states is championed as the solution to humanitarian crises, and if the normative perspective on the evolution of Western action involves a progression from media reportage to public outrage to political action, then there are clear incentives on the part of subordinate groups to escalate the scale of the violence within their respective area. Media coverage, however, will be inconsistent and will not necessarily reflect those cases of greatest need. Finally, as demonstrated in Chapter 5, it is not at all clear that domestic pressure to intervene will necessarily result in military intervention and therefore conflicts will be worsened in the expectation of external intervention which fails to materialize.

Conclusion

On 19 March 2003, the day the invasion of Iraq began, UN Secretary General Kofi Annan stated, 'we must all feel that this is a sad day for the UN and the International community.'[78] The UN had, in many respects, performed its functions to the best of its ability in the pre-invasion diplomacy, yet the invasion was a clear blow to its status and credibility. Prior to the invasion the UN had acted as a forum for debate between the various interested parties and states and regularly updated the Security

Council, the General Assembly and the wider international community on the situation in Iraq, especially through the work of Hans Blix and the Atomic Energy Committee. In the end the UN's efforts were unsuccessful as both its power and perspective were ignored. It seems clear that the great effort made by the US and the UK to gain UN assent for the invasion was born from a perspective which viewed the UN as no more than a welcome, but ultimately unnecessary, stamp of approval.

Many of Operation Iraqi Freedom's most vociferous opponents were supporters of Operation Allied Force four years earlier. The logic of NATO's actions in 1999, however, evidenced a similar attitude to the UN. Clearly, it would be an exaggeration to suggest that Operation Iraqi Freedom was a consequence of Operation Allied Force. The continuities between the two operations are, however, quite clear. It is indisputable that advocates of the invasion of Iraq often pointed out that the intervention in Kosovo had also been illegal but legitimate. The perspective widely avowed in March 1999 would thus seem to have contributed to the erosion of the status of the UN and international law which were characteristic of the later invasion of Iraq. As Orford notes, 'Legal literature discussing the legitimacy of the actions undertaken by NATO appears to indicate a loss of faith in international law as a repository of the values that should underpin the actions of international organisations.'[79] This loss of faith in international law and the attendant acceptance that the UN was not the world's only legitimate authority was a central aspect of the pro-invasion perspective in 2003. The normative thesis' position on the UN and the attempts to find 'legitimate' alternatives to the organization would appear, therefore, to have contributed to the UN's contemporary predicament.

The rhetoric supportive of the normative thesis is often didactic and paternalistic premised on an emphatic vision of a sharply bifurcated world characterized by extreme moral contrasts. The West, undoubtedly the most powerful group of states in the world, is characterized as the repository of the most enlightened system and imbued with the most benevolent outlook. Western states are thus implored by the normative thesis to transcend international law and reach out to support the oppressed around the world languishing in the so-called 'zones of incivility'.[80] Edward Said noted that central to imperialism was the conviction that 'certain territories and peoples require and beseech domination'.[81] This logic of benevolent hegemony is readily evident in the prescriptions advanced by the normative thesis and evident in the discourse supportive of both intervention and state-building.[82] Aside from the questionable morality of such a view, history suggests that a world organized by powerful states on the basis of a perceived equation between ethics and rights is more unstable and violent than one built on the notion of sovereign equality. Replacing contemporary international law and the 'equalitarian regime' conceived at San Francisco in 1945 with a hierarchical system based on moral rather than positive law thus poses significant risks for international peace and stability. Reus-Smit argues that such a development would

> only exacerbate already widespread feelings about inequities of the present international order, reduce the sense of investment of many states in the institutional architecture and rules of international society, and, as a consequence, heighten rather than diminish conflict and discord.[83]

According to Hayden the realist inspired world of sovereign states is marked by 'the instability of power struggles [and] the casual resort to armed conflict'.[84] Yet, the vision of a world without sovereign equality ordered according to moral rather than positive law would seem to have the potential to increase these negatives.

Finally, the normative perspective on the means by which humanitarian crises will be addressed risks escalating intra-state conflicts. States are ostensibly compelled to act by their outraged citizenry and these citizens become mobilized by emotive images or descriptions of slaughter they are exposed to through the media. It is clear, therefore, that conflicts which generate extreme violence will be addressed first, provided, of course, that the media deems these conflicts worthy of coverage. As the war in the DRC demonstrates certain conflicts are evidently deemed too costly or of insufficient public interest to cover. Additionally, the centrality of the mass media and its need to broadcast and publish shocking (and hence interesting) news creates an escalation imperative. Subordinate groups may conclude, as the KLA did, that they require external support to achieve their aims and that this support can only be achieved by generating external revulsion at mass murder and extreme violence. Conflicts may thus be deliberately escalated by subordinate groups to provoke state repression and external intervention. While this will definitely result in more lives being lost it need not necessarily compel external actors to intervene, leading to the phenomenon of 'optimistic miscalculation'.

The power of global civil society and its representative nature convinced some that it should be seen as the primary source of authority and legitimacy to which the UN, in fact, must be made accountable.[85] This expressed desire for the diminution of the UN's importance does not derive, however, from a desire to destroy either it or international law. As Vaclav Havel stated regarding Operation Allied Force, 'although it has no direct mandate from the UN, it did not happen as an act of aggression or out of disrespect for international law'.[86] It is also very clear that adherents to the normative perspective do not wish to compromise international peace and security or cause the escalation of intra-state crises. This Chapter has sought to demonstrate that the normative thesis, despite the intentions of its advocates, has in fact articulated proposals and ideas which have contributed to the rapid decline in the UN's status and the deterioration of international peace and stability. This irony – the adverse consequence of good intentions – was highlighted by Hedley Bull, who warned,

> Particular states or groups of states that set themselves up as the authoritative judges of the world common good, in disregard of the views of others, are in fact a menace to international order, and thus to effective action in that field.

Chapter 4 demonstrated the extent to which the normative prescriptions and predictions have not equated with international relations since 1999, and this Chapter has highlighted the adverse effects of the normative position. The following Chapter advances a means by which the goals advanced by the normative thesis, and many others, regarding the alleviation of human suffering could be achieved while maintaining the integrity of the UN and international law.

7
Regulating Humanitarian Intervention: The Need for Redirection

Introduction

The situation in Kosovo in 1999 propelled the issue of humanitarian intervention to top of the international political agenda. Writing at the time Kai Ambos declared, 'The Kosovo crisis dramatically shows the limits of international law.'[1] NATO did offer a legal justification for its intervention but few endorsed their reading of international law. Far more persuasive however were the moral justifications articulated by NATO and its supporters. The dominant view was that Operation Allied Force, as famously asserted by the Independent International Commission on Kosovo, was illegal but legitimate. This gap between legitimacy and legality clearly highlighted a deficiency in positive international law.

Tom Farer notes that humanitarian intervention as a concept 'has subsisted on the shadowy periphery of international law, episodically invoked with varying degrees of hypocrisy, more as a political/ethical than a legal justification for usually short-term military operations across frontiers'.[2] This description of humanitarian intervention existing in the 'shadowy periphery' is indeed accurate as is Farer's reference to its dubious historical record. The history of humanitarian intervention does not inspire confidence and it is clear that there are very few, if indeed any, cases considered to be unequivocal instances of such action.[3] The rise in concern for 'human security' in the post-Cold War era focused renewed attention on the status of humanitarian intervention, and proponents of the normative thesis have essentially sought to drag this issue from the periphery to the very centre of international relations.

The solution offered by the normative thesis to the perennial problem of humanitarian intervention has been outlined in Chapter 3 and critiqued in the three subsequent chapters. This chapter offers an alternative means by which humanitarian intervention can become an accepted practice in international relations. The aim here is not to provide a detailed, comprehensive proposal; such an undertaking would constitute a book in itself. Rather this chapter demonstrates that one's view on the status of humanitarian intervention does not necessarily constitute either the normative thesis or the realist perspective; an alternative, based on reforming international law, exists.

According to Andrew Hurrell, 'The degree to which international society is affected morally and practically by humanitarian catastrophe means that we need new rules on humanitarian intervention.'[4] The old status of humanitarian intervention – that of the shadowy periphery – can no longer be sustained and the issue must be clarified or the ambiguity and subjectivity surrounding it will continue to cause division and paralyse efforts to halt mass suffering. International law since 1945 has established ever more treaties on human rights and codified the responsibilities states have towards their citizens. It has not, however, clarified the conditions under which the violation of these rights would justify external intervention. Clear rules would serve to remove the subjectivity currently inherent in humanitarian intervention, as detailed in Chapter 6. This in itself, however, would not be a sufficiently comprehensive amendment. Again, Hurrell argues, 'a new rule on humanitarian intervention would [not] obviate the need for institutions and for institutional debate. Even if a rule is agreed and even if the background criteria for evaluation are agreed, all rules have to be interpreted and applied to the circumstances of a particular case'.[5] The prescriptions advanced here seek to address both the need for legal clarity regarding the relationship between human rights and sovereign inviolability and the institutional reforms required to make such clarification effective. This chapter begins by arguing that the normative thesis has addressed the wrong aspect of the 'problem' of humanitarian intervention and has undermined the effectiveness of the only viable means by which the actions of states can be consistently constrained in the long term, namely, international law. Having outlined the reforms required this chapter then proceeds to defend these reforms against the dominant counterpoints which have, historically and in the contemporary era, marginalized this approach to the issue.

Misdiagnosing the problem

In the early years of the post-Cold War era many supporters of the principle of humanitarian intervention became increasingly frustrated with the constraints imposed by international law, the impotence of international institutions and the evident reluctance of states, including Western states, to act altruistically. The obstacles to humanitarian intervention were therefore perceived as both institutional and attitudinal.

The institutional obstacles manifest as the status of sovereignty in positive international law and the UN's stasis caused by the (increasingly highlighted) veto powers of the permanent five members (P5). Given the scale of the problems presented by the structure of the UN, the complexity of international law and not least the attitudes of the veto-wielding P5, the most plausible solution to the problem of humanitarian inaction was deemed to be addressing the attitudinal obstacle. Driven by cosmopolitan principles the 'new humanitarians' thus focused on mobilizing global civil society to pressurize Western states to behave morally in their foreign affairs, even if this action was not strictly legal. Humanitarian advocates, convinced that democracies were naturally receptive to domestic pressure, felt they could exercise a moral leverage on Western political leaders previously impossible during the Cold War when the fear of nuclear Armageddon naturally curtailed foreign policy options. Therefore the conscious disregard for international law in favour of cultivating a change in attitude among Western states was deemed to be the strategy required to achieve the realization of the humanitarian's vision.[6]

The role of international law, therefore, has been consciously marginalized through the strategy adopted by the normative perspective. International law's restrictive view of sovereignty and disregard for 'domestic issues' ostensibly enabled despotic regimes to massacre civilians with impunity, and the international legal regime has been conceptualized as part of the problem and an obstacle to the vision of the humanitarians. The principle of sovereign inviolability, enshrined in the Charter, prevented, and prevents, effective action and this flaw inherent in the basic element of international law – the sovereign state – supposedly undermined the entire legal regime.[7] International law has, consequently, been increasingly portrayed as anachronistic, overly restrictive and a barrier to the realization of human rights.

The notion that international law has been integral to the lack of effective action in response to intra-state humanitarian crises is, however, fundamentally flawed. The idea that international law has prevented willing saviours from helping suffering innocents is a fiction. As Simon Chesterman notes,

> Implicit in many arguments for a right of humanitarian intervention is the suggestion that international law currently prevents interventions

> that should take place. This is simply not true. Interventions do not take place because states choose not to undertake them.[8]

The problem is not that international law exercises a constraining influence over the actions of states, but rather that states have been able to act outside of the present legal framework. States have *chosen* whether or not to intervene and the influence of international law on this choice has been marginal and certainly secondary to state's conceptions of their national interest. The problem, as such, has been the inability of international law to compel or prevent intervention due to its limited capacity to override state interest. It is difficult to think of any case where a state wanted to intervene but didn't purely because it would be illegal to do so. State power and interest have, therefore, been the key variables influencing whether intervention takes place.

As noted in Chapter 3, advocates of the normative perspective have sought to constrain state power through the mobilization of global civil society. The logic driving this strategy is based on the idea that if states can be made to act more morally and socialized into a cosmopolitan disposition, humanitarian crises will be halted. States will act morally in their foreign affairs and be prevented from abusing the new scope for illegal action by the constraining influence of global civil society. As Chapter 4 demonstrated, however, the capacity of global civil society has been significantly overestimated. In effect, the limited constraints previously acting upon state action – namely, international law – have been lessened and the alternative constraints – namely, global civil society – have proved largely impotent.

Proponents of the normative thesis have argued that their cosmopolitan perspective 'decentres the state'.[9] In fact the strategy of the normative thesis has, both consciously and unconsciously, accentuated the asymmetrical relationship between powerful states and international law. Having determined that international law was a problem to be overcome, proponents of the normative thesis, as outlined in Chapter 3, have sought to compel Western states to literally take the law into their own hands and intervene when morality demands it. This increases the power of certain states at the expensive of international law. Therefore the 'modest constraints of international law' have been significantly diminished by the normative strategy.[10]

The normative thesis has, therefore, effectively misdiagnosed the problem. Buoyed by a misconceived perception of its own capacity, global civil society has sought not to address the weaknesses inherent in international law's enforcement mechanisms but to catalyse a fundamental attitudinal sea change in Western perceptions of their foreign policy interests. The problem has been conceived as one involving the need to lift the legal restrictions on state action and increase the capacity of certain states to exercise their independent judgement, albeit a judgement largely moulded by global civil society. In fact the real problem central to the spectacle of what Chesterman describes as 'inhumanitarian non-intervention'[11] relates to the weakness of international law and the ability of states to act without significant constraint.

The idea of strengthening international law has, however, been rejected by many proponents of the normative approach. According to Terry Nardin the basis for regulating humanitarian intervention must be 'common morality' rather than international law because the latter 'rests on custom and agreement, not moral reasoning'.[12] This preference for moral reasoning over international law evidences a great faith in both the objective existence of universal morality and the efficacy of moral norms. Alex Bellamy explicitly rejects reformulating positive law, instead advocating a policy orientated towards constructing criteria which will act as constraints on state action. If states abuse the new scope for intervention, global civil society will 'expose the abuse as such, and... confront the perpetrators with the unjustness of their actions in order to constrain potential abusers through normative pressure at the domestic and international level'.[13] Nardin's privileging of common morality and Bellamy's faith in normative pressure appear misplaced and idealistic in light of the events since Operation Allied Force, which has been identified in Chapter 4. Universal common morality, accepting there is such a thing, is clearly more subjective and malleable than Nardin suggests while states are evidently largely untroubled by popular moral outrage and unlikely to view Bellamy's punitive measures as a major deterrent.

The seminal report *The Responsibility to Protect* of ICISS similarly puts great emphasis on altering the disposition of states rather than the law acting upon them. *The Responsibility to Protect* acknowledges the mixed record of the Security Council but nonetheless offers a prescription dependent on the goodwill of the five permanent members. The five are implored to observe a voluntary 'code of conduct'.

> The idea essentially is that a permanent member, in matters where its vital national interests were not claimed to be involved, would not use its veto to obstruct the passage of what would otherwise be a majority resolution.[14]

This prescription does nothing, however, to address the fundamental problem with humanitarian intervention, namely, the influence of power and state interest on the determination of when and where to intervene. The voluntary nature of this code is clearly problematic but aside from this the essence of the proposal contributes nothing new. It is difficult to conceive of a situation where the interests of one of the five members are not at least tangentially at stake but, if such a situation were to arise, then why would the veto be used? Clearly if, as in the ICISS's scenario, a crisis erupts which none of the P5 have any national interests in, it is likely that the P5 will agree at least that the situation comes under Chapter VII of the UN Charter, if not necessarily that it warrants external intervention. Historically, Security Council inertia has been a function of situations involving national interest when the response to humanitarian tragedy has become politicized. The idea that the P5 will adhere to a non-binding, voluntary code which is ultimately dependent on their subjective interpretations of their own national interest appears hopelessly idealistic in light of actual state practice.

The proposals advanced by Nardin, Bellamy and the ICISS are therefore indicative of a broader trend, namely, the attempt to make states moral actors and the belief in the ability of moral pressure to achieve this goal. This strategy ostensibly worked in 1999 when NATO intervened in Kosovo, yet the record since suggests that at best Operation Allied Force was an aberration, a moment when state interests and humanitarian advocacy coincided. As noted in Chapter 6, the attempt to repeal international law and undermine the UN's authority in favour of moral advocacy and a faith in the benevolence of Western foreign policy has done little to address the problem of 'inhumanitarian non-intervention', as evidenced by the situation in Darfur. The moral approach has in fact created increased scope for abusing the rhetoric of humanitarian intervention, as evidenced by the US-led invasion of Iraq. The project to change the behaviour of states – to alter their conceptions of national interest and constrain their action – has evidently failed.

The need for legal clarity

The regulatory capacity of global civil society is manifestly incapable of acting as a sufficiently robust constraint on state behaviour. The solution to the problem of what to do when a humanitarian crisis erupts within an uncooperative or incapable state should therefore be sought via international law rather than nebulous and ineffective moral aspirations. This section outlines the deficiencies of the status quo and suggests a means by which these deficiencies could be overcome which, unlike the normative thesis' proposals, do not necessarily undermine international law.

The deficiencies of the status quo

The debate surrounding humanitarian intervention derives from the question of what to do when a humanitarian crisis occurs within a state which is either unwilling or unable to halt the suffering of its own citizens. Whether or not an 'answer' or solution *is* required is, of course, a matter of some contention. While calls for intervention have increasingly been made in the post-Cold War era, the desire to contrive means to address humanitarian crises is not universally held.

Support for, and the promotion of, humanitarian intervention is born from a moral judgement. The relationship between morality and international relations is one of significant concern for realists. E. H. Carr's famous assertion, 'Theories of morality are... the product of dominant nations or groups of nations'[15] became totemic for later realists such as Hans Morgenthau who argued that 'universal moral principles cannot be applied to the actions of states.'[16] Neo-realists, emphasizing the structural constraints compelling states to act, 'do not even bother with morality' disregarding it entirely as a factor in international relations.[17] The application of morality to international relations, manifest in this instance as the attempt to facilitate humanitarian intervention, is thus fundamentally rejected by the realist position. This is not to say that realism is immoral but rather that it conceives of morality as inherently destabilizing and ultimately not a genuine compulsion for state action.

Previous chapters have potentially added credence to this view. It is certainly clear that the humanitarian rhetoric espoused by states, even Western democracies, since Operation Allied Force has often been hypocritical and occasionally spurious. Research suggests that when humanitarian justifications have been articulated by intervening states they have invariably been, if not always, outright lies, at least not as important a motive as the rhetoric espoused has suggested.[18] Carl Schmidt's famous assertion – 'He who invokes humanity wants to cheat'[19] – thus appears to have contemporary applicability.[20]

It is my contention, however, that despite the historical record of humanitarian intervention in actual state practice it is both right and necessary to attempt to contrive means by which humanitarian crises can be halted. This is, of course, a normative perspective and thus may appear incongruous in the context of my earlier critique of the 'normative thesis'. The critique advanced in earlier chapters, however, did not focus on the *principle* of normative theorizing or the notion of 'saving strangers' but rather on the *strategy* adopted by the dominant normative perspective.

It is inevitable that humanitarian crises will erupt in the future, and it is both impractical and morally indefensible to countenance inertia in the face of mass humanitarian tragedy. Impractical because the global media can generate immense public disquiet at human rights violations, which can develop into significant pressure to assist victims of oppression. A survey carried out in 1999 among 1000 UN officials with experience in Yugoslavia found that over three-quarters believed that the media had influenced the course of events in the region.[21] The media impacts significantly on the calls for humanitarian intervention and this influence strengthens the argument for amending the current status of intervention. The media, though a beneficial source of information, are not a suitable judge for determining when and where interventions should occur. The ability of the media to highlight certain human rights abuses and ignore others suggests that journalists cannot be relied upon to impartially and equitably assess when intervention is warranted.[22] In addition to problems of access and availability of information, there is the potential fear that media sources may be biased advocates, either covertly or overtly, of certain policy objectives. Additionally, the nature of media is that it must engage, if not titillate, otherwise uninformed sections of society and, to that end, journalistic enquiry must conform to certain stylistic requirements. In relation to intra-state conflicts this reportage often takes the form of what Bentham describes as the 'fairy story'.[23] This manipulation of the truth firstly involves a hapless victim, secondly, a clear villain and thirdly, a potential or active saviour, usually NATO or individual Western powers. This simplification has meant, according to Philip Hammond, that 'our understanding of these conflicts has been distorted by simplistic narratives of good versus evil' which distort the true picture.[24] Given that media reportage is not necessarily immune from bias, and is, in certain instances, explicitly partisan, mechanisms for determining when and where to intervene should not be based on media reportage. As the ICISS notes, 'Thanks to the modern media, some humanitarian crises receive a surfeit of attention, while others languish in indifference and neglect. Some crises are exaggerated by media coverage and ill-considered calls for action skew the response of the international community in an inconsistent and undisciplined manner.'[25]

Additionally, given the reality of human rights abuses and the increased, albeit selective, awareness of both states and citizens to these abuses, it is naive to expect that states will refrain from acting to prevent human rights abuses, or alleged human rights abuses, because international law is deficient in this area. As the ICISS notes, 'if the Security Council fails to discharge its responsibility in conscience-shocking situations crying out for action, then it is unreasonable to expect that concerned states will rule out other means and forms of action to meet the gravity and urgency of these situations.'[26] Indeed, at its Fiftieth Anniversary NATO announced, 'Even though all NATO member states undoubtedly would prefer to act with such mandates [from the Security Council] they must not limit themselves to acting only when such a mandate can be agreed.'[27] The present status of humanitarian intervention will, therefore, lead to unilateral determinations that 'something has to be done' and the ICISS warns, 'such interventions will not be conducted for the right reasons or with the right commitment to the necessary precautionary principles'.[28] Therefore, an acceptance that certain violations of human rights are unacceptable demands a means by which these violations can be halted and the perpetrators punished and thus a clarification of a right of intervention.

The status quo is morally indefensible for the simple, albeit possibly subjective, reason that one cannot be content with an international system that lacks the means by which to halt egregious human suffering quickly and consistently. It is, of course, a matter of personal opinion but it is difficult to believe that anyone who has read the reports of the events in Rwanda in 1994 could conclude that, awful as it was, nothing should, or can, be done to prevent such a tragedy from reoccurring.

Enforcing existing laws

As Chapter 2 noted, humanitarian intervention is considered by the majority of observers to be illegal. International law is not, however, silent on the issue of human rights and there are many international treaties outlining the basic human rights all individuals are entitled to. The problem lies, therefore, with the lack of clear legal guidelines as to the enforcement mechanisms available to maintain or compel compliance with these rights especially within the UN Charter.

The UN Charter outlines certain aspirations regarding human rights; Article 55(3) states that the UN will promote 'universal respect for, and observance of, human rights and fundamental freedoms for all without distinction as to race, sex, language, or religion'. Under Article 56 all member states 'pledge themselves to take joint and separate action in co-operation with the Organization for the achievement of the purposes set forth in Article 55'. The Charter, however, does not identify the specific obligations all member states have to their citizens. Arguably more importantly, the Charter does not specify the obligations upon states when one state consciously violates the human rights of its own citizens.

Instead the Charter articulates 'loose formulas' containing often contradictory and ambiguous provisions.[29] This legal lacuna coupled with the lack of political will has contrived to create the situation we face today.

During the drafting of the Charter three groups formed with differing perspectives on how to include human rights in the Charter. The first group, made up predominately of Latin American states, sought to have clear obligations noted in the Charter. A second group of Western states strongly objected to the specification of obligations especially obligations relating to states not directly involved in a humanitarian crisis. The third group of socialist states largely adhered to the Western perspective but sought specific provisions regarding the right to self-determination. The outcome of the discussions between these groups constituted a compromise between the Western and the socialist groups with the Latin American perspective largely ignored.[30] The provisions agreed removed any reference to human rights obligations, described the right of self-determination only as a 'guiding principle' and limited the General Assembly's power in the area of human rights. Ultimately, according to Antonio Cassese, 'the Charter provisions on human rights were inspired by the conviction that respect for human rights should only be furthered as a means of safeguarding peace.'[31] Thus, the UN Charter, the fulcrum of international law, fails to provide clear guidelines regarding human rights and this failure is, in large part, a consequence of the concerted efforts of Western states.

Many major human rights treaties have been signed since the UN Charter came into force in October 1945, though the impact of these treaties has been limited. States have demonstrated a willingness to publicly support human rights, increasingly so in the post-Cold War era but as David Armstrong, Theo Farrell and Helene Lambert note, 'we should be cautious in inferring increasing compliance from increasing rhetorical commitment to human rights.'[32] Indeed, the proliferation of these expressions of concern for, and commitment to, human rights have not been accompanied by an attendant alteration in the Charter's provisions for dealing with violations of human rights. The result is a large body of both treaty and customary law related to human rights which lacks clear means by which these laws can be enforced. As noted by Armstrong, Farrell and Lambert,

> many human rights treaties, especially at the international level, do not contain enforcement mechanisms. States are merely obliged to self-validate compliance with these treaties through period reports and even this reporting obligation is poorly complied with'.[33]

States are subject to scrutiny by UN bodies such as the Human Rights Council (formerly the UN Commission on Human Rights), the Human Rights Committee and the Office of the UN High Commissioner for Human Rights. Compliance with even just the supervisory role of these organizations, however, is poor and the enforcement capacity and effectiveness of these organizations is minimal.

The nature of human rights differentiates this area of international law from the laws governing inter-state relations. As Malgozia Fitzmaurice states, 'Human rights treaties are not contractual in nature and do not create rights and obligations between States on the traditional basis of reciprocity; they establish relationships between States and individuals.'[34] In this respect, as Louis Henkin notes, 'compliance with human rights law…is wholly internal.'[35] States, therefore, may well agree among themselves as to the standards they should uphold domestically but ultimately the necessarily domestic nature of compliance with these agreements limits the effect the inter-state context of the original treaty can have. Non-compliance with these treaties results in negative consequences only for the domestic citizenry and not other signatories to the treaty. Highlighting this situation, the DIIA states:

> There is an asymmetry between the means of enforcement and the potential for violations of international legal norms. Violators of, for instance, human rights norms are protected by the high standards of international law concerning state sovereignty and the non-use of force, whereas enforcement action against them is dependant on political organs and conditions and they need not accept compulsory international jurisdiction.[36]

The gap between treaty (and customary) law in this area and enforcement mechanisms is obviously problematic and central to the debate surrounding humanitarian intervention.

The provisions of Chapter VII of the UN Charter have been identified as a means by which this gap can be closed. As noted in Chapter 2, however, while the interpretation of Chapter VII has expanded to facilitate intervention in a number of cases since the end of the Cold War, these cases do not evidence any consistency but appear rather more like instances when humanitarian need and political expediency coincided.[37] Cassese notes that the Security Council has 'considerably enlarged' the concept of threat to the peace noted in Article 39 of the UN Charter so as to include intra-state humanitarian crises. However, he also observes that

> The SC is eager to retain discretionary power in this matter and tends to avoid explaining the nature of the link and the reasons for its action. As a result its practice lacks consistency and turns out to be selective... African countries have railed against the fact that some humanitarian disasters in Africa...have not motivated the SC so strongly as some previous cases.[38]

Additionally, Chapter VII does not advance clear guidelines on how a domestic crisis can come to be considered a threat to international peace and stability, and there are limits to the Security Council's competencies in invoking Chapter VII.[39] While various treaties and conventions since the Charter was implemented have specified what rights individuals should enjoy, they have not articulated enforcement measures and procedures outside the UN Charter.

This leads to a key problem with the existing system. The vast corpus of human rights treaties lack attendant means of enforcement and are reliant upon the Charter's provisions. These provisions, covered under Chapter VII, are essentially ill-suited to being applied to intra-state crises. Even if one maintains that Chapter VII, imperfect as it is, *can* be applied to intra-state crises there remains a key barrier to enforcement, namely, the interests of the P5. Unless the P5 agree to it, no enforcement action can be ordered under Chapter VII. An example is provided by the provisions of the 1948 Genocide Convention. Article 8 of the Convention states 'Any Contracting Party may call upon the competent organs of the United Nations to take such action under the Charter of the United Nations as they consider appropriate for the prevention and suppression of acts of genocide or any of the other acts enumerated in article III.' In practice, the 'competent organ' of the UN is the Security Council. Thus if states believe that genocide is occurring and wish to stop it, the matter is referred to the Security Council. The crisis in Darfur has been described as genocide by many states, including the US and UN missions to the region. The matter was referred to the Security Council and while it determined that the situation constituted a threat to international peace and stability, and certain members agreed that the Sudanese government was orchestrating the genocide, no effective action was taken by the P5.[40] Additionally, as noted in Chapter III, the manner in which the provisions of *The Responsibility to Protect* were adopted at the 2005 World Summit stipulated that the Security Council had to sanction the action leading some to argue that the original Report had lost its potency.[41] The Security Council may conclude that a situation constitutes a threat to international peace and stability but ultimately this determination means little and is a declaration which compels no further action. The argument that new laws are not required because of the Security Council's capacity to use Chapter VII creatively is thus flawed. Use of Chapter VII can mean nothing more than a collective designation.

As noted earlier, the ICISS suggested a voluntary 'code of conduct' for the Security Council which appears to have little hope of success. In a similar vein the 2004 UN High-Level Panel on Threats, Challenges and Change articulated 'five basic criteria of legitimacy' which the Security Council 'should always address' in considering whether to authorize the use of force.[42] Yet these are advisory prescriptions which do not address the fundamental, and perennial, problem of the P5's interests. Hurrell notes that the Security Council has significant competencies and scope to interpret the provisions of Chapter VII and apply them when they see fit. 'The problem' however 'concerns the structural obstacles that work against effective collective action'.[43] These obstacles manifest as the difficulty involved in achieving consensus among the P5, a difficulty born from their respective, and often mutually exclusive, national interests. Hurrell thus charges the Panel with evading the crucial issue, namely, 'what status are these "criteria for legitimacy" supposed to have in precisely those difficult cases when the Council is unable to act?'.[44] The Security Council has no record of acting in the interests of common humanity to the determent of any of its members own national interests[45] and it is difficult to imagine that the blandishments of this UN panel or the ICISS will alter this disposition.

The enforcement of the plethora of existing human rights treaties is, therefore, dependant on strained interpretations of Chapter VII and the whims of the P5. This has led to the emergence of the normative perspective; frustrated with the restrictions and inconsistencies of international law and ultimately despairing of the Security Council's centrality and disposition, many have looked to global civil society and the ostensible benevolence of Western states to close the gap between law and enforcement. While I agree that the status quo is untenable, the solution need not be that proffered by the normative thesis.

Legal reform

Supporters of Operation Allied Force obviously welcomed the finding of the Independent International Commission on Kosovo (IICK) that the intervention was 'illegal but legitimate'. One aspect of the IICK's report which received less publicity was the corollary; 'Allowing this gap between legality and legitimacy to persist is not healthy.'[46] The status quo is, as I have suggested above, acknowledged to be unsatisfactory by many who advocate fundamental legal reform on the basis of the damage done by the persistence of the gap between legitimacy and legality identified by the IICK. According to the ICISS,

> the issue of international intervention for human protection is a clear and compelling example of concerted action urgently being needed to bring international norms and institutions in line with international needs and expectations. [47]

Similarly Bruno Simma noted that the obstacles to addressing human suffering 'could only be removed by changing the law of the UN Charter',[48] while Catherine Guicherd advocates a 'focus on consolidating embryonic practices into a clear and strong body of law to allow intervention on humanitarian grounds'.[49]

The basis for the need for legal reform derives from two key deficiencies; first, the lack of clear guidelines outlining the circumstances under which states forfeit their right to sovereign inviolability and an objective assessment mechanism for determining when these conditions have been reached. Second, the lack of any means by which intervention can take place automatically when intra-state crises are deemed to have degenerated to a certain level. In light of these problems with the status quo, effective reform needs to comprise two elements. First the authorization of intervention would have to become the sole preserve of an international body, within the UN, comprising officials elected by the General Assembly to represent the UN and not individual states. This group would be tasked with determining, on the basis of existing international law and reports from objective observers on the ground, when a situation required external intervention. A declaration that intervention was required would obviously legitimize any subsequent intervention. Simply calling for intervention would not overcome the second problem; states could ignore the call. Therefore the second aspect of the reform would require the establishment of an international force commanded by the UN which could be deployed once the authorization for intervention has been given but state willingness to intervene is lacking.

The scale of such reform is clearly enormous and the obstacles to its realization myriad and immense. While it is highly unlikely that these provisions will be adopted anytime soon, I would argue that this legal route is nonetheless *more* likely to materialize than the prescriptions advanced by the normative thesis. Given the evolution of international law even in the short period since the end of World War II it is surely an exaggeration to argue that further codification and the creation of enforcement mechanisms is utterly impossible. Given the history of international relations since the Peloponnesian War, however, it seems fair to argue that moral pressure, the articulation of ethical aspirations and the dissemination of non-binding criteria for the 'just' use of force will never constitute effective constraints on the actions of states. Accepting, however, the reality that these proposals are highly unlikely to come to pass, the following sections will justify the *principle* of such reform and defend it against the primary objections to this hypothetical development.

Defending legal reform

Having discussed these proposals with many experts in the field, the initial reaction to the solution articulated above focuses on the fact that such a radical alteration of the existing system would be highly unlikely. It would be foolish to challenge this view. It is, however, not necessarily incumbent upon academics to limit themselves to positivist observation, and similarly, once one accepts the merits of normative theorizing, it seems counterintuitive to limit oneself to prescriptions deemed 'realistic' by others. If the proposal or prescriptions can be defended in principle then the fact that they are ambitious or unlikely to manifest need not undermine the entire exercise. The proposals can be challenged, however, on grounds other than that they are unlikely to manifest. The following sections aim to address these concerns.

The realist position

Realists argue that international organizations have no independent capacity to influence the behaviour of states[50] and that morality has no place in international relations.[51] Proponents of these principles would thus clearly oppose a proposal aimed at regulating humanitarian intervention exclusively through the UN.

In terms of the first position, John Mearsheimer's assertion – 'institutions are basically a reflection of the distribution of power in the world. They are based on the self-interested calculations of the great powers, and they have no independent effect on state behaviour'[52] – is, I would suggest, presently largely true, certainly in the case of the UN. The Security Council is, as Nigel White notes, 'a Realist core in an institutionalist framework'[53] and was created as a means by which the victorious powers could consolidate their power in the aftermath of World War II. Under the proposals outlined above, however, the power vested in this organ of the UN would be diminished and hence the capacity of power to influence the determination of when to intervene would be less pronounced. Organizations which delegate competencies to non-state-based institutions, such as many EU institutions, clearly constitute examples of international organizations which do operate, at least constitutionally, without the interference or influence of power. Individual members of the EU no longer have exclusive power over many competencies traditionally the sole preserve of sovereign states. States will join, or remain members of, organizations which exercise control over aspects of their domestic system if they are convinced that the benefits outweigh the sacrifices.

Additionally, it is questionable whether realists articulate a coherent position on morality and normative theorizing. While realists disavow normative theorizing, the realist position on state behaviour in many respects constitutes a normative position; a set of prescriptions on how states *ought* to behave based on normative assumptions regarding sovereignty.[54] Additionally, the idea that key realist thinkers have consistently disavowed the domestic relationship between the state and its citizens is untrue. Hobbes, the 'archetypal proponent of "realism"'[55] certainly didn't neglect the issue of the state's duty to its own citizens. According to William Bain Hobbes's famous statement on national security – 'the safety of the people is the supreme law' – was not a narrow prescription limiting sovereigns to concern themselves only with 'national security' but rather refers to,

> an explicitly normative safety... For the word 'safety', Hobbes explains, should be understood to mean, not a base condition of mere survival, but 'a happy life so far as that is possible'.[56]

Sovereigns are thus expected to provide the means by which their citizens can enjoy 'domestic peace, acquisition of wealth, and enjoyment of liberty'. Given that these prescriptions were articulated by the iconic Hobbes one might wonder whether modern adherents to his views have ignored a significant aspect of his theory. Indeed Chris Brown further highlights the misuse of Machiavelli by twentieth-century realists and argues that 'the realists' use of the European tradition of state-craft was actually much more selective than they themselves seem to have acknowledged'.[57]

Additionally, the total disregard for domestic issues and human morality, particularly evident in Kenneth Waltz's landmark study *Theory of International Politics*,[58] is no longer tenable in light not only of the political and social changes of the past 20 years but also the emergence of the post-positivist perspectives on security within the discipline of International Relations. The question of a state's responsibilities to its citizens is a key debate in international politics and International Relations and any attempt to remove this issue from the agenda of either discourse is futile.

It is impossible to achieve international consensus on human Rights

Since the ratification of the UN Charter, international law has become increasingly based on treaty law. As per Article 38 of the Statute of the International Court of Justice, treaties are not the only sources of international law, but it is clear that they have become the more popular source of legality. Since 1945, over 33,000 treaties have been registered with the UN, many drafted with the help of the International Law Commission, established to facilitate the codification of international law. Todd Landman describes the plethora of human rights treaties in the post-Charter era as the 'international human rights legal regime'. His statistical analysis finds that 'there has been an expansion in both the breadth and depth of the regime'. Additionally Landman notes, 'the proliferation of human rights treaties has meant an increasingly larger set of human rights has found positive legal expression, while on the other hand a larger number of states have ratified these main instruments'.[59] It is clear, therefore, that states, at least since 1945, have been willing and able to agree on certain human rights laws.

The precise determination of the violations of human rights that would necessitate an international response is a more contentious issue. In the 1970s, attempts by the International Law Commission to formulate a means by which intervention could be legitimized faltered on this issue. Cassese suggests that intervention is permissible when 'Gross and egregious breaches of human rights occur, involving the loss of hundreds or thousands of innocent lives.'[60] Yet as a definition this is imprecise; 'Gross' and 'egregious' are both subjective terms and 'hundreds or thousands' is inexact and focuses on scale rather than motives or systematic intent. Superlatives, such as 'serious', 'grave', 'large', 'massive' and 'terrible', articulated in an attempt to clarify the circumstances under which intervention should take place, are ultimately unhelpful and do not guard against the potential for abuse and manipulation.

The Rome Statute of the International Criminal Court (ICC) constitutes a potential source of intervention criteria. Article 5 states:

> The Court has jurisdiction in accordance with this Statute with respect to the following crimes: (a) The crime of genocide (b) Crimes against humanity (c) War crimes (d) Crimes of aggression.

The Preamble of the ICC details its commitment to working in tandem with the UN and determines that it is concerned only with crimes 'of concern to the international community as a whole'. Thus, there is an explicit commitment to the notion of internal sovereignty, as outlined in the UN, with the proviso that certain acts are the concern of the international community. These acts are then clearly defined in Part II of the Statute. The ICC's remit could become the basis for a definition of the circumstances that may trigger international involvement and possibly humanitarian intervention.

Those who argue that human rights are culturally specific and not applicable to universality are, in key respects, correct. Rights such as voting, private property, etc. are certainly not universally vaunted. Violation of these 'human rights' would not be grounds for intervention, however, and the basis for intervention would have to be the violation of certain universally recognized human rights. No nations can, or do, claim to hold culturally specific views on genocide, ethnic cleansing or mass rape. The plethora of human rights treaties suggests that the problem is not so much agreeing on what inalienable human rights are but rather enforcing these rights. As Guicherd states, 'Despite the now-recognized right of victims to assistance, it is not possible to derive a right of states to bring this assistance by all means, including force.'[61] Additionally, the remit of the ICC constitutes an example of what can be done, with the consent of states, in terms of identifying the circumstances under which the actions of a state becomes of international concern. It is clear, therefore, that states have been capable of agreeing upon certain inalienable human rights for all people and identifying the circumstances under which the domestic violation of these rights becomes an international issue.

Of course the articulation of commitments is not necessarily indicative of a genuine desire to uphold human rights laws. States may well declare their support for the expansion of Chapter VII's remit and human rights law generally but subsequent state practice and declarations have often undermined these commitments. The realist perspective clearly expects just such hypocrisy. As George Kennan wrote,

> It is true that there are certain words and phrases sufficiently high-sounding the world over so that most governments, when asked to declare themselves for against, will cheerfully subscribe to them, considering that such is their vagueness that the mere act of subscribing to them carries with it no danger of having one's freedom of action sufficiently impaired.[62]

Kennan's archetypal realist perspective is, I would suggest, largely true. However, this situation arises because, as he suggests, states are aware that the current enforcement mechanisms are flawed and inconsistently applied. Clearly with the creation of a new UN force this problem would be addressed.[63]

Codification will increase potential for abuse

History has demonstrated the willingness of states to assert that their actions are in accordance with international law when clearly they are not and this has led some to conclude that creating a new legal right of humanitarian intervention would be counterproductive. According to Richard Falk, 'any authorization of intervention creates a manipulative nexus that can itself be used as a justification for abusive intrusion upon the legitimate orbit of autonomy of another state'.[64] In a similar vein Jane Stromseth argues, 'a risk exists that creating a clear legal right of humanitarian intervention would encourage more frequent resort to the practice in less compelling circumstances than at present by creating an additional doctrinal basis for justifying the use of force'.[65] One may look at the extent to which states have invoked the right to self-defence as evidence for this caution. Cassese notes that historically states have invoked Article 51 'in cases which hardly amounted to self-defence or even in cases that were clearly not covered by the provision at issue'.[66] It has been, additionally, an abuse perpetrated in the majority of cases by the major powers, particularly, as Cassese notes the United States.[67]

Undoubtedly there is the potential for a new formal right of intervention to be abused, but compared to the normative thesis' prescriptions codification appears to present significantly less scope for abuse. The argument that codification will create a new means by which humanitarian intervention can be illegitimately invoked as justification for the use of force is ultimately illogical. It is difficult to understand how legal clarity is more open to abuse than subjective interpretation. As Michael Burton asserts,

> While no legal norm is entirely free from potential abuse... the use of codified criteria will diminish rather than exacerbate the problem of pre-textual interventions. A codified rule of intervention is less prone to abuse than is the current 'sublegal' status accorded unilateral humanitarian intervention.[68]

The clearest way to prevent states abusing the right of humanitarian intervention is to declare that such a right does not exist. However, the normative thesis clearly does not wish to eliminate the right to intervene but seeks to articulate guidelines and criteria *rather* than legal codes believing the former to be less open to abuse than the latter. Clearly this view has proven to be incorrect.

Of course, contriving a suitable and acceptable definition and attendant right of humanitarian intervention presents significant difficulties. This does not, however, negate the need to do so. Weiss and Chopra acknowledge the potential for abuse in any new law but point to the adverse consequence derived from the argument that codification should be avoided:

> Since no definition could be sufficiently comprehensive, it was argued ... that potential aggressors would be able to navigate between provisions and circumvent the letter of any prohibition. Instead, without any defined parameters states found that they did not have to navigate at all to contravene the spirit of the prohibition.[69]

Thus, viewed in the context of its current status, codifying a right to intervene for humanitarian reasons, though potentially open to abuse, would constitute a significant diminution of the scope for abuse. Whereas today, powerful states can determine that a situation necessitates intervention, both formally through the Security Council and unilaterally, codification would transfer these decision-making responsibilities to an impartial organization. The capacity of powerful states and coalitions to claim legality derives from humanitarian interventions confused status and the capacity of powerful states to currently claim legitimate authority in determining what is legal. The codification advocated above would help to clarify this status and transfer authority to an impartial body thus mitigating these concerns.

Oscar Scachter also opposes codification suggesting instead, 'It would be better to acquiesce in a violation that is considered necessary and desirable in the particular circumstances.'[70] Chesterman is similarly inclined arguing that legal reform 'would increase the number of interventions undertaken in bad faith'.[71] With respects to what should be done he writes,

> In the event of an intervention alleged to be on humanitarian grounds the better view is that such an intervention is illegal but that the international community may, in extreme circumstances, tolerate the delict. In judicial terms this might translate to a finding of illegality but the imposition of only a nominal penalty.[72]

This logic is predicated on his assertion, 'There is a mechanism for legal regulation of such military [humanitarian] interventions: Chapter VII [of the Charter]',[73] yet his prior analysis of Chapter VII usage in the post-Cold War era finds that this provision of the Charter has been widely abused and politicized. He argues that the determination of a threat to international peace and security under Chapter VII has become a matter of political exigencies rather than legal objectivity and criticizes the Council's use of Chapter VII for allowing the Council's 'authorization [to] become viewed as a formal step towards legitimate intervention, [therefore the Security Council's] substantive role in decisions on international peace and security has been diminished'.[74] It is questionable then, on the basis of these findings, that the maintenance of the Security Council's authority over the use of force for humanitarian intervention, under Chapter VII, should be maintained. The toleration of illegal action, on the basis of the ill-defined acquiescence of the 'international community' appears both imprecise and open to precisely the politicization Chesterman earlier criticizes. It is additionally difficult to accept that an issue as important as humanitarian intervention should be designated beyond the scope of international law. A legal system based on rules and procedures widely acknowledged as inadequate in respects to one of the most pressing issues of our age is surely one which must be changed. Paul Christopher states,

> surely in those cases where we find our legal and moral rules at odds, we should endeavor to reconcile these differences...Clearly the law in this case is not responsive to policy or in agreement with our moral sensibilities. If one accepts that the prohibition against intervention is prima facie rather than absolute, inherent in this recognition is an obligation at least to attempt to articulate the grounds for when the prohibition may justifiably be overridden. Ideally, of course, one would like the legal code to include any overriding criteria.[75]

Negates sovereignty

Absolutist notions of sovereignty, as espoused by Bodin and Hobbes, clearly no longer have relevance. The separation of powers within many states and the willingness of states to cede certain power to international or regional entities is clear evidence that contemporary sovereignty is not characterized by complete independence, if indeed it ever was. According to Jean Cohen,

> The theory and practice of modern constitutionalism demonstrates that limited sovereignty is not an oxymoron; and that sovereignty, constitutionalism, and the rule of law are not incompatible. It also

> shows that functions or prerogatives once ascribed to the unitary sovereign can be divided and/or ascribed to other bodies... without the abolition of sovereignty or the disaggregation of the state.[76]

Key to many of the criticisms of the normative thesis and the idea of humanitarian intervention is the claim that these ideas and prescriptions undermine sovereignty. In the early chapters I articulated a similar argument. However, the key aspect of my earlier discussion of sovereignty was the fact that the normative thesis articulated a proposal which would undermine the sovereignty of *some* states. This assault on sovereign equality constitutes a much more destructive scenario than a reinterpretation of universal sovereign inviolability.

As previously highlighted, developing states have been hostile to increased Western intervention and the normative thesis. The opposition to these developments, however, would seem to stem from the manner in which interventions are being executed and regulated. Indicatively, Soliman Awaad, from the Egyptian foreign ministry, stated '[The legitimacy of humanitarian intervention depends upon] norms and criteria [being] indiscriminately applied to all cases without double standards or politicization'.[77] The problem, then, is not so much with the principle of humanitarian intervention but rather with a system where the decision to intervene is dependent on the whims of powerful Western states and there is a lack of clear guidelines as to precisely what constitutes legitimate grounds for external intervention. States in the developing world have suffered the negative consequences of such a system prior to the codification of sovereign equality and naturally do not want to jeopardize the gains they have made under international law. According to Hedley Bull, the tenets of sovereignty enable weaker states to 'combat the foreign domination to which they were subjected when they lacked these rights'.[78] Yet while Bull defends sovereignty and highlights its importance, he acknowledges that it need not be absolute and must be a product of consensus and subject to broader systemic regulation:

> Whatever rights are due to states or nations or other actors in international relations, they are subject to and limited by the rights of the international community. The rights of sovereign states, and of sovereign peoples or nations, derive from the rules of the international community or society and are limited by them... the idea of sovereign rights existing apart from the rules laid down by international society itself and enjoyed without qualification has to be rejected in principle.[79]

The key tenets of sovereignty need not be casualties in the development of clear rules on humanitarian intervention. Cohen argues that the normative goods that sovereignty provides essentially relate to the relationship between the citizenry and the government and the capacity of these actors to operate without fear of domination or intervention.[80] The fear of domination is currently prevalent because the arbitrary nature of the present regulation of humanitarian intervention and the parallels between the rhetoric of conditional sovereignty and 'enlightened states' espoused by global civil society and the 'standards of civilization' discourse used to legitimate colonialism in the pre-Charter era. The clarification of the circumstances under which intervention is deemed necessary and the creation of an impartial body with sole authority to make this determination would go a long way towards alleviating the concerns presently expressed in the developing world. As Karen Feste states, 'If an intervention is authorized by an international body and has specific stated purposes, these concerns are far less relevant.'[81]

Indeed, Article 4(h) of the Constitutive Act of the African Union recognizes 'the right of the Union to intervene in a Member State pursuant to a decision of the Assembly in respect of grave circumstances, namely: war crimes, genocide and crimes against humanity'. This aspect of the African Union's constitution again highlights that, even among those states most suspicious and critical of the idea of humanitarian intervention, there is an acceptance that sovereignty does not imbue states with the right of complete domestic impunity. In its findings the ICISS noted, 'even in states where there was the strongest opposition to infringements on sovereignty, there was a general acceptance that there must be limited exceptions to the non-intervention rule for certain kinds of emergencies'.[82] Again this suggests that there isn't widespread opposition to the principle of upholding universally agreed human rights domestically. Clearly, however, there is widespread opposition to the creation of a two-tiered system. Henkin argues that those principles of international law that prohibit unilateral humanitarian intervention

> do not reflect a conclusion that the 'sovereignty' of the target state stands higher in the scale of values of contemporary international society than the human rights of its inhabitants to be protected from genocide and massive crimes against humanity... rather they reflect, above all, the moral-political conclusion that no individual state can be trusted with authority to judge and determine wisely.[83]

Sovereign inviolability is meant, therefore, to prevent powerful states from interfering in the affairs of weaker states and not necessarily to prevent collective intervention authorized by an internationally recognized body.

The assurances of Western statesmen and academics will never allay the suspicions of the developing world regardless of how eloquently articulated. More than rhetorical promises are required if the developing world is to accept that humanitarian intervention is not a contemporary manifestation of the white mans burden.

Will never work against powerful states

The establishment of a UN force, to be used if states decline to provide troops, is a proposal designed to address the problem of 'inhumanitarian non-intervention' which has been a more prevalent phenomena than 'inhumanitarian intervention'. It would mean that a designation by the international body that intervention was warranted would not go unheeded due to the unwillingness of states to deploy their troops to certain regions. It is clear that had any state wished to do so they could have intervened in Rwanda in 1994 or Sudan in 2004 and claimed legitimacy, if not legality, on the basis of the UN's own reports which stated clearly that genocide was occurring. Few would have disputed that there were objectively acknowledged grounds for intervening in either case, unlike the invasion of Iraq in 2003. Had the UN had the independent capacity to deploy troops during these situations, then it surely would have done so.

The inability of the UN to compel states to act is certainly a problem and one which has hampered a number of peace-keeping operations.[84] If the UN had a standing force trained specifically to intervene in humanitarian crises then this would clearly increase its capacity to act on its own findings, as was manifestly not the case regarding Darfur in 2004.

It is clear, however, that such a force would have definite limitations. In particular, it is difficult to imagine that such a force would ever be deployed to halt the activities of the Chinese, American or Russian armies. The power of a state's military and its own international status would clearly influence the decision to intervene. In this sense the proposal advocated above would be ineffective against certain states. This is a significant problem. Wheeler asserts, 'if these states are seen to be able to abuse human rights with impunity, the dangerous signal is sent that the way to avoid becoming a target for humanitarian intervention is to develop the military capabilities that make the costs of outside intervention too prohibitive.'[85]

Events in Tiananmen Square, Chechnya and Guantánamo Bay have demonstrated that major powers are willing to systematically violate human rights. The capacity of any new UN organ and military force to compel these states to cease these activities will always be limited. It is important to note, however, that this would certainly not constitute deterioration relative to the present system. Currently, these states, and their major allies, can, and often do, trump international organizations including the International Court of Justice and the UN. The best one could hope for would be that if the new institutions outlined above were created and activated compliance with them would become a key factor in a state's international prestige. States, regardless of size, do not want to be seen as pariahs. As Cassese notes, 'The international community is less anarchic and individualistic, and far more integrated than in the past. Consequently, community pressure on individual States, including Great Powers, is such that it proves difficult for a state to avoid being bound by a new general rule.'[86] Of course, this is a highly hypothetical scenario and the actions of China, Russia and the US since the end of the Cold War suggests that they are capable of withstanding international outrage. This is, therefore, ultimately a valid weakness of the proposal.

Conclusion

According to Cassese, 'the system envisaged in the UN Charter for the maintenance of international peace and security...has substantially failed'.[87] Provided one has an interest in international peace and stability and upholding the role of international law, it is clear that this failure requires substantive action. The normative thesis has articulated a prescription which, I believe, has not only demonstrably failed, and will continue to fail, but which will also further jeopardize international peace and stability. This chapter has outlined a solution aimed at redressing the deficiencies in contemporary positive international law which does not undermine sovereign equality or replace law with morality.

These proposals are ambitious and certainly unlikely to manifest in the near future. According to Parsi, 'to consider a reform of the United Nations that could reduce the power of the United States is pure fantasy'.[88] It is difficult to disagree with this view, especially in light of the US's increasing unwillingness to ratify international treaties such as Kyoto and Rome. These proposals, though radical, are not, however, entirely divorced from reality or completely out of step with international relations in the post-Charter era. They are ambitious but I believe they are more realistic than those prescriptions based on the idea that Western states, in defiance of their history, will develop a moral conscious.

The provisions outlined could be added to the existing canon of international law without requiring a wholesale rewriting of either the Charter, the status of sovereignty or international law. What actually needs to be done is not especially ambiguous and one can compile a list of the required procedures.[89] While sovereignty would have to be amended to the extent that external interference would be legal under certain clearly defined circumstances, the principle of non-interference would essentially be maintained, as, for an intervention to be legitimized, it would have to both meet the codified criteria for a serious crime, as detailed by the ICC, or constitute a situation of systemic inertia in the face of a humanitarian catastrophe, and have the support of the UN. The right of a state to independently decide its own internal system would be maintained. Intervention would not be permissible under any circumstances other than the serious violation of human rights, which would itself be determined by a non-partisan actor. The idea that sovereignty imbues states with absolute domestic autonomy does not reflect either legal developments, such as the 1993 Vienna Declaration on Human Rights, or the practice of the Security Council in the 1990s and therefore domestic humanitarian issues are currently already of international concern.

International law does not emerge in a vacuum and the proposals articulated in this Chapter recognize that law is, as Frank Berman suggests, 'a system of codified morality'.[90] In the area of human rights, an extensive canon of laws has been constructed which delineates the responsibilities incumbent on states towards their citizens. It is unsatisfactory, however, to simply articulate rights in the absence of effective enforcement mechanisms. It is additionally unsatisfactory to create treaties determining the human rights which states must uphold domestically, but which impose no duties on states to, collectively, uphold these rights internationally. As Berman notes, 'the moral calculus must necessarily end up with the identification of duties to act (and who bears them) and cannot have as its concluding point no more than a discretionary entitlement'.[91]

The normative thesis has, at times, presented the debate on humanitarian intervention as a choice between 'those who stand for internationalist, Europeanist, democratic values, including human rights, and those who remain wedded to national or exclusivist thinking'.[92] There are others perspectives however, and the 'Europeanist' element of the righteous path is questionable. The third way – advocacy in favour of legal reform – has tended to focus on the need to reform the Security Council. While increasing the number of permanent members of the Security Council would address the Council's obviously unrepresentative nature, this would not constitute a solution to the problem of the veto; in fact it would likely make it harder to achieve unanimity. The non-binding codes of conduct advocated by both the ICISS and the 2004 UN High Level Panel on Threats, Challenges and Change are unlikely to have a significant influence on the behaviour of the Security Council if the history of P5 practice is indicative. Therefore, while the Security Council acting under Chapter VII can legitimately authorize a humanitarian intervention, it is only likely to do so when the national interests of the major powers are in unison.

Given that the politicization of the Security Council's approach towards humanitarian intervention has led to inconsistent responses in the post-Cold War era it has been suggested that 'we will have to look for and live with unilateral interventions'.[93] While it is tempting to look to certain liberal democracies to solve the enforcement gap, this has two major drawbacks. First, there is no real evidence to suggest that liberal democracies are inclined to act when their national interests are not involved. Second, the majority of states are opposed to special dispensation being granted to certain ostensibly 'enlightened' states acting as self-appointed guardians of international human rights. The acceptance of unilateralism arguably influenced the invasion of Iraq and will certainly continue to undermine international law. As noted by the United Nations High Level Panel on Threats, Challenges and Changes,

> in a world full of perceived potential threats, the risk to the global order and the norm of non-intervention on which it continues to be based is simply too great for the legality of unilateral preventative action, as distinct from collectively endorsed action, to be accepted. Allowing one to so act is to allow all.[94]

The preference throughout this chapter has been for international law to regulate the actions of states. Law is a reflection of morality but constitutes a more robust framework for regulating state behaviour than the inherently malleable and subjective Just War theory or cosmopolitan ethics which are inherently weak on the question of authority.[95] Fred Dallmayr argues that it is vitally important to determine who has the right of interpretation and authority to act.

> This right or competence cannot simply be left to 'universal' theorists or intellectuals – in the absence of an explicitly political delegation or empowerment. These considerations indicate that it is insufficient – on moral and practical grounds – to throw a mantle of universal rules over humankind without paying simultaneous attention to public debate and the role of political will formation.[96]

The moral guidelines triumphantly proffered by proponents of global civil society are of little practical utility unless they are translated into binding, positive law. As Cohen argues, 'Only international law can mediate between the moral and the political so as to establish clear limits and rules while affording legality and legitimacy to appropriate action.'[97] Additionally, however, legal rules and treaties are themselves impotent if they lack attendant enforcement mechanisms. There is as such pressing need to reform the enforcement mechanisms available to the UN. 'The challenge facing the international community', as Michael Byers notes, 'is to maintain rules on military action that are reasonable, effective and widely accepted – including by the most powerful state, at least most of the time.'[98] The proposals articulated in this chapter are an attempt to reconcile the moral argument for intervention with international law accepting that this requires significant changes in the enforcement mechanisms currently operable.

The increasingly prevalent focus on the ills allegedly accruing from sovereignty overlooks the extent to which unilateral moral interventionism has historically proved both highly divisive and, in the main, a cover for more nefarious interests. As Berman argues,

> 'sovereignty' is not the only cloak behind which wrong can hide; self-anointment can serve just as well, even if in the latter case the ill consequences may be less consciously willed than in the former. The saving grace must thus lie in collective international authority, and more particularly in building up its regularity, predictability modes of operation, and most of all its accountability.[99]

The prescriptions advanced in this chapter seek to address this need for collectivity, predictability and accountability. The demonization of sovereignty, the reification of Western liberal democracy and the exaggeration of global civil society's capacity are the bases of the normative thesis, a thesis that has demonstrably failed to positively influence international relations. The increasing asymmetry between 'enlightened' Western states and the abandonment of international law do not constitute positive developments. It is necessary, therefore, to develop imaginative solutions which can bolster international law's regulatory and enforcement capabilities.

8

Conclusion: Sovereignty, Human Rights and the Integrity of International Law

Introduction

This study has outlined the record of the normative thesis since NATO's seminal intervention in Kosovo in 1999. This record indicates that the ambitious prescriptions advanced before, during and after Operation Allied Force failed to materialize. Worse still, evidence suggests that the normative prescriptions have contributed to a deterioration in respect for international law and the UN, and increased the asymmetry between Western and non-Western states. While the normative thesis constitutes the dominant perspective on how to address humanitarian crises effectively and consistently, clearly new thinking is urgently required.

Expressions of wounded surprise, commonly articulated after the invasion of Iraq, are indicative of the naïve and misplaced belief in the power of 'moral' codes to affect the behaviour of states, which is central to the normative position. The necessarily subjective and malleable criteria, based on the Just War theory, have failed to significantly influence Western interventionism. They have, rather, created an expansive, easily manipulated justificatory framework which facilitates inhumanitarian intervention and does nothing to address the problem of inhumanitarian non-intervention. This book has argued, therefore, that the status of humanitarian intervention must be clarified in international law and that there is a need to contrive innovative means to enable the UN to consistently and effectively address humanitarian crises.

Global civil society and the normative thesis

The basis of the normative thesis, as outlined in Chapter 3, constitutes a belief in cosmopolitanism and the capacity of global civil society to influence the behaviour of Western states. The Western democratic state is portrayed as embodying liberal values and naturally inclined towards respect for human rights. Democracy, it has been argued, facilitates bottom-up policy formation and thus domestic pressure, derived from international solidarity with humanitarian need, compels Western states to act morally in their international affairs. Proponents of the West's eminence, building on the basic tenets of the 'End of History' thesis, have argued that the West should no longer be afraid to proliferate its values. According to Vittorio Emmanuel Parsi, 'The positive effects of living under a democratic regime are so obvious and deep as to permit the claim that cultural relativism must succumb to the universal values of human dignity.'[1] This disdain for pluralism and relativism – described by Gerry Simpson as 'liberal anti-pluralism'[2] – necessarily led to calls for increased interventionism and extensive engagement with international affairs.

'We' in the West have thus been portrayed as key to the dissemination of the good life for all. 'We' as members of global civil society and citizens of receptive liberal states are empowered to halt the suffering of others. The rhetoric espoused by proponents of the normative thesis in this regard often threads a fine line between impassioned advocacy and emotive hysteria. John Janzekovic, for example, recalling the horrors of the genocide in Rwanda, declares, 'It is not enough to simply blame belligerents for atrocities. We are all to blame for not responding directly and effectively to stop such activities ... Everyone is responsible for allowing severe violations of human rights to occur.'[3] This is, to put it mildly, somewhat exaggerated. My 92-year-old Grandmother would have been surprised indeed to discover that she was to blame for the massacre of 800,000 people in a country she quite possibly never heard of. This almost messianic belief in Western capacity is not entirely due to a faith in Western states, however. Key to the power of the West is the power of global civil society. Proponents of the normative thesis have argued that this new global force acts as both a restraint on and a catalyst for Western action and therefore genuine humanitarian interventions will be initiated while nefarious interest-led interventions constrained.

NATO's intervention in Kosovo was greeted with jubilation by proponents of global civil society who clearly believed it heralded a new era. Within two months of Operation Allied Force, however, the international community demonstrated a pronounced unwillingness to intervene in East Timor in the wake of the violence sparked by the results of the independence referendum. Not until Indonesia had given its consent did an international force deploy by which time thousands of people had been killed.

The election of George Bush suggested that the US was posed to regress into isolationism. September 11, 2001, however, catalysed the 'War on Terror' which, in tandem with a determination to wipe out 'the evil doers', saw the US lead a campaign to promote liberty, freedom and democracy. This mantra, in addition to the counter-terrorism argument, formed a key rhetorical basis for the invasion of Afghanistan and the toppling of the Taliban. Up to this point supporters of humanitarian intervention found the Bush administration, to their surprise, to be amenable to their agenda; the invasion of Iraq, however, destroyed the tentative coalition between Bush, Blair and the humanitarians. The invasion 'broke the Kosovo liberal intervention consensus'[4] and suggested a regression to self-interested interventionism, and worse, the appropriation of humanitarian rhetoric for this very cause. In addition to the damage done by the invasion of Iraq, the crisis in Darfur further dashed notions of progress when the world watched a massive humanitarian tragedy go unaddressed despite extensive media coverage and the highly successful mobilization of NGOs and Western democratic publics. The 2005 World Summit additionally undermined hopes of progress; while the principle of the 'responsibility to protect' was formally incorporated into the *Outcome Document*, the provisions of Paragraph's 138 and 139 constituted a significant diminution of the original proposals proffered by the ICISS.

The capacity of global civil society – this 'rival superpower'[5] – has thus proved very limited. This is not surprising, however, given the nature of this entity. As David Chandler observes, 'The problem is that "civil society" and "cosmopolitan democracy" are not political institutions, they are moral aspirations.'[6] The power of moral aspirations is obviously limited and thus the calls for greater Western interventionism and the rejection of international law has lessened the restraints previously acting upon the West without creating effective alternative means of restraint.

The normative thesis has additionally clearly underestimated the importance of interests in Western foreign policy. The prevalence of national interest in the determination of whether to intervene is evident in the historical record outlined in Chapter 3. According to Nicholas Wheeler and Justin Morris,

> in no case have states intervened when there were no vital interests at stake and/or where there were perceived to be high risks to the lives of intervening forces. This produces a pattern of intervention that is highly selective, frequently driven by considerations of national self-interest rather than humanitarian need. It also ensures that when intervention does take place it is widely viewed as morally hypocritical,

> a rhetorical instrument that rationalizes the projection of force by the powerful. Iraq is only the latest intervention where this long-standing critique can be strongly heard.[7]

This appraisal of the role of state interest in foreign policy would appear to be accurate. It is difficult to reconcile this analysis, however, with Wheeler's views as articulated ten years earlier,

> Domestic publics and the media have the potential to hold Western state leaders accountable for greater humanitarian responsibility...it is only through the mobilisation of intense pressures on the part of domestic publics that governments will be prepared to embark upon humanitarian policies which they would normally regard as electorally disastrous.[8]

The capacity of domestic public opinion and global civil society was at this time considered sufficiently powerful to trump the self-interested inclinations of Western states which, again according to Wheeler, appeared to embrace the agenda of these activists.

> a new norm of intervention has developed that supports the use of force to protect civilians from genocide, mass murder, and ethnic cleansing. This norm is the strongest in Western states, which were the key players throughout the 1990s in establishing this new principle in international society.[9]

The evolution in Wheeler's perspective captures the demise of the high expectations articulated in the late 1990s. While at that juncture the West was considered to be wedded to the project of global civil society, with Blair's government heralded as a 'norm entrepreneur',[10] developments in the post-Kosovo era have underscored the reality of the prevalence of national interest.[11] As the situation in Darfur degenerated throughout 2004 it was increasingly clear that the mobilization of global civil society and domestic opinion within the West had limited impact.

Additionally, the 'illegal but legitimate' route has created a means by which the justifications for intervention have become easier. As Martin Wight observed, 'The fundamental problem of politics is the justification of power...Power is not self-justifying; it must be justified by reference to some source outside or beyond itself, and thus be transformed into "authority".'[12] The diminution of the importance of the UN and the creation of the 'illegal but legitimate' rhetorical framework has had a number of unintended consequences for the normative thesis, most evidently Operation Iraqi Freedom.

While this study has been highly critical of global civil society it would be an exaggeration to suggest that it is entirely impotent or that its effect can only be negative. Clearly, global civil society can act as a means by which moral concerns are raised, norms articulated and guidelines formed. It therefore constitutes a viable source for the foundational tenets of a regulatory framework. It does not, however, constitute this framework in itself.

Sovereignty, human rights and the integrity of international law

In 1984 Hedley Bull asked,

> Is the gap between the rule of non-intervention and the facts of intervention now so vast that the former has become a mockery with which it would be better to dispense altogether, or does the proscription of intervention remain a vital part of the normative structure on which international order depends?[13]

This question returned in a much different context in the early years of the post-Cold War era and the viability and usefulness of sovereignty remains a contested issue. Clearly this study has argued that there is still merit to the idea of sovereignty, though the rights enjoyed by sovereign states must be qualified.

International law has evolved substantially in the post-World War II era and today an enormous corpus of legal rules exists on a wide variety of issues. This includes many treaties relating to human rights, an area long considered a domestic issue beyond the reach of international law. Law's 'ceaseless quest for organization and institutionalization'[14] has accelerated markedly and positive international law has never been as comprehensive as it is at present.

International law may comprise more rules and treaties than ever before but the perennial problem of enforcing these laws remains, especially since the invasion of Iraq. The perspective on international law articulated in this book is one based on respect for the necessity and potential of international law but also an acknowledgement that, as presently structured, the international legal system is incapable of dealing sufficiently with humanitarian intervention.

Sovereign equality constitutes a progressive principle in international relations, one which should not easily be abandoned. Equality enables states to engage in constructive dialogue without fear of subordination and constitutes a legal prohibition against both colonialism and empire. This prohibition on external interference need not, and in legal terms arguably does not, mean that states can treat their domestic population with impunity. A vast body of international law now outlines the duties incumbent upon states and there is no basis for absolutist conceptions of sovereign inviolability. While Bull articulated the positive contribution made by sovereignty he also acknowledged that it was a right contingent on the wider society of states. The emergence of what has become termed 'human security' thus need not necessarily constitute either an affront to, or the end of, sovereignty. Bull asserts,

> The spread of the doctrine that states are not the only subjects of international law would be likely to represent a strengthening of the contribution of international law to international order only if it were accompanied by agreement among states as to what the rights and duties of these other subjects are, comparable at least to the minimal agreement that exists among states about their own rights and duties.[15]

Key to this view is the notion of agreement among states. For similar reasons the basis of the prescriptions articulated in Chapter 7 was the need for an inclusive, accountable process for determining the dynamics of any new relationship between states and their citizens. As William Bain argues, 'To hold stubbornly to an abstract principle of equality in the face of great human suffering is to refuse to make contact with the real problems of the real world.'[16] But, Bain argues, we cannot pretend that subverting equality, regardless of any professed humanitarian motivations, does not constitute a deviation from existing international law and a policy with clear parallels to 'its imperial past because it belongs to a mode of conduct that is imperial by nature'.[17] Thus, the key challenge, and impetus behind the prescriptions in Chapter 7, is to contrive a new conception of sovereignty which does not undermine sovereign equality.

Michael Reisman, argues, 'The insistence on the integrity of procedures is not arid formalism' and highlights the adverse consequences that can accrue from subverting the law:

> Lawyers know that however noble the impulse, action in the common interest that is taken without formal authority may have incalculable public costs. Group security and individual liberty depend, in no small part, on orderly decision preceded by due deliberation; actions

> inconsistent with the procedures of the law erode their authority and increase the probability of abuse.[18]

The negative consequences of the normative thesis' dismissal of international law and specifically the subversion of sovereign equality were outlined in Chapter 6. Cleary, the costs of this strategy outweigh any potential benefits. One alternative strategy is to look to increase the Security Council's willingness to act under Chapter VII of the Charter. Questions remain as to whether the provisions of Chapter VII can reasonably be said to cover intra-state humanitarian crises but, as Reisman also states, it is necessary to sometimes be creative with legal texts as 'a constitution is not a suicide pact'.[19] While the remit of the Security Council under Chapter VII holds out a compelling means by which the deficiencies in international law regarding enforcement of human rights *could* be surmounted, it is clear that the nature of the Security Council means this is highly unlikely to happen in practice. The key issue is not so much whether the Security Council can use the enabling language of Chapter VII creatively – it already have done so, particularly with respect to Haiti in 1994 – but rather does this constitute a viable legal means by which humanitarian intervention can be enforced? As Chesterman warns, 'The plasticity of Chapter VII is suggestive of more traditional motives',[20] indicating that the fact that the provisions can be applied to almost all cases but lack any stipulation regarding responsibilities facilitates selective invocation. It is for this reason that Chapter 7 advocates not only the clarification of the exact circumstances under which sovereign states loose their right to inviolability and the creation of an impartial body to determine whether such circumstances have been reached, but also the creation of a force commanded by the UN capable of being deployed whenever it is determined that intervention is warranted.

In addition to the support articulated for international law, this study has expressed a preference for the enforcement of human rights. The support for human rights articulated here, however, is more modest than some have afforded the idea. For example, according to Patrick Hayden,

> the expectations are that human rights will promote political liberties, lead to the enhancement of the social bases of human welfare and increased security, as well as to international relations characterized by peaceful cooperation and constructive independence.[21]

I do not conceive of human rights as a means by which international peace or stability can be achieved, but rather as a necessary condition for domestic civility. Additionally, actual state practice and the thrust of the normative thesis suggest that Anne Orford is correct when she describes human rights as 'an apology for state violence'.[22] The promotion of human rights in the absence of international law and basic principles of sovereign equality leads to subjective interpretation, selective enforcement and domination. Human rights do exist – as the vast corpus of international laws related to the subject attests – but only insofar as they are based on consent and expressed in legal form.

Conclusion: Reality and perception

The likelihood of the prescriptions advanced in Chapter 7 manifesting is slim. According to Chesterman, 'Humanitarian intervention will remain in a legal penumbra – sometimes given legitimacy by the Security Council, sometimes merely tolerated by states.'[23] This pessimistic prediction would appear to be the most realistic. The potential for international agreement on issues as divisive and major as intervention and an international force must reasonably be considered minimal, especially in the wake of the polarization caused by the invasion of Iraq. Yet, once we accept that there is some merit to normative theorizing, as I do, then it is a question of determining which normative approach is more likely to be effective and less deleterious to international peace and stability. I have suggested that the 'normative thesis' is a prescription based on flawed assumptions which is not only doomed to continue to fail but will also further polarize the international system and threaten international peace.

The primary barrier to the realization of the prescriptions I advance in Chapter 7 is undoubtedly the likelihood that such proposals will divide the international community. It is a cause for regret that an issue as important as humanitarian intervention has proved so intractable. Regardless of who or what was to blame the spectacle of international dithering and hand wringing while thousands die in Rwanda and Darfur can surely only be considered unedifying and a damming indictment of mankind's collective capacity to overcome difference in the interest of the common good. NATO's intervention brought the issue of humanitarian intervention to the centre of international relations and it is surely to be regretted that despite the prominence now afforded to the subject it continues to occupy the 'shadowy periphery'. As noted by Kofi Annan, 'The inability in the case of Kosovo to unify these two equally compelling interests of the international community – universal legitimacy and effectiveness in defence of human rights – can only be viewed as a tragedy.'[24] Tzvetan

Todorov offers perhaps a more damming analysis of the controversy caused by NATO's intervention:

> The complete fragmentation of opinion on the Kosovo campaign, even inside one country, is really depressing for anyone who would rather believe in the intellect. It makes it seem as if our opinions depended not at all on the information that we have, on our ability to reason, or on the values we adhere to, but on murkier grounds – on our infinitely variable identities as individuals, on our life histories, and on unconscious allegiances. Information and reasoned argument seem to serve only to give a rational shell to choices made deeper down.[25]

This study has championed international law because I believe enforceable law is the only effective means by which we can constrain and address humanity's darker compulsions. The fact that law rather than moral reasoning is required to stop humanitarian suffering is a poor reflection of our being; the fact that such a law remains elusive is far worse.

Ultimately, perhaps the more pertinent issue is what the promotion of humanitarian intervention at this time in human history tells us about the motivations and character, not of the international system, but of the people and states driving this agenda. Orford speculates,

> perhaps the idea that we are now one with the rest of humanity, that we are close to these suffering masses, inspires our fear as much as our compassion ... Intervention texts can thus be read as a response to this threat, an attempt simultaneously to locate and thus distance the colonised from the coloniser.[26]

The discourse of humanitarian intervention is superficially benevolent but arguably contains an essence which belies different motivations. Orford suggests this motivation derives from a process of Western self-affirmation, the attempt to distinguish between a barbarous 'them' and a civilized 'us'.[27] Of course, such discussion, though worthwhile, is of little comfort to those suffering. This study has sought to address the empirical aspect of humanitarian intervention rather than the more cerebral questions of motivation and identity.

The crisis in Darfur constitutes the single greatest humanitarian disaster since NATO launched Operation Allied Force. The situation, it is claimed, 'provides an important test case of international society's commitment to an emerging norm of humanitarian intervention and the ideas set out in the Responsibility to Protect'.[28] When Kofi Annan was asked how future generations would judge the world's reaction to the tragedy in Darfur for which he replied, 'quite likely that we were slow, hesitant, uncaring and that we have learnt nothing from Rwanda'.[29] The UN Secretary General further described the response as 'pathetic and inexcusable'.[30] If Darfur is indeed 'an important test case' then Annan's judgement, echoed by many others, constitutes a damming verdict on the record of the normative thesis and the power of global civil society. For those concerned with alleviating human suffering the period since the intervention in Kosovo has clearly been a major disappointment.

This book has sought to explain why the events since Operation Allied Force must be seen to conclusively demonstrate the flaws inherent in the normative approach to humanitarian intervention rather than the mere misapplication of, or deviation from, the normative prescriptions. If there is a solution to the perennial problem posed by humanitarian intervention it must be sought beyond the blandishments of global civil society and the moral character of Western states.

Notes

1 Introduction: The Humanitarian Intervention Controversy

1. See P. de Cuellar, 'Report of the Secretary General', UN Yearbook, 1991, paragraph 11.
2. Quoted in J. Mayall, 'Non-Intervention, Self-Determination and the "New World Order"', *International Affairs*, 67, 3 (1991), p. 427.
3. T. Landman, *Studying Human Rights* (London: Routledge, 2006), p. 8.
4. G. Robertson, *Crimes against Humanity* (London: Penguin, 2002), p. 220.
5. T. Nardin, 'The Moral Basis of Humanitarian Intervention', in Anthony Lang (ed.), *Just Intervention* (Washington: Georgetown University Press, 2003), pp. 11–27.
6. R. Miller, 'Respectable Oppressors, Hypocritical Liberators', in Deen Chatterjee and Don Scheid (eds), *Ethics and Foreign Intervention* (Cambridge: Cambridge University Press, 2003), pp. 215–50.
7. R. Thakur, 'Intervention, Sovereignty and the Responsibility to Protect: Experiences from ICISS', *Security Dialogue*, 33, 3 (2002), pp. 327–28.
8. E. Herman and D. Peterson, 'Morality's Avenging Angels: The New Humanitarian Crusaders', in David Chandler (ed.), *Rethinking Human Rights* (Basingstoke: Palgrave Macmillan, 2002), pp. 196–216.
9. J. Chopra and T. Weiss, 'Sovereignty is no Longer Sacrosanct', *Ethics and International Affairs*, 6 (1992), p. 95.
10. M. Shaw, *Global Society and International Relations* (Cambridge: Cambridge University Press, 1994).
11. S. Hoffmann, 'Intervention: Should It Go On? Can It Go On?' in Chatterjee and Scheid (eds), *Ethics and Foreign Intervention* (Cambridge: Cambridge University Press, 2003), p. 22.
12. A. Linklater, 'The Good International Citizen and the Crisis in Kosovo', summary in Albrecht Schnabel and Ramesh Thakur (eds), *Kosovo and the Challenge of Humanitarian Intervention* (New York: United Nations University Press, 2000).
13. See A. Arend and R. Beck, *International Law and the Use of Force* (London: Routledge, 1993).
14. T. Pangle and P. Ahrensdorf, *Justice among Nations* (Lawrence KS: University of Kansas Press, 1999), p. 3.
15. N. Wheeler, *Saving Strangers* (Oxford: Oxford University Press, 2002), p. 11.
16. J. Gow, *Defending the West* (Cambridge: Polity, 2006); Hoffmann, 'Intervention', p. 24.
17. E. H. Carr, *The Twenty Years Crisis, 1919–1939* (Basingstoke: Palgrave Macmillan, 2001).
18. S. Chesterman, 'Hard Cases Make Bad Law', in Anthony Lang (ed.), *Just Intervention* (Washington: Georgetown University Press, 2003), p. 54.
19. J. Mertus, 'Back to the Drawing Board: Human Rights Should Know No Boundaries', *Washington Post*, April 11, 1999, p. B01.

20. Nardin, 'The Moral Basis for Humanitarian Intervention', p. 23.
21. International Commission on Intervention and State Sovereignty, *The Responsibility to Protect: Research, Bibliography, Background* (Ottawa: International Development Research Centre, 2001), p. vii.
22. Independent International Commission on Kosovo, *Kosovo Report* (Oxford: Oxford University Press, 2000), p. 4.
23. N. Gardels, 'The Paradox of Post-Heroic Warfare', *New Perspectives Quarterly*, 16, 4 (1999), p. 2.
24. Robertson, *Crimes against Humanity*, p. 451.
25. See Vaclav Havel's speech to the Canadian Parliament, 29 April 1999, quoted in Robertson, *Crimes against Humanity*, p. 433.
26. Further clarification and detail is provided in Chapter 7.
27. The 'normative thesis' is not a homogeneous theory. Its genesis and manifestation variously in solidarism and cosmopolitanism are dealt with in Chapter 3.
28. D. Chatterjee and D. Scheid, 'Introduction', in Chatterjee and Scheid (eds), *Ethics and Foreign Intervention* (Cambridge: Cambridge University Press, 2003), p. 5.
29. M. Ignatieff, *Virtual War* (London: Vintage, 2001), p. 210.
30. N. Wheeler, 'Agency, Humanitarianism and Intervention', *International Political Science Review*, 18, 1 (1997), p. 22.
31. M. Waltzer, 'The Politics of Rescue', *Dissent* (1995), pp. 35–41.
32. M. Kaldor, *Global Civil Society: An Answer to War* (Cambridge: Polity, 2003), p. 13.
33. B. Kouchner, 'The Right to Intervention: Codified in Kosovo', *New Perspectives Quarterly*, 16, 4 (1999), pp. 4–6.
34. Shaw, *Global Society and International Relations*, p. 181.
35. For example, Nardin, 'Moral Basis for Humanitarian Intervention', p. 23; Wheeler, *Saving Strangers*, p. 34; J. Stromseth, 'Rethinking Humanitarian Intervention: The Case for Incremental Change', in Jeff Holzgrefe and Robert Keohane (eds), *Humanitarian Intervention: Ethical, Legal and Political Dilemmas* (Cambridge: Cambridge University Press, 2003), p. 248.
36. Stromseth, 'Rethinking Humanitarian Intervention', p. 257.
37. A. Bellamy, 'Ethics and Intervention: The "Humanitarian Exception" and the Problems of Abuse in the Case of Iraq', *Journal of Peace Research*, 41, 2 (2004), p. 134.
38. B. Parekh, 'Rethinking Humanitarian Intervention', *International Political Science Review*, 18, 1 (1997), p. 49.
39. See A. Buchanan and R. Keohane, 'The Preventive Use of Force: A Cosmopolitan Institutional Proposal', *Ethics and International Affairs*, 18, 1 (2004), pp. 1–22.
40. D. Chandler, 'Introduction: Rethinking Human Rights', in Chandler (ed.), *Rethinking Human Rights*, p. 3.
41. J. Donnelly, 'Twentieth Century Realism', in Terry Nardin and David Mapel (eds), *Traditions of International Ethics* (Cambridge: Cambridge University Press, 1992), p. 85.
42. H. Morgenthau, *Scientific Man versus Power Politics* (Chicago, IL: Phoenix Books, 1965), p. 195.
43. C. Krauthammer, 'In Bosnia Partition Might Do', *International Herald Tribune*, 9 September 1992, p. 18.

44. T. B. Knudsen, 'Humanitarian Intervention Revisited: Post Cold War Responses to Classical Problems', in Michael Pugh (ed.), *The UN, Peace and Force* (London: Frank Cass, 1997), p. 150.
45. T. Franck and N. Rodley, 'After Bangladesh: The Law of Humanitarian Intervention by Force', *American Journal of International Law*, 67 (1973), pp. 275–305.
46. A. Lang, 'Humanitarian Intervention: Definition and Debates', in Lang (ed.), *Just Intervention* (Washington: Georgetown University Press, 2003), p. 2.
47. Carr, *The Twenty Years Crisis, 1919–1939*, p. 74.
48. See Wheeler, 'Agency, Humanitarianism and Intervention', p. 13; C. Lu, *Just and Unjust Interventions in World Politics* (Basingstoke: Palgrave Macmillan, 2006), Chap. 3.
49. Danish Institute of International Affairs, *Humanitarian Intervention* (Copenhagen: Danish Institute of International Affairs, 1999), p. 34.
50. See F. Hampson, 'Law and War', in Alex Danchev and Thomas Halverston (eds), *International Perspectives on the Yugoslav Crisis* (New York: St Martin's Press, 1996), p. 149; Danish Institute of International Affairs, *Humanitarian Intervention*, p. 20.
51. M. Burton, 'Legalising the Sublegal', *Georgetown Law Journal*, 85 (1996), p. 422.
52. S. Chesterman, *Just War or Just Peace?* (Oxford: Oxford University Press, 2002), p. 87.
53. C. Reus-Smit, 'Liberal Hierarchy and the Licence to Use Force', in David Armstrong, Theo Farrell and Bice Maiguashca (eds), *Force and Legitimacy in World Politics* (Cambridge: Cambridge University Press, 2005), p. 72.

2 International Law, Sovereignty and Humanitarian Intervention

1. See Chapter 3.
2. The proportion of civilians killed in conflicts rose from 1:10 in 1900 to 9:10 in 2000. Cited in International Commission on Intervention and State Sovereignty, *The Responsibility to Protect*, p. 13.
3. Ibid., p. VII.
4. Independent International Commission on Kosovo, *Kosovo Report*, p. 4.
5. A. Roberts, 'The So-Called "Right" of Humanitarian Intervention', in *Yearbook of International Humanitarian Law 2000*, 3 (The Hague: T.M.C Asser, 2002), p. 5.
6. Quoted in D. Chandler, *From Kosovo to Kabul* (London: Pluto, 2002), p. 123.
7. D. Chandler, 'International Justice', *New Left Review*, 6, (2000), p. 59.
8. C. Guicherd, 'International Law and the War in Kosovo', *Survival*, 41, (1999), p. 21.
9. International Commission on Intervention and State Sovereignty, *The Responsibility to Protect*, p. 53.
10. Danish Institute of International Affairs, *Humanitarian Intervention*, p. 61.
11. Quoted in Danish Institute of International Affairs, *Humanitarian Intervention*, p. 86.
12. Ibid., p. 83.
13. Quoted in J. Holbrook, 'Humanitarian Intervention', in David Chandler (ed.), *Rethinking Human Rights* (Basingstoke: Palgrave Macmillan, 2002), pp. 140–1.

14. Quoted in M. Burton, 'Legalising the Sublegal', p. 428.
15. Simon Chesterman, *Just War or Just Peace?*, p. 5.
16. Chesterman further notes, with respect to the broadening of the provisions of Chapter VII in the 1990s, that these developments, '...by blurring the boundaries of the exception to the prohibition of the use of force established by Chapter VII...threaten to undermine this cardinal principle of the international legal order.' Ibid., p. 112.
17. Ibid., p. 165.
18. In 1993 China stated its position on intervention for the purpose of human rights protection; 'In essence the issue of human rights falls within the sovereignty of each country...China values human rights...However, it is opposed to interference in the internal affairs of other countries using the human rights issue as an excuse.' Quoted in Danish Institute of International Affairs, *Humanitarian Intervention*, p. 54.
19. Danish Institute of International Affairs, *Humanitarian Intervention*, p. 62. Chesterman similarly notes, '[Actions undertaken under Chapter VII during the 1990s] would never have been contemplated by the founders of the UN in 1945'. S. Chesterman, 'Hard Cases Make Bad Law', p. 48.
20. Independent International Commission on Kosovo, *Kosovo Report*, p. 168.
21. Ibid., p. 196.
22. Quoted in Chesterman, *Just War or Just Peace?*, p. 130.
23. Danish Institute of International Affairs, *Humanitarian Intervention*, p. 71.
24. R. Caplan, 'Humanitarian Intervention: Which Way Forward?', *Ethics and International Affairs*, 14 (2000), p. 27.
25. S. Chesterman, *Just war or Just Peace?*, p. 128.
26. C. Guicherd, 'International Law and the War in Kosovo', p. 19.
27. Quoted in Holbrook, 'Humanitarian Intervention', p. 141.
28. The one page note is reprinted in full in A. Roberts, 'NATO's "Humanitarian War" Over Kosovo', *Survival*, 41 (1999), pp. 102–23.
29. Ibid., p. 107.
30. Ibid., p. 107. Additionally, the motivation behind the new legal opinion expressed in this report is questionable. Throughout 1998 the UK had consistently questioned the legality of acting outside the UN. When Robin Cook reported to Madeleine Albright that the UK's lawyers had concluded that such an act would be illegal, Albright replied, 'Get new lawyers.' The October report appears to have been a product of this advice. Quoted in M. Glennon, 'How War Left the Law Behind', *New York Times*, November 21 (2002), p. 37.
31. Report No. HC 28-1 of 7 June 2000, paragraph 1138, available at www.publications.parliament.uk/pa/cm199900/cmselect/cmfaff/28/2802.htm [accessed June 2007].
32. T. Dunne and N. Wheeler, 'Blair's Britain: A Force for Good in the World?', in Karen Smith and Margot Light, *Ethics and Foreign Policy* (Cambridge: Cambridge University Press, 2001), p. 183.
33. S. Chesterman and M. Byers, 'Has US Power Destroyed the UN?', *London Review of Books*, 21, 9, 29 April (1999).
34. B. Simma, 'NATO, the UN and the Use of Force', *European Journal of International Law*, 10, 1 (1999), p. 14.
35. Ibid., p. 14.
36. The justification offered by the UK Foreign Office comprises elements of each.

37. According to Chesterman, 'Anthony D'Amato is one of the strongest contemporary advocates [of this interpretation' and he cites Fernando Tesón and Oscar Schachter as other adherents to this view. See Chesterman, *Just War or Just Peace?*, pp. 48–51.
38. T. Weiss, *Humanitarian Intervention* (London: Polity, 2007), p. 17.
39. Ibid., p. 53.
40. R. Lillich, 'Forcible Self-Help by States to Protect Human Rights', *Iowa Law Review*, 53 (1967), pp. 325–51.
41. G. Robertson, *Crimes against Humanity*, p. 434.
42. Danish Institute of International Affairs, *Humanitarian Intervention*, p. 82.
43. Ibid., p. 82.
44. In 1986 the International Court of Justice ruled that the Geneva Convention applied to all states, even those who had not signed it had become a norm of customary international law.
45. Quoted in Chesterman, 'Hard Cases Make Bad Law', p. 49.
46. Quoted in W. Gaberson, 'Conflict in the Balkans', *New York Times*, March 27 (1999), p. 8.
47. Chesterman, *Just War or Just Peace?*, p. 24.
48. Ibid., p. 25.
49. Danish Institute of International Affairs, *Humanitarian Intervention*, p. 88.
50. A. Arend and R. Beck, *International Law and the Use of Force*, p. 137.
51. P. Hilpold, 'Humanitarian Intervention: Is There a Need for a Legal Reappraisal?', *European Journal of International Law*, 12, 3 (2001), p. 445.
52. International Commission on Intervention and State Sovereignty, *The Responsibility to Protect*, p. 12. The Danish Institute of International Affairs also found 'state practice after the end of the Cold War concerning humanitarian intervention is neither sufficiently substantial nor has there been sufficient acceptance in the international community to support the view that a right of humanitarian intervention without Security Council authorisation has become part of customary international law', Danish Institute of International Affairs, *Humanitarian Intervention*, p. 93.
53. K. Ambos, 'Comment – NATO, the UN and the Use of Force: Legal Aspects', *European Journal of International Law*, 10, 1 (1999), p. 114.
54. See Chesterman, *Just war or Just Peace?*, pp. 84–5.
55. Holbrook, 'Humanitarian Intervention', p. 143.
56. Danish Institute of International Affairs, *Humanitarian Intervention*, p. 123.
57. Quoted in M. Finnemore, 'Fights about Rules: The Role of Efficacy and Power in Changing Multilateralism', in David Armstrong, Theo Farrell and Bice Maiguashca (eds), *Force and Legitimacy in World Politics* (Cambridge: Cambridge University Press, 2005), p. 193.
58. Ambos, 'Comment – NATO, the UN and the Use of Force: Legal Aspects', p. 114.
59. J. Chopra and T. Weiss, 'Sovereignty is no Longer Sacrosanct', p. 103.
60. G. Simpson, *Great Powers and Outlaw States* (Cambridge: Cambridge University Press, 2004), p. 41.
61. D. Held, *Democracy and the Global Order* (London: Polity, 1995), p. 268.
62. J. Hertz, 'Rise and Demise of the Territorial State', *World Politics*, 9, 4 (1957), p. 474.
63. See W. Bloom, *Personal Identity, National Identity and International Relations* (Cambridge: Cambridge University Press, 1990), p. 60.

64. Quoted in Weiss, *Humanitarian Intervention*, p. 16.
65. See International Peace Academy, 'Humanitarian Intervention: Perspectives from Africa', Report by Simon Chesterman on International Consultation on Humanitarian Intervention in Gabrone, Botwana 12 December 2001.
66. H. Bull, *Justice in International Relations: Hagey Lectures* (Ontario: University Publications Distribution Service, 1984), p. 6.
67. A. Lang, 'Humanitarian Intervention: Definition and Debates', p. 2.
68. A. Hurrell, 'Legitimacy and the Use of Force: Can the Circle be Squared?', in Armstrong, Farrell and Maiguashca (eds), *Force and Legitimacy in World Politics* (Cambridge: Cambridge University Press, 2005), p. 18.
69. C. Reus-Smit 'Liberal Hierarchy and the License to Use Force', p. 71.
70. See J. Locke 'The Second Treatise of Government', in Peter Laslett (ed.), *Two Treatises of Government* (Cambridge: Cambridge University Press, 1988).
71. Quoted in Simpson, *Great Powers and Outlaw States*, p. 27.
72. A. Bellamy, 'Ethics and Intervention', pp. 141 and 132.
73. W. Bain, 'The Political Theory of Trusteeship and the Twilight of International Equality', *International Relations*, 17, 1 (2003), p. 63.
74. Ibid., p. 66.
75. Reus-Smit, 'Liberal Hierarchy and the License to Use Force', p. 72.
76. D. Chandler, *From Kosovo to Kabul*, p. 136.
77. Bain, 'The Political Theory of Trusteeship and the Twilight of International Equality', p. 75.
78. G. Lyons and M. Mastanduno, 'Introduction', in Gene Lyons and Michael Mastanduno (eds), *Beyond Westphalia: State Sovereignty and International Intervention* (Baltimore: John Hopkins University Press, 1995), p. 8.
79. Chesterman and Byers, 'Has US Power Destroyed the UN?'.
80. E. H. Carr, *The Twenty Years Crisis, 1919–1939*, p. 74.
81. Ibid., p. 14.
82. Bellamy, *Just Wars: From Cicero to Iraq* (London: Polity, 2007), p. 118.
83. H. Bull, *The Anarchical Society* (London: Macmillan, 1995), p. 92.
84. Bull, *Justice in International Relations*, p. 12.
85. Simpson, *Great Powers and Outlaw States*, p. 68.
86. A. Orford, *Reading Humanitarian Intervention* (Cambridge: Cambridge University Press, 2003).
87. A. Roberts, 'Beyond Dictatorial Interference', in William Bain (ed.), *The Empire of Security and the Safety of the People* (London: Routledge, 2007), p. 163.
88. Chesterman and Byers, 'Has US Power Destroyed the UN?'.
89. D. Armstrong and T. Farrell, 'Introduction', in Armstrong, Farrell and Maiguashca (eds), *Force and Legitimacy in World Politics* (Cambridge: Cambridge University Press, 2005), p. 5.
90. Ibid., p. 10.
91. Chesterman, *Just War or Just Peace?*, p. 97.

3 The Normative Thesis and Operation Allied Force

1. R. Kaplan, 'The Coming Anarchy', *Atlantic Monthly*, February, 2 (1994), pp. 44–76.
2. J. Mearsheimer, 'Back to the Future', *International Security*, 19, 3 (1990), p. 7.

3. M. Shaw, *Global Civil Society and International Relations* (Cambridge: Polity, 1994), p. 155.
4. Editorial, 'Everybody's Business', *Wall Street Journal*, 24 August (1992).
5. F. Fukuyama, 'Nation-building and the Failure of International Memory', in Francis Fukuyama (ed.), *Nation-Building* (New York: John Hopkins University Press, 2006), p. 2.
6. M. Kaldor, *New and Old Wars* (London: Polity, 1999), pp. 1–2.
7. B. Kouchner, 'The Right to Intervention', p. 20.
8. S. Hoffman, 'Intervention', p. 23.
9. UN Commission on Global Governance, *Our Global Neighbourhood* (Oxford: Oxford University Press, 1995), p. 81.
10. See M. Duffield, *Global Governance and the New Wars* (London: Zed Books, 2006).
11. Described as such by E. Herman and D. Peterson, 'Morality's Avenging Angels', in David Chandler (ed.), *Rethinking Human Rights* (Basingstoke: Palgrave Macmillan, 2002), p. 199.
12. Kaldor, *New and Old Wars*, pp. 10–11.
13. Ibid., pp. 115 and 147.
14. K. Hutchings, *International Political Theory* (London: Sage, 1999), p. 154.
15. Ibid., pp. 154–5.
16. D. Chandler, 'New Rights for Old?', *Political Studies*, 51 (2003), p. 332.
17. T. Landman, *Studying Human Rights*, pp. 8–14.
18. M. Kaldor, 'Transnational Civil Society', in Tim Dunne and Nicholas Wheeler (eds), *Human Rights in Global Politics* (Cambridge: Cambridge University Press, 2001), p. 198.
19. G. Robertson, *Crimes against Humanity*, p. 220.
20. Danish Institute for International Affairs, *Humanitarian Intervention* (Copenhagen, Danish Institute for International Affairs, 1999), p. 39.
21. Robertson, *Crimes against Humanity*, p. xvi.
22. N. Wheeler, 'Agency, Humanitarianism and Intervention', p. 9.
23. See D. Chandler, *From Kosovo to Kabul*, pp. 21–52.
24. Quoted in J. Mayall, 'Non-Intervention, Self-Determination and the "New World Order"', p. 427.
25. D. Malone, *The International Struggle over Iraq* (Oxford: Oxford University Press, 2006), p. 11.
26. Figures quoted in Malone, *The International Struggle over Iraq*, p. 11.
27. M. Kaldor, *Global Civil Society*, p. 2.
28. See D. Chandler, *Constructing Global Civil Society: Morality and Power in International Relations* (Basingstoke: Palgrave Macmillan, 2004), p. 82.
29. Ibid., p. 1.
30. Kaldor, *Global Civil Society*, p. 2.
31. J. Grugel, 'Democratisation Studies Globalisation: the Coming Age of a Paradigm', *British Journal of Politics and International Relations*, 5, 2 (2003), p. 275.
32. Kaldor, *Global Civil Society*, p. 12.
33. K. Booth, 'Human Wrongs and International Relations', *International Affairs*, 71, 1 (1995), pp. 103–26.
34. C. Brown, *International Relations Theory: New Normative Approaches* (Hemel Hempstead: Harvester Wheatsheaf, 1992), p. 3.

35. See Chandler, *From Kosovo to Kabul*, pp. 89–91; K. Booth, 'Critical Explorations', in Ken Booth (ed.), *Critical Security Studies and World Politics* (London: Lynne Rienner, 2005).
36. Booth, 'Human Wrongs and International Relations', p. 103.
37. M. Kaldor, 'What is Human Security?', in David Held (ed.), *Debating Globalization* (London: Polity, 2005), p. 177.
38. N. Thomas and W. Tow, 'The Utility of Human Security: Sovereignty and Humanitarian Intervention', *Security Dialogue*, 33, 2 (2002), p. 178.
39. See R. Falk, *On Humane Governance: Toward a New Global Politics* (Cambridge: Polity, 1995), p. 82.
40. P. Hayden, *Cosmopolitan Global Politics* (Aldershot: Ashgate, 2005), p. 70.
41. Janzekovic in fact suggests, 'The realist position ... is immoral and not as realists assert amoral.' J. Janzekovic, *The Use of Force in Humanitarian Intervention* (Hampshire: Ashgate, 2006), p. 48.
42. A. Linklater, 'The Good International Citizen and the Crisis in Kosovo'.
43. J. T. Mattews, 'Redefining Security', *Foreign Affairs*, 68, 2 (1989), p. 162; I. Kaul, 'Peace Needs no Weapons', *Ecumenical Review*, 47, 3, July (1995), p. 313.
44. H. Kung, *Global Responsibility* (New York, Crossroad, 1991), p. 28.
45. T. Nardin, 'The Moral Basis of Humanitarian Intervention', p. 18.
46. Ibid., p. 18.
47. Ibid., p. 19.
48. H. Morgenthau, *Politics among Nations* (New York: Knopf, 1985), p. 12.
49. T. Farer, 'The Ethics of Intervention in Self Determination Struggles', in Deen Chatterjee and Don Scheid (eds), *Ethics and Foreign Intervention* (Cambridge: Cambridge University Press, 2003), p. 146.
50. Chandler, *Constructing Global Civil Society*, p. 4.
51. Margaret Keck and Kathyrn Sikkink, *Activists beyond Borders: Advocacy Networks in International Politics* (Ithaca: Cornell University Press, 1998), p. 203.
52. Kaldor, *Global Civil Society*, p. 2.
53. Ibid., p. 102.
54. R. Falk, 'Recovering Normative Consciousness', *International Relations*, 19, 1 (2005), p. 87.
55. Shaw, *Global Civil Society and International Relations*, p. 24.
56. H. Hensel, 'Introduction', in Howard Hensel (ed.), *Sovereignty and the Global Community* (Aldershot: Ashgate, 2004), p. ix.
57. E. Moxon-Browne, 'A Future for Peacekeeping?', in Edward Moxon-Browne (ed.), *A Future for Peacekeeping?* (New York: St Martin's Press, 1998), p. 192.
58. Wheeler, 'Agency, Humanitarianism and Intervention', p. 22.
59. Shaw, *Global Civil Society and International Relations*, pp. 180–1.
60. UK Government Strategic Defence Review, 8 July 1998, Cm 3999, para 21, available online, http://www.parliament.the-stationery-office.co.uk/pa/cm199798/cmselect/cmdfence/138/13809.htm#n263, [accessed June 2007].
61. C. Brown, 'Ethics, Interests, and Foreign Policy', in Karen Smith and Margot Light (eds), *Ethics and Foreign Policy* (Cambridge: Cambridge University Press, 2001), pp. 15–32.
62. K. Sikkink, 'Human Rights, Principled Issue-Networks, and Sovereignty in Latin America', *International Organisation*, 47, 3 (1993), p. 475.
63. See Chapter 2.
64. N. Wheeler, 'Guardian Angel or Global Gangster?', *Political Studies*, 44, 1 (1997), pp. 123–35.

65. K. Booth, 'Three Tyrannies', in Dunne and Wheeler (eds), *Human Rights in Global Politics* (Cambridge: Cambridge University Press, 2001), p. 65.
66. D. Held, *Democracy and the Global Order* (London: Polity, 1995), p. 268.
67. A. Cassese, '*Ex iniuria ius oritur*: Are We Moving Towards International Legitimisation of Forcible Humanitarian Countermeasures in the World Community?', *European Journal of International Law*, 10, 1 (1999), p. 26.
68. T. Weiss, *Humanitarian Intervention*, p. 89.
69. A. Linklater, *The Transformation of Political Community* (Oxford: Polity, 1998), p. 109.
70. Robertson, *Crimes against Humanity*, p. 372.
71. Hoffmann, 'Intervention', p. 22.
72. D. Chatterjee and D. Scheid, 'Introduction', p. 5.
73. M. Barnett, 'Bureaucratizing the Duty to Aid: The United Nations and the Rwandan Genocide', in Anthony Lang (ed.), *Just Intervention*, p. 175.
74. Robertson, *Crimes against Humanity*, p. 382.
75. Shaw, *Global Civil Society and International Politics*, p. 186.
76. Danish Institute of International Affairs, *Humanitarian Intervention*, p. 103.
77. M. Burton, 'Legalising the Sublegal', p. 418.
78. There are many sets of such criteria, see, for example, S. Hoffman, *The Ethics and Politics of Humanitarian Intervention* (Notre Dame, IN: Notre Dame University Press, 1996), p. 23; G. Lucas, 'From Jus ad Bellum to Jus ad Pacem', in Chatterjee and Scheid (eds), *Ethics and Foreign Intervention*, pp. 72–96; J. Stromseth, 'Rethinking Humanitarian Intervention', pp. 232–72; N. Wheeler, *Saving Strangers*, p. 34; T. Nardin, 'The Moral Basis of Humanitarian Intervention', pp. 11–27.
79. B. J. Hehir, 'Intervention: From Theory to Cases', *Ethics and International Affairs*, 9, (1995), p. 5.
80. Wheeler, *Saving Strangers*, p. 309.
81. Stromseth, 'Rethinking Humanitarian Intervention', pp. 233 and 234.
82. Ibid., p. 267.
83. Danish Institute of International Affairs, *Humanitarian Intervention*, pp. 99 and 105.
84. Ibid., p. 104.
85. Tony Blair quoted in W. Clark, *Waging Modern War* (Oxford: Public Affairs, 2001), p. xx.
86. G. Fuller, 'Two, Three, Many Kosovars', *New Perspectives Quarterly*, 16, 4 (1999), p. 12.
87. Robertson, *Crimes against Humanity*, pp. 451 and 387.
88. C. Guicherd, 'International Law and the War in Kosovo', pp. 19–34.
89. Stromseth, 'Rethinking Humanitarian Intervention', p. 243.
90. Quoted in Robertson, *Crimes against Humanity*, p. 433.
91. Independent International Commission on Kosovo, *Kosovo Report*, pp. 4 and 185.
92. A. Coll, 'Kosovo and the Moral Burdens of Power', in Andrew Bacevich and Eliot Cohen (eds), *War over Kosovo* (New York: Columbia University Press, 2001), p. 128.
93. A. Bellamy, *Kosovo and International Society* (Hamphshire: Palgrave Macmillan, 2002), pp. 211–12 and 214.
94. I. Daalder and M. O'Hanlon, *Winning Ugly* (Washington, DC: Brookings Institute, 2000), p. 13.

95. T. Dunne and N. Wheeler, 'Blair's Britain', p. 177.
96. T. Weiss, 'The Sunset of Humanitarian Intervention?', *Security Dialogue*, 35, 2 (2004), p. 137.
97. International Commission on Intervention and State Sovereignty, *The Responsibility to Protect*, p. 9.
98. Ibid., p. 31.
99. Ibid., p. 31.
100. There has been some dissonance regarding the criteria. Bellamy, for example, criticized them for being too restrictive, A. Bellamy, *Just Wars*, p. 208.
101. International Commission on Intervention and State Sovereignty, *The Responsibility to Protect*, p. 48.
102. Ibid., p. 49.
103. Ibid., p. 51.
104. Ibid., p. 50.
105. Ibid., p. 53.
106. Wheeler, *Saving Strangers*, p. 28.
107. International Commission on Intervention and State Sovereignty, *The Responsibility to Protect*, p. xi.
108. Ibid., p. 136.
109. International Commission on Intervention and State Sovereignty, *The Responsibility to Protect*, p. 136.
110. Ibid., p. 11.
111. Quoted in Kaldor, *Global Civil Society*, p. 149.
112. A. Roberts, 'The Role of Humanitarian Issues in International Politics in the 1990s', *International Review of the Red Cross*, 81, 833 (1999), p. 19.
113. L. Gelb, 'The Rise of Ethics in Foreign Policy', *Foreign Affairs*, 82, 3 (2003), p. 5.
114. Kaldor, *Global Civil Society*, p. 132.
115. Quoted in Chandler, *Constructing Global Civil Society*, p. 47.
116. Robertson, *Crimes against Humanity*, p. 82.
117. Wheeler, *Saving Strangers*, p. 41.
118. J. Mertus, 'Back to the Drawing Board', p. B01.

4 Humanitarian Intervention after Kosovo

1. Figures quoted in T. Seybolt, *Humanitarian Military Intervention* (Oxford: Oxford University Press, 2007), p. 88.
2. T. Samuel, 'East Timor: The Path to Self-Determination', in Chandra Lekha Sriram and Karin Wermester (eds), *From Promise to Practice: Strengthening UN Capacities for the Prevention of Violent Conflict* (London: Lynne Rienner, 2003), p. 205; S. Chesterman, *You the People* (Oxford: Oxford University Press, 2005), p. 61.
3. Report of the Security Council Mission to Jakarta and Dili, (S/1999/976), 8 to 12 September 1999, Annex I, para. 1.
4. See J. Chopra, 'Building State Failure in East Timor', in Aidan Hehir and Neil Robinson (eds), *State-Building: Theory and Practice* (London: Routledge, 2007), p. 146.
5. Samuel, 'East Timor: The Path to Self-Determination', p. 215.
6. A. Bellamy, *Just Wars*, p. 201.

7. Report of the Secretary-General, 'Question of East Timor', (S/1999/862), 9 August 1999, para 5 (emphasis added).
8. Human Rights Watch, 'Indonesian Government Must Prevent East Timor Bloodbath', 3 September 1999. Available online, http://hrw.org/english/docs/1999/09/03/eastti1662.htm, [accessed August 2007].
9. N. Wheeler and T. Dunne, 'East Timor and the New Humanitarian Interventionism', *International Affairs*, 77, 4 (2001), p. 813.
10. See A. Orford, *Reading Humanitarian Intervention*, pp. 1–37.
11. Wheeler and Dunne, 'East Timor and the New Humanitarian Interventionism', p. 822.
12. Ibid., p. 818.
13. Ibid., p. 821.
14. Ibid., p. 807.
15. A. Bellamy, 'Whither the Responsibility to Protect? Humanitarian Intervention and the 2005 World Summit', *Ethics and International Affairs*, 20, 2 (2006), p. 150.
16. Wheeler and Dunne, 'East Timor and the New Humanitarian Interventionism', p. 806.
17. Ibid., p. 808.
18. Ibid., p. 825.
19. S. Chesterman, *Just War or Just Peace?*, p. 225.
20. Ibid., p. 150.
21. Ibid., p. 150.
22. Ibid., p. 219.
23. Ibid., p.181.
24. Quoted in G. Robertson, *Crimes against Humanity*, p. 461.
25. Chesterman, *Just War or Just Peace?*, p. 151.
26. G. Gonzalez-Foerster, 'East Timor: Better Late Than Never', in Fabrice Weissman (ed.), *In the Shadow of "Just Wars"* (London: Hurts and Co., 2004), p. 26.
27. A. Roberts, 'The So-Called "Right" of Humanitarian Intervention', p. 5 (emphasis added).
28. See P. Bergen, *The Osama Bin Laden I Knew* (New York: The Free Press, 2006), p. 164; M. A. Zahab and O. Roy, *Islamist Networks* (London: Hurst and Co., 2004), p. 13.
29. Quoted in N. Wheeler, 'Humanitarian Intervention after September 11, 2001', in Anthony Lang (ed.), *Just Intervention* (Washington, DC: Georgetown University Press, 2003), p. 198.
30. Department of Defense News Briefing: General Tommy Franks, January 18, 2002. Quoted in Jim Garamone, 'Humanitarian Success Story in Afghanistan', US Department of Defense, American Forces Press Service: News Articles, January 18, 2002. Available online, http://www.defenselink.mil/news/newsarticle.aspx?id=43839 [accessed September 2007].
31. Quoted in Wheeler, 'Humanitarian Intervention after September 11, 2001', p. 202.
32. F. Calas and P. Salignon, 'Afghanistan: From "Militant Monks" to Crusaders', in Weissman (ed.), *In the Shadow of "Just Wars"* (London: Hurts and Co., 2004), p. 82.

33. Quoted in Calas and Salignon, 'Afghanistan: From "Militant Monks" to Crusaders', p. 82.
34. Ibid., p. 83.
35. N. Wheeler, 'Humanitarian Intervention after September 11, 2001', p. 198.
36. Calas and Salignon, 'Afghanistan: From "Militant Monks" to Crusaders', p. 86.
37. Y. Dinstein, *War, Aggression and Self-Defence* (Cambridge: Cambridge University Press, 2005), p. 237.
38. D. Chandler, *From Kosovo to Kabul*, p. 1.
39. Wheeler, 'Humanitarian Intervention after September 11, 2001', p. 207.
40. J.-H. Bradol, 'The Sacrificial International Order and Humanitarian Action', in Weissman (ed.), *In the Shadow of "Just Wars"* (London: Hurts and Co., 2004), p. 12.
41. Wheeler, 'Humanitarian Intervention after September 11, 2001', p. 208.
42. For such a study see D. Malone, *The International Struggle over Iraq*.
43. G. Bush, 'President Discusses Beginning of Operation Iraqi Freedom', White House Press Release, March 22 (2003). http://www.whitehouse.gov/news/releases/2003/03/20030322.html, [accessed October 4, 2007] (Emphasis added).
44. 'Transcript: Bush's Speech to the UN on Iraq', *The New York Times*, 12 September 2002.
45. Quoted in G. Hinsliff 'Blair stakes his political future on beating Iraq', *The Observer*, 16 February, 2003.
46. N. Wheeler and J. Morris, 'The Iraq War as a Humanitarian Intervention: The Cure is Worse than the Disease', in Ramesh Thakur and Wahegura Pal Singh Sidhu (eds), *The Iraq Crisis and World Order: Structural, Institutional and Normative Challenges* (New York: United Nations University, 2006), p. 453.
47. Ibid., p. 454.
48. John Howard, 'Transcript of the Prime Minister's Address to the National Press Club', 14 March 2003, http://www.pm.gov.au/media/Speech/2003/speech74.cfm [accessed 4 October 2007].
49. George Bush, 'State of the Union Address', 28 January 2003. http://www.whitehouse.gov/news/releases/2003/01/20030128-19.html, [accessed 4 October 2007].
50. "President Says Saddam Hussein Must Leave Iraq Within 48 Hours: Remarks by the President in Address to the Nation", 17 March 2003, www.whitehouse.gov/news/releases/2003/03/20030317-7.html, [accessed July 2007].
51. See A. Bellamy, 'Ethics and Intervention', pp. 136–37.
52. Ibid., p. 145.
53. See C. Lu, *Just and Unjust Interventions in World Politics,* p. 145.
54. R. Brauman and P. Salignon, 'Iraq: In Search of a "Humanitarian Crisis"', in Weissman (ed.), *In the Shadow of "Just Wars"*, p. 278.
55. Tony Blair, 'Speech to the Labour Party Conference', 28 September 2004. http://www.labour.org.uk/ac2004news?ux_news_id=ac04tb [accessed October 2004].
56. Tony Blair, 'Blair Terror Speech in Full', BBC News, 5 March 2004. http://news.bbc.co.uk/1/hi/uk_politics/3536131.stm, [accessed 4 October 2007].
57. George Bush, 'President Addresses the Nation in Prime Time Press Conference', 13 April 2004. http://www.whitehouse.gov/news/releases/2004/04/20040413-20.html, [accessed 4 October 2007].

58. George Bush, 'President Bush Discusses Global War on Terror', 10 April 2006. http://www.whitehouse.gov/news/releases/2006/04/20060410-1.html, [accessed 4 October 2007].
59. R. Melanson, 'Unravelling the Domestic Foreign Policy Consensus', in John Dumbrell and David Ryan (eds), *Vietnam in Iraq* (London: Routledge, 2007), p. 59.
60. Richard Clarke, quoted in D. Malone, *The International Struggle over Iraq*, p. 187.
61. Jack Straw, quoted in Malone, *The International Struggle over Iraq*, p. 191.
62. Quoted in D. Cortright, 'The World Says No: The Global Movement against War in Iraq', in Ramesh Thakur and Wahegura Pal Singh Sidhu (eds), *The Iraq Crisis and World Order: Structural, Institutional and Normative Challenges* (New York: United Nations University, 2006), p. 89.
63. Malone, *The International Struggle over Iraq*, p. 191.
64. In early 1998 the group wrote an open letter to President Clinton calling for 'the removal of Saddam Hussein's regime from power' arguing that further weapon inspections would be futile and military action was therefore required. Project for a New American Century, 'Open Letter to President William J. Clinton', 26 January 1998. http://www.newamericancentury.org/iraqclintonletter.htm [accessed 4 October 2007].
65. Quoted in L. Gardner, 'The Final Chapter?', in Dumbrell and Ryan (eds), *Vietnam in Iraq* (London: Routledge, 2007), p. 19.
66. H. Blix, 'The Importance of Inspections', Carnegie Endowment for International Peace, Proliferation Brief, 7, No. 11, (2004). http://www.carnegieendowment.org/publications/index.cfm?fa=viewandid=1591, [accessed 4 October 2007].
67. Malone, *The International Struggle over Iraq*, p. 212.
68. M. Kaldor, 'From Just War to Just Peace', in Charles Reed and David Ryall (eds), *The Price of Peace* (Cambridge: Cambridge University Press, 2007), p. 263.
69. See M. Wheeler, 'A US Political Perspective', in Reed and Ryall (eds), *The Price of Peace* (Cambridge: Cambridge University Press, 2007), pp. 277–85.
70. See J. Tyner, *The Business of War* (Aldershot: Ashgate, 2006).
71. Human Rights Watch, 'Human Rights News: Crisis in Darfur', 18 September 2007. http://www.hrw.org/english/docs/2004/05/05/darfur8536.htm [accessed 8 October 2007].
72. P. Williams and A. Bellamy, 'The Responsibility to Protect and the Crisis in Darfur', *Security Dialogue*, 36, 1 (2005), p. 30.
73. Ibid., p. 31.
74. Ibid., p. 31.
75. UNHCR, 'Report of the United Nations High Commissioner for Human Rights and Follow-Up to the World Conference on Human Rights: Situation of Human Rights in the Darfur region of Sudan', E/CN.4/2005/3, 7 May (2004), pp. 6, 3 and 22. http://www.unhchr.ch/huridocda/huridoca.nsf/AllSymbols/863D14602AA82CAEC1256EA80038E268/$File/G0414221.doc?OpenElement [accessed 12 October 2007].
76. United Nations Security Council, 5015th Meeting (S/PV.5015), 30 July 2004, p. 4, http://daccessdds.un.org/doc/UNDOC/PRO/N04/445/15/PDF/N0444515.pdf?OpenElement [accessed 11 October 2007].
77. Bellamy, *Just Wars*, p. 224.

78. Quoted in W. Hoge, 'U.N. Council Threatens to Punish Sudan Over Militia Killings', *New York Times*, 31 July 2004.
79. T. Weiss, *Humanitarian Intervention*, p. 55.
80. Ibid., p. 56.
81. Ibid., p. 58.
82. Human rights Watch 'Human Rights News: Crisis in Darfur', 18 September(2007), http://www.hrw.org/english/docs/2004/05/05/darfur8536.htm [accessed 8 October 2007].
83. Bellamy, *Just Wars*, p. 222.
84. H. Slim, 'Dithering over Darfur?', *International Affairs*, 80, 5 (2004), p. 811.
85. Ibid., p. 815.
86. R. Dallaire, 'Looking at Darfur, Seeing Rwanda', *New York Times*, 4 October 2004.
87. Quoted in P. Williams, 'Military Responses to Mass Killing: The African Union Mission to Sudan', *International Peacekeeping*, 13, 2 (2006), p. 181.
88. J. Mueller, 'Legitimacy, Success and Iraq', in David Armstrong, Theo Farrell and Bice Maiguashca (eds), *Force and Legitimacy in World Politics* (Cambridge: Cambridge University Press, 2005), pp. 122–3.
89. Slim, 'Dithering over Darfur?', pp. 811–28.
90. US Department of State, 'The Crisis in Darfur: Secretary Colin Powell, Testimony before the Senate Foreign Relations Committee', 9 September 2004. http://www.state.gov/secretary/former/powell/remarks/36042.htm [accessed 11 October 2007].
91. Dinstein, *War, Aggression and Self-Defence*, pp. 72–3.
92. Bellamy, *Just Wars*, p. 223.
93. Weiss, *Humanitarian Intervention*, p. 54.
94. Slim, 'Dithering over Darfur?', p. 815.
95. Quoted in D. Fisher, 'Humanitarian Intervention', in *The Price of Peace*, Reed and Ryall (eds) (Cambridge: Cambridge University Press, 2007), p. 103.
96. K. Annan, 'In Larger Freedom: Decision Time at the UN', *Foreign Affairs*, 84, 3 (2005), p. 66.
97. United Nations General Assembly, 'Draft resolution referred to the High-Level Plenary Meeting of the General Assembly by the General Assembly at its fifty-ninth session: 2005 World Summit Outcome', A/60/L.1, 15 September 2005, p. 31. http://www.who.int/hiv/universalaccess2010/worldsummit.pdf [accessed 22 October 2007].
98. International Commission on Intervention and State Sovereignty, *The Responsibility to Protect*, p. 51.
99. A. Bellamy, 'Whither the Responsibility to Protect? Humanitarian Intervention and the 2005 World Summit', p. 155.
100. John Bolton, 'Letter to President Ping', 30 August 2005. www.responsiblity-toprotect.org/index.php?module=uploadsandfunc=downloadand-fileld=219 [accessed 22 October 2007].
101. Bellamy, 'Whither the Responsibility to Protect? Humanitarian Intervention and the 2005 World Summit', p. 153.
102. Weiss, *Humanitarian Intervention*, p. 117.
103. Bellamy, 'Whither the Responsibility to Protect? Humanitarian Intervention and the 2005 World Summit', pp. 145–6.
104. Ibid., p. 167.

105. N. Wheeler, 'A Victory for Common Humanity? The Responsibility to Protect after the 2005 World Summit', paper presented at the conference 'The UN at Sixty: Celebration or Wake?', Faculty of Law, University of Toronto, Canada, 6–7 October, 2005, p. 2. Available at www.una.org.uk/humanrights/R2P%5B1%5D.pdf [accessed 11 October 2007].
106. Ibid., p. 9.
107. Quoted in Wheeler, 'A Victory for Common Humanity? The Responsibility to Protect after the 2005 World Summit', p. 2.
108. Weiss, *Humanitarian Intervention*, p. 122.
109. T. Weiss, 'The Sunset of Humanitarian Intervention?', pp. 135–53.

5 The Normative Flaws

1. C. Brown, 'Ethics and Foreign Policy', in Margot Light and Karen Smith (eds), *Ethics and Foreign Policy* (Cambridge: Cambridge University Press, 2001), p. 32.
2. Tony Blair quoted in W. Clark, *Waging Modern War* (Oxford: Public Affairs, 2001), p. xx.
3. See F. Zakaria, 'Is Realism Finished?', *The National Interest*, Winter, 30 (1992).
4. N. Wheeler, *Saving Strangers*, p. 363.
5. N. Wheeler, 'Humanitarian Intervention after September 11, 2001', p. 207.
6. M. Frost, 'The Ethics of Humanitarian Intervention', in Smith and Light (eds), *Ethics and Foreign Policy* (Cambridge: Cambridge University Press, 2001), p. 42.
7. Ibid., p. 51.
8. M. Kaldor, *Global Civil Society*, p. 12.
9. T. Weiss, *Humanitarian Intervention*, p. 100.
10. A. Buchanan and R. O. Keohane, 'The Preventive Use of Force', pp. 1–22.
11. A. Bellamy, *Kosovo and International Society*, p. 212.
12. 'Special Report: The International Arms Trade to Indonesia', *The Guardian*, 9 September 1999.
13. S. Chesterman, *Just War or Just Peace?*, p. 185.
14. Weiss, *Humanitarian Intervention*, p. 119.
15. John Bolton, 'Letter to President Ping', August 30, www.responsiblitytoprotect.org/index.php?module=uploads&func=download&fileld=219 [accessed 22 October 2007].
16. J. Mueller 'Force, Legitimacy, Success, and Iraq', p. 109.
17. Ibid., p. 123.
18. As alleged by both Human Rights Watch and Amnesty International.
19. See D. Chandler, *From Kosovo to Kabul*, p. 85.
20. The White House, 'National Strategy for Combating Terrorism', September 2006. http://www.whitehouse.gov/nsc/nsct/2006/index.html [accessed 1 November 2007].
21. See Kaldor, *Global Civil Society*; M. Keck and K. Sikkink, *Activists beyond Borders: Advocacy Networks in International Politics* (Ithaca: Cornell University Press, 1998).
22. Wheeler and Morris describe the response to Darfur as a 'Dismal failure.... The international community remained stubbornly passive in the face of what was at the time the world's worst humanitarian crisis'. N. Wheeler and J. Morris, 'Justifying the Iraq War as a Humanitarian Intervention', p. 457.

23. D. de Bréadún, 'A Defiant Bush Defends Iraq Strategy before the UN', *Irish Times*, 22 September 2004, p. 11.
24. SaveDarfur, 'About US: Frequently Asked Questions', (2007) http://www.savedarfur.org/pages/faq/#1 [accessed November 2007].
25. H. Chmela, 'Thousands Rally in Washington for More U.S. Aid to Darfur', *The New York Times*, 1 May 2006.
26. A. Meixner, 'Darfur: A Problem Worth Solving', SaveDarfur, 1 November 2007, http://www.savedarfur.org/blog/entries/darfur_a_problem_worth_solving/ [accessed November 2007].
27. According to data from Freedom house of the 52 member states of the African Union, 11 are classed as 'Free', 21 as 'Partially Free' and 20 as 'Not Free'. Freedom House, 'Freedom in the World 2007: Sub Scores', http://www.freedomhouse.org/template.cfm?page = 372 [accessed November 2007].
28. D. Cortright, 'The World Says No', p. 75.
29. P. Tyler, 'Threats and Responses: News Analysis; A New Power in the Streets', *New York Times*, 17 February 2003.
30. Cortright, 'The World Says No', p. 75.
31. D. Malone, *The International Struggle over Iraq*, pp. 185–221.
32. A. Bellamy, 'Whither the Responsibility to Protect? Humanitarian Intervention and the 2005 World Summit', p. 150.
33. Independent International Commission on Kosovo, *Kosovo Report*, p. 4.
34. M. Burton, 'Legalising the Sublegal', p. 418.
35. International Commission on Intervention and State Sovereignty, *The Responsibility to Protect*, p. 32.
36. See Wheeler, *Saving Strangers*, p. 309.
37. Assembly of the African Union, 'Decision on Darfur', Third Ordinary Session, 6–8 July 2004, Addis Ababa, Ethiopia, para. 2. http://www.africa-union.org/DARFUR/homedar.htm# [accessed November 2007]. Medecins Sans Frontieres, 'MSF Condemns Violence in Darfur', *Medecins Sans Frontieres Article*, 8 April 2005. http://www.msf.org/msfinternational/invoke.cfm?component=article&objectid=2260FE2B-E018-0C72-09DACE85BB3176F8&method=full_html [accessed November 2007].
38. Bellamy, 'Whither the Responsibility to Protect? Humanitarian Intervention and the 2005 World Summit', p. 159.
39. G. Bardos, 'International Policy in Southeast Europe: A Diagnosis', in Raju Thomas (ed.), *Yugoslavia Unravelled: Sovereignty, Self Determination, Intervention* (Oxford: Lexington Books, 2003), p. 57.
40. T. Garton-Ash, 'The War We Almost Lost', *The Guardian*, 4 September 2000, p. 2.
41. P. Hilpold, 'Humanitarian Intervention', p. 458.
42. Regarding this aspect of the debate on Kosovo, see A. Hehir, 'The Impact of Analogical Reasoning on US Foreign Policy Towards Kosovo', *Journal of Peace Research*, 43, 1 (2005), pp. 67–81. Regarding Iraq see Malone, *The International Struggle over Iraq*, pp. 185–221.
43. See Clark, *Waging Modern War*, pp. 240–1.
44. See A. Roberts, 'NATO's "Humanitarian War" over Kosovo', p. 114.
45. K. Roth, 'Bombs Report off Target', *The Guardian*, 12 January 2000, p. 21; Amnesty International (2000) 'NATO/Federal Republic of Yugoslavia: "Collateral Damage" or Unlawful Killings?', http://web.amnesty.org/library/index/ENGEUR700182000 [accessed September 2004].

46. See Malone, *The International Struggle over Iraq*.
47. Buchanan and Keohane, 'The Preventative Use of Force', p. 19.
48. N. Wheeler, 'A Victory for Common Humanity? The Responsibility to Protect after the 2005 World Summit', p. 7. Available at www.una.org.uk/human-rights/R2P%5B1%5D.pdf [accessed 11 October 2007].
49. As Alan Greenspan, former Chairman of the United States Federal Reserve has noted, 'I am saddened that it is politically inconvenient to acknowledge what everyone knows: the Iraq war is largely about oil'. Quoted in H. Davies, 'Political Currency Examined', *The Guardian Review*, 6 October 2007.
50. Brown, 'Ethics, Interests, and Foreign Policy', p. 23; Weiss, *Humanitarian Intervention*, p. 7.
51. See Chesterman, *Just War or Just Peace?*, pp. 7–8.
52. Bellamy, *Just Wars*, p. 5.
53. According to Hayden, '... any legitimate military action can only be justified from a cosmopolitan perspective that integrates human security and the right to peace with the criteria of Just War'. P. Hayden, *Cosmopolitan Global Politics*, p. 90. See also, Buchanan and Keohane, 'The Preventive Use of Force', pp. 1–21.
54. R. Myers, 'Notes on the Just War Theory', *Ethics and International Affairs*, 10 (1996), p. 118.
55. Bellamy, *Just Wars*, p. 26.
56. R. L. Holmes, *On War and Morality* (Princeton, NJ: Princeton University Press, 1989), p. 141.
57. See D. Boucher and P. Kelly, *Political Thinkers: From Socrates to the Present* (Oxford: Oxford University Press, 2003), p. 113.
58. Aquinas quoted in J. Finnis, *Aquinas* (Oxford: Oxford University Press, 1998), p. 290.
59. John Tooke, *The Just War in Aquinas and Grotius* (London: SPCK, 1965), p. 26.
60. Ibid., p. 27.
61. Aquinas quoted in D. Boucher, *Political Theories of International Relations* (Oxford: Oxford University Press, 1998), p. 198.
62. Bellamy, *Just Wars*, p. 50.
63. Ibid., p. 54.
64. Ibid., p. 55.
65. A. J. Coates, *The Ethics of War* (Manchester: Manchester University Press, 1997), p. 123.
66. N. Rengger, 'The Judgement of War', in Armstrong, Farrell and Maiguashca (eds), *Force and Legitimacy in World Politics* (Cambridge: Cambridge University Press, 2005), p. 160.
67. C. Reed and D. Ryall, 'Introduction', in Charles Reed and David Ryall (eds), *The Price of Peace* (Cambridge: Cambridge University Press, 2007), pp. 1–2.
68. G. Weigel, 'The Development of Just War Thinking in the post–Cold War World', in Reed and Ryall (eds), *The Price of Peace* (Cambridge: Cambridge University Press, 2007), p. 23.
69. M. Evans, 'In Humanity's Name: Democracy and the Right to Wage War', in Mark Evans (ed.), *Just War Theory: A Reappraisal* (Edinburgh: Edinburgh University Press, 2005), p. 77.
70. Ibid., p. 75.
71. A. Orford, *Reading Humanitarian Intervention*, pp. 34–6.

72. D. Chandler, 'International Justice', pp. 55–66.
73. Bellamy, 'Whither the Responsibility to Protect? Humanitarian Intervention and the 2005 World Summit', p. 151.
74. Bellamy, *Just Wars*, pp. 223–4.
75. Bellamy, 'Whither the Responsibility to Protect? Humanitarian Intervention and the 2005 World Summit', p. 33.
76. Quoted in A. Bellamy, 'Responsibility to Protect or Trojan Horse? The Crisis in Darfur and Humanitarian Intervention after Iraq', *Ethics and International Affairs*, 19, 2 (2005), p. 45.
77. Bolton, 'Letter to President Ping'.
78. Bellamy, 'Whither the Responsibility to Protect? Humanitarian Intervention and the 2005 World Summit', p. 169.
79. J. Tanguy, 'Redefining Sovereignty and Intervention', *Ethics and International Affairs*, 17, 1 (2003), p. 142.
80. Evans, 'In Humanity's Name', p. 75; Tyler, 'Threats and Responses'; Robertson, *Crimes against Humanity*, p. 450.
81. M. Kaldor, 'Transnational Civil Society', p. 210.
82. Human Rights Watch, 'World Report 2000', quoted in Orford, *Reading Humanitarian Intervention*, p. 8.
83. B. Altunbas, 'Darfur has Become and Even Greater Challenge for Humanitarian Action', *Medecins Sans Frontieres Article*, 26 October 2007. http://www.msf.org/msfinternational/invoke.cfm?objectid=DCAD5415-15C5-F00A-25AC4B9C6129E0E7&component=toolkit.article&method=full_html [accessed November 2007].
84. Weiss, *Humanitarian Intervention*, p. 154.
85. Kaldor admits, 'The concept of transnational civil society is less a descriptive or analytical term and more a political project'. Kaldor, 'Transnational Civil Society', p. 195.
86. Myers, 'Notes on the Just War Theory', p. 127.

6 The Dangers of Unregulated Humanitarian Intervention

1. D. Armstrong and T. Farrell, 'Introduction', p. 13.
2. F. Teson, 'Collective Humanitarian Intervention', *Michigan Journal of International Law*, 17 (1996), p. 342.
3. A. Linklater, 'The Good International Citizen and the Crisis in Kosovo'.
4. C. Brown, 'Selective Humanitarianism: In Defense of Inconsistency', in Deen Chatterjee and Don Scheid (eds), *Ethics and Foreign Intervention* (Cambridge: Cambridge University Press, 2003), p. 48.
5. Kofi Annan quoted in G. Lyons and M. Mastanduno (eds), *Beyond Westphalia*, p. 2.
6. F. Teson, 'The Liberal Case for Humanitarian Intervention', in Larry May, Eric Rove and Steve Viner (eds), *The Morality of War* (Upper Saddle River, NJ: Pearson, 2005), p. 358.
7. See S. Chesterman and M. Byers, 'Changing the Rules About Rules?', in J. L. Holzgrefe and Robert Keohane (eds), *Humanitarian Intervention* (Cambridge: Cambridge University Press, 2003), pp. 177–8.
8. T. Dunne and N. Wheeler, 'Blair's Britain', p. 183.

9. President Clinton described NATO's intervention as a 'moral imperative'. Foreign Desk, 'Conflict in the Balkans', *The New York Times*, March 25 1999, p. 15.
10. W. J. Rockler, 'War Crimes Law Applies to U.S. Too', *Chicago Tribune*, 23 May 1999.
11. D. Clark, 'Iraq has wrecked our case for humanitarian wars', *The Guardian*, 12 August 2003, p. 20.
12. A. Cassese, '*Ex iniuria ius oritur*', p. 25.
13. Dunne and Wheeler, 'Blair's Britain', p. 177.
14. See W. Bain, 'The Political Theory of Trusteeship and the Twilight of International Equality', pp. 59–77.
15. M. Glennon, 'The New Interventionism', *Foreign Affairs*, 78, 3 (1999), p. 4.
16. N. Lemann, 'The Next World Order', *The New Yorker*, 1 April 2002, pp. 42–8.
17. See T. Frank, 'Legality and Legitimacy in Humanitarian Intervention', in Terry Nardin and Melissa Williams (eds), *Humanitarian Intervention* (New York: New York University Press, 2006), p. 143.
18. M. Byers, 'Not yet Havoc', in Armstrong, Farrell and Maiguashca (eds), *Force and Legitimacy in World Politics* (Cambridge: Cambridge University Press, 2005), p. 51.
19. See Thomas Weiss, *Humanitarian Intervention*, p. 135.
20. R. Perle, 'Thank God for the Death of the UN', *The Guardian*, 21 March 2003. According to John Bolton, ironically the US Ambassador to the UN for a period under President Bush, 'There is no such thing as the United Nations. There is only the international community, which can only be led by the only remaining superpower, which is the United States'. Quoted in R. Watson, 'Bush Deploys Hawk as New UN Envoy', *Timesonline*, 8 March 2005. http://www.timesonline.co.uk/article/0,,11069-1515816,00.html [accessed January 2008].
21. Clark, 'Iraq has wrecked our case for humanitarian wars', p. 20.
22. Frank, 'Legality and Legitimacy in Humanitarian Intervention', p. 144.
23. Quoted in Simon Chesterman (2002), *Just War or Just Peace?*, pp. 144–5.
24. S. Chesterman, *Just War or Just Peace?*, p. 146.
25. D. Held, *Democracy and the Global Order* (London: Polity, 1995), p. 273.
26. Ibid., pp. 273–4.
27. International Commission on Intervention and State Sovereignty, *The Responsibility to Protect*, p. 49.
28. Ibid., p. 53.
29. Quoted in N. White, 'The Will and Authority of the Security Council after Iraq', *Leiden Journal of International Law*, 17, 4 (2004), p. 660.
30. M. Wesley, 'The New Interventionism and the Invasion of Iraq', in Michael Heazle and Iyanatul Islam, *Beyond the Iraq War: The Promises, Pitfalls and Perils of External Interventionism* (Cheltenham: Edward Elgar, 2006), p. 20.
31. White, 'The Will and Authority of the Security Council after Iraq', p. 655.
32. See Clark, 'Iraq has wrecked our case for humanitarian wars', p. 20; Weiss, *Humanitarian Intervention*, p. 124.
33. R. Falk, 'Legality and Legitimacy', in Armstrong, Farrell and Maiguashca (eds), *Force and Legitimacy in World Politics* (Cambridge: Cambridge University Press, 2005), p. 42.
34. M. Evans, 'In Humanity's Name', p. 71.
35. See R. Melanson, 'Unravelling the Domestic Foreign Policy Consensus', pp. 48–65.

36. S. Chesterman and M. Byers, 'Changing the Rules About Rules?', p. 194.
37. This reading of international law should not be exaggerated, however, as some elements of hierarchy remain. See A. Orford, *Reading Humanitarian Intervention*; G. Simpson, *Great Powers and Outlaw States*.
38. A. Hurrell, 'Legitimacy and the Use of Force', p. 18.
39. V. E. Parsi, *The Inevitable Alliance* (Basingstoke: Palgrave Macmillan, 2006), p. 136.
40. C. Reus-Smit, 'Liberal Hierarchy and the Licence to Use Force', p. 71.
41. Ibid., p. 72.
42. Bain, 'The Political Theory of Trusteeship and the Twilight of International Equality', p. 66.
43. Simpson, *Great Powers and Outlaw States*, pp. 280 and 78.
44. Ibid., p. 72.
45. G. Gong, *The Standard of Civilisation in International Society* (Oxford: Oxford University Press, 1984).
46. Reus-Smit, 'Liberal Hierarchy and the Licence to Use Force', p. 87.
47. M. Kaldor, *Global Civil Society*, p. 6.
48. M. Kaldor, *New and Old Wars*, pp. 120 and 122.
49. M. Glennon, 'The New Interventionism', p. 2; R. Cooper, 'The New Liberal Imperialism', *The Observer*, 7 April 2002.
50. Cooper, 'The New Liberal Imperialism'.
51. T. Farer quoted in Orford, *Reading Humanitarian Intervention*, p. 173.
52. Orford, *Reading Humanitarian Intervention*, p. 34.
53. Both quoted in J. Tyner, *The Business of War* (Aldershot: Ashgate, 2006), pp. 35 and 36.
54. Simpson, *Great Powers and Outlaw States*, p. 283.
55. Falk, 'Legality and Legitimacy', p. 37.
56. Quoted in Nardin, 'The Moral Basis for Humanitarian Intervention', p. 16.
57. A. Bellamy, 'Ethics and Intervention', p. 132.
58. Quoted in R. Myers, 'Notes on the Just War Theory', *Ethics and International Affairs*, 10 (1996), p. 119.
59. Weiss, *Humanitarian Intervention*, p. 37.
60. M. Pugh, 'Peacekeeping and Critical Theory', in Alex Bellamy and Paul Williams (eds), *Peace Operations and the Global Order* (London: Routledge, 2005), p. 40.
61. Reus-Smit, 'Liberal Hierarchy and the Licence to Use Force', p. 91.
62. Speech Given by President Hugo Chavez at 60th UN General Assembly. New York September 15th 2005. Available online, http://www.embavenez-us.org/news.php?nid=1745 [accessed January 2008].
63. Group of 77 South Summit, 'Declaration of the South Summit', Havana, Cuba, 10–14 April 2000, para. 54. Available online, http://www.g77.org/summit/Declaration_G77Summit.htm [accessed January 2008].
64. See B. Harff and T. Gurr, 'Towards an Empirical Theory of Genocides and Politicides', *International Studies Quarterly*, 32 (1988), pp. 359–71; H. Fein 'Genocide: A Sociological Perspective', *Current Sociology*, 38, 1 (1990), pp. 1–126.
65. A. Kuperman, 'Suicidal Rebellions and the Moral Hazard of Humanitarian Intervention', in Timothy Crawford and Alan Kuperman (eds), *Gambling on Humanitarian Intervention* (London: Routledge, 2006), p. 3.
66. Ibid., pp. 1–2.

67. M. Weller, *The Crisis in Kosovo 1989–1999: International Documents and Analysis* (Cambridge: Documents and Analysis Publishing, 1999), p. 29.
68. T. Judah, *Kosovo: War and Revenge* (New Haven: Yale University Press, 2000), pp. 124–5.
69. C. Hodge, 'Casual War: NATO's Intervention in Kosovo', *Ethics and International Affairs*, 14 (2000), p. 26.
70. J. Gow, *The Serbian Project and its Adversaries: A Strategy of War Crimes* (Montreal: McGill-Queens University Press, 2003), p. 256.
71. Quoted in Kuperman, 'Suicidal Rebellions and the Moral Hazard of Humanitarian Intervention', p. 12.
72. Ibid., p. 12.
73. Quoted in A. Kuperman, 'Transnational Causes of Genocide', in Raju Thomas (ed.), *Yugoslavia Unravelled: Sovereignty, Self Determination, Intervention* (Oxford: Lexington Books, 2003), p. 57.
74. Ibid., p. 57.
75. Chapter 7 will advance a possible solution to this problem.
76. C. Chinkin, 'Kosovo: A Good or Bad War?', *American Journal of International Law*, 93, 4 (1991), p. 847.
77. N. Mandela, 'Address by Former President Nelson Mandela', in Independent International Commission on Kosovo, *Kosovo Report*, pp. 15–16.
78. D. Malone, *The International Struggle over Iraq*, p. 204.
79. Orford, *Reading Humanitarian Intervention*, p. 5.
80. Kaldor, *Global Civil Society*, p. 6.
81. E. Said, *Culture and Imperialism* (London: Chatto and Windus, 1993), p. 9.
82. See Bain, 'The Political Theory of Trusteeship and the Twilight of International Equality', pp. 59–77.
83. Reus-Smit, 'Liberal Hierarchy and the Licence to Use Force', in Armstrong, Farrell and Maiguashca (eds), *Force and Legitimacy in World Politics*, p. 72.
84. P. Hayden, *Cosmopolitan Global Politics*, p. 70.
85. M. Shaw, *Global Society and International Relations*, p. 175.
86. Quoted in Robertson, *Crimes against Humanity*, p. 433.

7 Regulating Humanitarian Intervention: The Need for Redirection

1. K. Ambos, 'Comment – NATO, the UN and the Use of Force: Legal Aspects', pp. 114–15.
2. T. Farer, 'The Ethics of Intervention in Self Determination Struggles', p. 143.
3. See S. Chesterman, *Just War or Just Peace?*, Chap. 1; A. Arend and R. Beck, *International Law and the Use of Force*, Chap. 8.
4. A. Hurrell, 'Legitimacy and the Use of Force', p. 30.
5. Ibid., p. 30.
6. N. Wheeler, 'Agency, Humanitarianism and Intervention', p. 22.
7. T. Frank, 'Legality and Legitimacy in Humanitarian Intervention', p. 144.
8. S. Chesterman, 'Hard Cases Make Bad Law', p. 54.
9. P. Hayden, *Cosmopolitan Global Politics*, p. 91.
10. S. Chesterman and M. Byers, 'Has US Power Destroyed the UN?'.
11. S. Chesterman, 'Hard Cases Make Bad Law', p. 54.

12. T. Nardin, 'The Moral Basis for Humanitarian Intervention', p. 19.
13. A. Bellamy, 'Ethics and Intervention', p. 134.
14. International Commission on Intervention and State Sovereignty, *The Responsibility to Protect*, p. 51.
15. E. H. Carr, *The Twenty Years Crisis, 1919–1939*, p. 74.
16. H. Morgenthau, *Politics among Nations*, p. 9.
17. J. Donnelly, 'Twentieth Century Realism', p. 107.
18. See T. Weiss, *Humanitarian Intervention*, p. 37.
19. C. Schmidt, *The Concept of the Political*, trans. George Schwabb (Chicago: Chicago University Press, 1996), p. 54.
20. Cohen suggests that publication of a new translation of Schmidt's *Nomos of the Earth* at the same time as the invasion of Iraq was more than a coincidence. Jean Cohen, 'Whose Sovereignty? Empire Versus International Law', *Ethics and International Affairs*, 18, 3 (2004), p. 1.
21. Cited in D. Johnstone, 'NATO and the New World Order – Ideals and Self-interest', in Philip Hammond and Edward Herman (eds), *Degraded Capability: The Media and the Kosovo Crisis* (London: Pluto Press, 2000), p. 7.
22. Herman and Peterson note that while the abuses of human rights occurring in Yugoslavia received media attention, 'massive human rights abuses in countries supported by the NATO powers, such as Turkey, Indonesia in East Timor, Colombia and Israel in its Occupied Territories, received slight or zero attention'. E. Herman and D. Peterson, 'Morality's Avenging Angels', p. 220.
23. Quoted in D. Chandler, *From Kosovo to Kabul*, p. 36.
24. P. Hammond, 'Moral Combat', in David Chandler (ed.), *Rethinking Human Rights*, p. 176.
25. International Commission on Intervention and State Sovereignty, *The Responsibility to Protect*, pp. 5–6.
26. Ibid., p. 55.
27. Quoted in R. Caplan, 'Humanitarian Intervention', p. 31.
28. International Commission on Intervention and State Sovereignty, *The Responsibility to Protect*, p. 55.
29. Antonio Cassese, *International Law* (Oxford: Oxford University Press, 2005), p. 379.
30. Ibid., pp. 378–9.
31. Ibid., pp. 378–9.
32. D. Armstrong, T. Farrell and H. Lambert, *International Law and International Relations* (Cambridge: Cambridge University Press, 2007), p. 157.
33. Ibid., p. 158.
34. M. Fitzmaurice, 'The Practical Working of the Law of Treaties', in Mark Evans (ed.), *International Law* (Oxford: Oxford University Press, 2006), pp. 205–6.
35. L. Henkin, 'Compliance with International Law in an Inter-State System', *Academie de droit international, Recueil des cours* 1989 (Dordrecht: Martinus Nijhoff, 1990), p. 250.
36. Danish Institute of International Affairs, *Humanitarian Intervention*, p. 97.
37. See Chesterman, *Just War or Just Peace?*, p. 128; Danish Institute of International Affairs, *Humanitarian Intervention*, p. 71.
38. Cassese, *International Law*, p. 347.
39. N. White, 'The Will and Authority of the Security Council after Iraq', p. 666.
40. See M. Finnemore, 'Fights About Rules', p. 223.

41. Weiss, *Humanitarian Intervention*, p. 117; N. Wheeler, 'A Victory for Common Humanity? The Responsibility to Protect after the 2005 World Summit', p. 2. Available at www.una.org.uk/humanrights/R2P%5B1%5D.pdf [accessed 11 October 2007].
42. UN High Level Panel on Threats, Challenges and Change (2004), 'A more secure world: Our shared responsibility', p. 67. Available at http://www.un.org/secureworld/report2.pdf [accessed February 2008].
43. Hurrell, 'Legitimacy and the Use of Force', p. 30.
44. Ibid., p. 30.
45. N. Wheeler and J. Morris, 'Justifying the Iraq War as a Humanitarian Intervention', p. 448.
46. Independent International Commission on Kosovo, *Kosovo Report*, p. 186.
47. International Commission on Intervention and State Sovereignty, *The Responsibility to Protect*, p. 3.
48. B. Simma 'NATO, the UN and the Use of Force', *European Journal of International Law*, 10, 1 (1999), p. 6.
49. C. Guicherd, 'International Law and the War in Kosovo', p. 20.
50. J. Mearsheimer, 'The False Promise of International Institutions', *International Security*, 19, 3 (1994), p. 8.
51. Morgenthau, *Politics among Nations*, p. 9.
52. Mearsheimer, 'The False Promise of International Institutions', p. 7.
53. White, 'The Will and Authority of the Security Council after Iraq', p. 666.
54. See S. Molloy, *The Hidden History of Realism* (Basingstoke: Palgrave Macmillan, 2006).
55. N. Malcolm, *Aspects of Hobbes* (Oxford: Oxford University Press, 2002), p. 432.
56. W. Bain, 'Introduction', in William Bain (ed.), *The Empire of Security and the Safety of the Peoples* (London: Routledge, 2006), p. 1.
57. C. Brown, *Sovereignty, Rights and Justice* (London: Polity, 2006), p. 69.
58. K. Waltz, *Theory of International Politics* (London: McGraw Hill, 1979).
59. T. Landman, *Studying Human Rights*, p. 14.
60. A. Cassese, '*Ex iniuria ius oritur*', p. 23.
61. Guicherd, 'International Law and the War in Kosovo', p. 23.
62. G. Kennan, 'Morality and Foreign Policy', *Foreign Affairs*, 64, 2 (1985), p. 207.
63. Though, of course, the creation of such an organ would be opposed precisely because it would reduce the power of states.
64. Quoted in M. Burton, 'Legalising the Sublegal', p. 421.
65. J. Stromseth, 'Rethinking Humanitarian Intervention', p. 257.
66. Cassese, *International Law*, p. 355.
67. Ibid., pp. 356–7.
68. Burton, 'Legalising the Sublegal', p. 422.
69. J. Chopra and T. Weiss, 'Sovereignty is no Longer Sacrosanct', p. 97.
70. O. Schachter, *International Law in Theory and Practice* (Dordrecht: Martinus Nijhoff, 1991), p. 126.
71. Chesterman, *Just War or Just Peace?*, p. 231.
72. Ibid., pp. 231–2.
73. Ibid., p. 227.
74. Ibid., p. 182.
75. P. Christopher, *The Ethics of War and Peace* (New Jersey: Pearson, 2004), p. 248.

76. J. Cohen, 'Whose Sovereignty? Empire Versus International Law', p. 14.
77. Quoted in Wheeler, 'Humanitarian Intervention After September 11, 2001', p. 194.
78. H. Bull, *Justice in International Relations*, p. 6.
79. Ibid., pp. 11–2.
80. Cohen, 'Whose Sovereignty? Empire Versus International Law', p. 16.
81. K. Feste, *Intervention* (London: Praeger, 2003), p. 61.
82. Independent International Commission on Intervention and State Sovereignty, *The Responsibility to Protect*, p. 31.
83. L. Henkin, 'Kosovo and the Law of "Humanitarian Intervention"', *American Journal of International Law*, 93, 4 (1999), pp. 824–5.
84. See D. Jett, *Why Peacekeeping Fails* (Basingstoke: Palgrave Macmillan, 2001).
85. N. Wheeler, *Saving Strangers*, p. 306.
86. Cassese, *International Law*, p. 155.
87. Ibid., p. 339.
88. V. E. Parsi, *The Inevitable Alliance* (Basingstoke: Palgrave Macmillan, 2006), p. 118.
89. Cohen, 'Whose Sovereignty? Empire Versus International Law', p. 23.
90. F. Berman, 'Moral Versus legal Imperatives', in Charles Reed and David Ryall (eds), *The Price of Peace* (Cambridge: Cambridge University Press, 2007), p. 159.
91. Ibid., p. 161.
92. M. Kaldor, 'Transnational Civil Society', p. 195.
93. M. Waltzer, 'The Politics of Rescue', p. 41.
94. UN High Level Panel on Threats, Challenges and Change (2004), 'A more secure world: Our shared responsibility', p. 63.
95. According to Coates, 'The criterion of legitimate authority has become the most neglected of all the criteria that have been traditionally employed in the moral assessment of war'. A. J. Coates, *The Ethics of War* (Manchester: Manchester University Press, 1997), p. 123.
96. F. Dallmayr, 'Cosmopolitanism: Moral and Political', *Political Theory*, 31, 3 (2003), p. 434.
97. Cohen, 'Whose Sovereignty? Empire Versus International Law', p. 23.
98. M. Byers, 'Not yet Havoc', p. 51.
99. Berman, 'Moral Versus legal Imperatives', p. 161.

8 Conclusion: Sovereignty, Human Rights and the Integrity of International Law

1. V. E. Parsi, *The Inevitable Alliance* (Basingstoke: Palgrave Macmillan, 2006), p. 87.
2. G. Simpson, *Great Powers and Outlaw States*, p. 280.
3. J. Janzekovic, *The Use of Force in Humanitarian Intervention*, pp. 32 and 74.
4. D. Clark, 'Iraq has wrecked our case for humanitarian wars', *The Guardian*, 12 August 2003, p. 20.
5. P. Tyler, 'Threats and Responses'.
6. D. Chandler, *From Kosovo to Kabul*, p. 113.
7. N. Wheeler and J. Morris, 'Justifying the Iraq War as a Humanitarian Intervention', p. 448.

8. N. Wheeler, 'Agency, Humanitarianism and Intervention', p. 22.
9. N. Wheeler, 'Humanitarian Intervention After September 11, 2001', p. 207.
10. T. Dunne and N. Wheeler, 'Blair's Britain', p. 177.
11. Wheeler never suggested, however, that humanitarian interventions only count as such if the intervening party had no interests at stake. See N. Wheeler, *Saving Strangers*, pp. 37–9.
12. M. Wight, *The Three Traditions* (Leicester: Leicester University Press, 1991), p. 99.
13. H. Bull (ed.), *Intervention in World Politics* (Oxford: Oxford University Press, 1984), p. 6.
14. M. Reisman, 'Kosovo's Antinomies', *American Journal of International Law*, 93, 4 (1999), p. 862.
15. H. Bull, *The Anarchical Society*, p. 146.
16. W. Bain, 'The Political Theory of Trusteeship and the Twilight of International Equality', p. 75.
17. Ibid., p. 75.
18. Reisman, 'Kosovo's Antinomies', p. 860.
19. Ibid., p. 860.
20. S. Chesterman, *Just War or Just Peace?*, p. 128.
21. Hayden, *Cosmopolitan Global Politics*, p. 37.
22. A. Orford, *Reading Humanitarian Intervention*, p. 35.
23. Chesterman, *Just War or Just Peace?*, p. 87.
24. UN Press Release SG/SM/7136, GA/9596, 20th September 1999.
25. T. Todorov, *Hope and Memory* (London: Atlantic Books, 2003), p. 238.
26. Orford, *Humanitarian Intervention*, p. 126.
27. Ibid., p. 205.
28. P. Williams and A. Bellamy, 'The Responsibility to Protect and the Crisis in Darfur', p. 30.
29. Ibid., p. 30.
30. BBC News 24, 'Kofi Annan interview transcript', 3 July 2005, available online http://news.bbc.co.uk/1/hi/programmes/panorama/4647177.stm [accessed January 2008].

Bibliography

Altunbas, B. 'Darfur Has Become and Even Greater Challenge for Humanitarian Action', *Medecins Sans Frontieres Article*, 26 October 2007, pp. 114–15.

Ambos, K. 'Comment – NATO, the UN and the Use of Force: Legal Aspects', *European Journal of International Law*, 10, 1 (1999).

Amnesty International, 'NATO/Federal Republic of Yugoslavia: "Collateral Damage" or Unlawful Killings?' (2000), http://web.amnesty.org/library/index/ENGEUR 700182000.

Annan, K. 'In Larger Freedom: Decision Time at the UN', *Foreign Affairs*, 84, 3 (2005).

Arend, A. and Beck, R. *International Law and the Use of Force* (London: Routledge, 1993).

Armstrong, D., Farrell, T. and Maiguashca, B. eds *Force and Legitimacy in World Politics* (Cambridge: Cambridge University Press, 2005).

Armstrong, D. and Farrell, T. 'Introduction', in *Force and Legitimacy in World Politics*, Armstrong, Farrell and Maiguashca, eds (Cambridge: Cambridge University Press, 2005).

Armstrong, D., Farrell, T. and Lambert, H. *International Law and International Relations* (Cambridge: Cambridge University Press, 2007).

Bacevich, A. and Cohen, E. eds *War over Kosovo* (New York: Columbia University Press, 2001).

Bain, W. 'The Political Theory of Trusteeship and the Twilight of International Equality', *International Relations*, 17, 1 (2003), pp. 59–77.

Bain, W. ed. *The Empire of Security and the Safety of the Peoples* (London: Routledge, 2006).

Bain, W. 'Introduction', in *The Empire of Security and the Safety of the Peoples*, Bain, ed. (London: Routledge, 2006).

Bardos, G. 'International Policy in Southeast Europe: A Diagnosis', in *Yugoslavia Unravelled: Sovereignty, Self Determination, Intervention*, Thomas, ed. (Oxford: Lexington Books, 2003).

Barnett, M. 'Bureaucratizing the Duty to Aid: The United Nations and the Rwandan Genocide', in *Just Intervention*, Lang, ed. (Washington, DC: Georgetown University Press, 2003).

Bellamy, A. *Kosovo and International Society* (Hampshire: Palgrave Macmillan, 2002).

Bellamy, A. 'Ethics and Intervention: The "Humanitarian Exception" and the Problems of Abuse in the Case of Iraq', *Journal of Peace Research*, 41, 2 (2004), pp. 131–47.

Bellamy, A. 'Responsibility to Protect or Trojan Horse? The Crisis in Darfur and Humanitarian Intervention after Iraq', *Ethics and International Affairs*, 19, 2 (2005), pp. 31–54.

Bellamy, A. 'Whither the Responsibility to Protect? Humanitarian Intervention and the 2005 World Summit', *Ethics and International Affairs*, 20, 2 (2006), pp. 143–69.

Bellamy, A. *Just Wars: From Cicero to Iraq* (London: Polity, 2007).

Bergen, P. *The Osama Bin Laden I Knew* (New York: The Free Press, 2006).

Berman, F. 'Moral Versus legal Imperatives', in *The Price of Peace*, Reed and Ryall, eds (Cambridge: Cambridge University Press, 2007).

Blair, T. 'Blair Terror Speech in Full', BBC News, 5 March 2004. http://news.bbc.co.uk/1/hi/uk_politics/3536131.stm.

Blair, T. 'Speech to the Labour Party Conference', 28 September 2004. http://www.labour.org.uk/ac2004news?ux_news_id=ac04tb.

Blix, H. 'The Importance of Inspections', Carnegie Endowment for International Peace, Proliferation Brief, 7, No. 11 (2004).

Bloom, W. *Personal Identity, National Identity and International Relations* (Cambridge: Cambridge University Press, 1990).

Booth, K. 'Human Wrongs and International Relations', *International Affairs*, 71, 1 (1995), pp. 103–26.

Booth, K. 'Three Tyrannies', in *Human Rights in Global Politics*, Dunne and Wheeler, eds (Cambridge: Cambridge University Press, 2001).

Booth, K. ed. *Critical Security Studies and World Politics* (London: Lynne Rienner, 2005).

Booth, K. 'Critical Explorations', in *Critical Security Studies and World Politics*, Booth, ed. (London: Lynne Rienner, 2005).

Boucher, D. *Political Theories of International Relations* (Oxford: Oxford University Press, 1998).

Boucher, D. and Kelly, P. *Political Thinkers: From Socrates to the Present* (Oxford: Oxford University Press, 2003).

Bradol, J. H. 'The Sacrificial International Order and Humanitarian Action', in *In the Shadow of "Just Wars"*, Weissman, ed. (London: Hurts and Co., 2004).

Brauman, R. and Salignon, P. 'Iraq: In Search of a "Humanitarian Crisis"', in *In the Shadow of "Just Wars"*, Weissman, ed. (London: Hurts and Co., 2004).

Brown, C. *International Relations Theory: New Normative Approaches* (Hemel Hempstead: Harvester Wheatsheaf, 1992).

Brown, C. 'Ethics, Interests, and Foreign Policy', in *Ethics and Foreign Policy*, Smith and Light, eds (Cambridge: Cambridge University Press, 2001).

Brown, C. 'Selective Humanitarianism: In Defense of Inconsistency', in *Ethics and Foreign Intervention*, Chatterjee and Scheid, eds (Cambridge: Cambridge University Press, 2003).

Buchanan, A. and Keohane, R. 'The Preventive Use of Force: A Cosmopolitan Institutional Proposal', *Ethics and International Affairs*, 18, 1 (2004), 1–22.

Bull, H. *Justice in International Relations: Hagey Lectures* (Ontario: University Publications Distribution Service, 1984).

Bull, H. *The Anarchical Society* (London: Macmillan, 1995).

Burton, M. 'Legalising the Sublegal', *Georgetown Law Journal*, 85 (1996), pp. 417–54.

Bush, G. 'State of the Union Address', 28 January 2003. http://www.whitehouse.gov/news/releases/2003/01/20030128-19.html.

Bush, G. 'President Discusses Beginning of Operation Iraqi Freedom', White House Press Release, 22 March 2003. http://www.whitehouse.gov/news/releases/2003/03/20030322.html.

Bush, G. 'President Addresses the Nation in Prime Time Press Conference', 13 April 2004. http://www.whitehouse.gov/news/releases/2004/04/20040413-20.html.

Bush, G. 'President Bush Discusses Global War on Terror', 10 April 2006. http://www.whitehouse.gov/news/releases/2006/04/20060410-1.html.

Byers, M. 'Not yet Havoc', in *Force and Legitimacy in World Politics*, Armstrong, Farrell and Maiguashca, eds (Cambridge: Cambridge University Press, 2005).

Calas, F. and Salignon, P. 'Afghanistan: From "Militant Monks" to Crusaders', in *In the Shadow of "Just Wars"*, Weissman, ed. (London: Hurts and Co., 2004).

Caplan, R. 'Humanitarian Intervention: Which Way Forward?', *Ethics and International Affairs*, 14 (2000), pp. 23–38.

Carr, E. H. *The Twenty Years Crisis, 1919–1939* (Hampshire: Palgrave Macmillan, 2001).

Cassese, A. '*Ex iniuria ius oritur*: Are We Moving Towards International Legitimisation of Forcible Humanitarian Countermeasures in the World Community?', *European Journal of International Law*, 10, 1 (1999), pp. 23–30.

Chandler, D. 'International Justice', *New Left Review*, 6 (2000), pp. 55–66.

Chandler, D. *From Kosovo to Kabul* (London: Pluto, 2002).

Chandler, D. ed. *Rethinking Human Rights* (Hampshire: Palgrave Macmillan, 2002).

Chandler, D. 'Introduction', in *Rethinking Human Rights*, Chandler, ed. (Hampshire: Palgrave Macmillan, 2002).

Chandler, D. 'New Rights for Old?', *Political Studies*, 51 (2003), pp. 339–56.

Chandler, D. *Constructing Global Civil Society: Morality and Power in International Relations* (Hampshire: Palgrave Macmillan, 2004).

Chatterjee, D. and Scheid, D. eds *Ethics and Foreign Intervention* (Cambridge: Cambridge University Press, 2003).

Chatterjee, D. and Scheid, D. 'Introduction', in *Ethics and Foreign Intervention*, Chatterjee and Scheid, eds (Cambridge: Cambridge University Press, 2003).

Chesterman, S. *Just War or Just Peace?* (Oxford: Oxford University Press, 2002).

Chesterman, S. 'Hard Cases Make Bad Law', in *Just Intervention*, Lang, ed. (Washington, DC: Georgetown University Press, 2003).

Chesterman, S. and Byers, M. 'Has US Power Destroyed the UN?', *London Review of Books*, 21, 9, 29 April (1999).

Chesterman, S. and Byers, M. 'Changing the Rules About Rules?', in *Humanitarian Intervention: Ethical, Legal and Political Dilemmas*, Holzgrefe and Keohane, eds (Cambridge: Cambridge University Press, 2003).

Chinkin, C. 'Kosovo: A Good or Bad War?', *American Journal of International Law*, 93, 4 (1991), pp. 841–7.

Chmela, H. 'Thousands Rally in Washington for More U.S. Aid to Darfur', *New York Times*, 1 May 2006.

Chopra, J. 'Building State Failure in East Timor', in *State-Building: Theory and Practice*, Hehir and Robinson, eds (London: Routledge, 2007).

Chopra, J. and Weiss, T. 'Sovereignty is no Longer Sacrosanct', *Ethics and International Affairs*, 6 (1992), 95–118.

Christopher, P. *The Ethics of War and Peace* (New Jersey: Pearson, 2004).

Clark, D. 'Iraq has wrecked our case for humanitarian wars', *Guardian*, 12 August 2003.

Clark, W. *Waging Modern War* (Oxford: Public Affairs, 2001).

Coates, A. J. *The Ethics of War* (Manchester: Manchester University Press, 1997).

Cohen, J. 'Whose Sovereignty? Empire versus International Law', *Ethics and International Affairs*, 18, 3 (2004), pp. 1–24.

Coll, A. 'Kosovo and the Moral Burdens of Power', in *War over Kosovo*, Bacevich and Cohen, eds (New York: Columbia University Press, 2001).

Cooper, R. 'The New Liberal Imperialism', *Observer*, 7 April 2002.

Cortright, D. 'The World Says No: The Global Movement against War in Iraq', in *The Iraq Crisis and World Order: Structural, Institutional and Normative Challenges*, Thakur and Sidhu, eds (New York: United Nations University, 2006).
Daalder, I. and O'Hanlon, M. *Winning Ugly* (Washington, DC: Brookings Institute, 2000).
Dallaire, R. 'Looking at Darfur, Seeing Rwanda', *New York Times*, 4 October 2004.
Dallmayr, F. 'Cosmopolitanism: Moral and Political', *Political Theory*, 31, 3 (2003), pp. 421–42.
Danish Institute of International Affairs, *Humanitarian Intervention* (Copenhagen: Danish Institute of International Affairs, 1999).
De Cuellar, P. 'Report of the Secretary General', UN Yearbook (1991).
De Bréadún, D. 'A Defiant Bush Defends Iraq Strategy Before the UN', *Irish Times*, 22 September 2004.
Dinstein, Y. *War, Aggression and Self-Defence* (Cambridge: Cambridge University Press, 2005).
Donnelly, J. 'Twentieth Century Realism', in *Traditions of International Ethics*, Terry Nardin and David Mapel, eds (Cambridge: Cambridge University Press, 1992).
Duffield, M. *Global Governance and the New Wars* (London: Zed Books, 2006).
Dumbrell, J. and Ryan, D. eds *Vietnam in Iraq* (London: Routledge, 2007).
Dunne, T. and Wheeler, N. eds *Human Rights in Global Politics* (Cambridge: Cambridge University Press, 2001).
Dunne, T. and Wheeler, N. 'Blair's Britain: A Force for Good in the World?', in *Ethics and Foreign Policy*, Smith and Light, eds (Cambridge: Cambridge University Press, 2001).
Evans, M. 'In Humanity's Name: Democracy and the Right to Wage War', in *Just War Theory: A Reappraisal*, Mark Evans, ed. (Edinburgh: Edinburgh University Press, 2005).
Falk, R. *On Humane Governance: Toward a New Global Politics* (Cambridge: Polity, 1995).
Falk, R. 'Recovering Normative Consciousness', *International Relations*, 19, 1 (2005), pp. 79–90.
Farer, T. 'The Ethics of Intervention in Self Determination Struggles', in *Ethics and Foreign Intervention*, Chatterjee and Scheid, eds (Cambridge: Cambridge University Press, 2003).
Fein, H. 'Genocide: A Sociological Perspective', *Current Sociology*, 38, 1 (1990), pp. 1–126.
Finnemore, M. 'Fights about Rules: The Role of Efficacy and Power in Changing Multilateralism', in *Force and Legitimacy in World Politics*, Armstrong, Farrell and Maiguashca, eds (Cambridge: Cambridge University Press, 2005).
Finnis, J. *Aquinas* (Oxford: Oxford University Press, 1998).
Fisher, D. 'Humanitarian Intervention', in *The Price of Peace*, Reed and Ryall, eds (Cambridge: Cambridge University Press, 2007).
Fitzmaurice, M. 'The Practical Working of the Law of Treaties', in *International Law*, Mark Evans, ed. (Oxford: Oxford University Press, 2006).
Franck, T. and Rodley, N. 'After Bangladesh: The Law of Humanitarian Intervention by Force', *American Journal of International Law*, 67 (1973), pp. 275–305.
Frank, T. 'Legality and Legitimacy in Humanitarian Intervention', in *Humanitarian Intervention*, Terry Nardin and Melissa Williams, eds (New York: New York University Press, 2006).

Frost, M. 'The Ethics of Humanitarian Intervention', in *Ethics and Foreign Policy*, Smith and Light, eds (Cambridge: Cambridge University Press, 2001).
Fukuyama, F. 'Nation-building and the Failure of International Memory', in *Nation-Building*, Francis Fukuyama, ed. (New York: John Hopkins University Press, 2006).
Fuller, G. 'Two, Three, Many Kosovars', *New Perspectives Quarterly*, 16, 4 (1999), 15–31.
Gaberson, W. 'Conflict in the Balkans', *New York Times*, 27 March 1999.
Gardels, N. 'The Paradox of Post-Heroic Warfare', *New Perspectives Quarterly*, 16, 4 (1999), pp. 2–3.
Gardner, L. 'The Final Chapter?' in *Vietnam in Iraq*, Dumbrell and Ryan, eds (London: Routledge, 2007).
Garton-Ash, T. 'The War We Almost Lost', *Guardian*, 4 September 2000.
Gelb, L. 'The Rise of Ethics in Foreign Policy', *Foreign Affairs*, 82, 3 (2003), pp. 2–7.
Glennon, M. 'The New Interventionism', *Foreign Affairs*, 78, 3 (1999), pp. 2–7.
Glennon, M. 'How War Left the Law Behind', *New York Times*, 21 November 2002.
Gong, G. *The Standard of Civilisation in International Society* (Oxford: Oxford University Press, 1984).
Gonzalez-Foerster, G. 'East Timor: Better Late Than Never', in *In the Shadow of "Just Wars"*, Weissman, ed. (London: Hurts and Co., 2004).
Gow, J. *The Serbian Project and Its Adversaries: A Strategy of War Crimes* (McGill-Queens University Press: Montreal, 2003).
Gow, J. *Defending the West* (Cambridge: Polity, 2006).
Grugel, J. 'Democratisation Studies Globalisation: The Coming Age of a Paradigm', *British Journal of Politics and International Relations*, 5, 2 (2003), pp. 258–83.
Guicherd, C. 'International Law and the War in Kosovo', *Survival*, 41, 2 (1999), pp. 19–34.
Hampson, F. 'Law and War', in *International Perspectives on the Yugoslav Crisis*, A. Danchev and T. Halverston, eds (New York: St Martin's Press, 1996).
Harff, B. and Gurr, T. 'Towards an Empirical Theory of Genocides and Politicides', *International Studies Quarterly*, 32 (1988), pp. 359–71.
Hayden, P. *Cosmopolitan Global Politics* (Aldershot: Ashgate, 2005).
Held, D. *Democracy and the Global Order* (London: Polity, 1995).
Hehir, A. 'The Impact of Analogical Reasoning on US Foreign Policy Towards Kosovo', *Journal of Peace Research*, 43, 1 (2005), pp. 67–81.
Hehir, A. and Robinson, N. eds *State-Building: Theory and Practice* (London: Routledge, 2007).
Hehir, B. J. 'Intervention: From Theory to Cases', *Ethics and International Affairs*, 9 (1995), pp. 1–13.
Henkin, L. 'Compliance with International Law in an Inter-State System', *Academie de droit international, Recueil des cours* 1989 (Dordrecht: Martinus Nijhoff, 1990).
Hensel, H. 'Introduction', in *Sovereignty and the Global Community*, Howard Hensel, ed. (Aldershot: Ashgate, 2004).
Herman, E. and Peterson, D. 'Morality's Avenging Angels: The New Humanitarian Crusaders', in *Rethinking Human Rights*, Chandler, ed. (Hampshire: Palgrave Macmillan, 2002).
Hertz, J. 'Rise and Demise of the Territorial State', *World Politics*, 9, 4 (1957), pp. 473–93.
Hinsliff, G. 'Blair stakes his political future on beating Iraq', *Observer*, 16 February 2003.

Hodge, C. 'Casual War: NATO's Intervention in Kosovo', *Ethics and International Affairs*, 14 (2000), pp. 39–54.

Hoffmann, S. 'Intervention: Should it go on? Can it go on?', in *Ethics and Foreign Intervention*, Chatterjee and Scheid, eds (Cambridge: Cambridge University Press, 2003).

Hoge, W. 'U.N. Council Threatens to Punish Sudan Over Militia Killings', *New York Times*, 31 July 2004.

Holbrook, J. 'Humanitarian Intervention', in *Rethinking Human Rights*, Chandler, ed. (Hampshire: Palgrave Macmillan, 2002).

Holmes, R. L. *On War and Morality* (Princeton, NJ: Princeton University Press, 1989).

Holzgrefe, J and Keohane, R. eds *Humanitarian Intervention: Ethical, Legal and Political Dilemmas* (Cambridge: Cambridge University Press, 2003).

Human Rights Watch, 'Indonesian Government Must Prevent East Timor Bloodbath', 3 September 1999. http://hrw.org/english/docs/1999/09/03/eastti 1662.htm.

Human Rights Watch, 'Human Rights News: Crisis in Darfur', 18 September 2007. http://www.hrw.org/english/docs/2004/05/05/darfur8536.htm.

Hurrell, A. 'Legitimacy and the Use of Force: Can the Circle be Squared?', in *Force and Legitimacy in World Politics*, Armstrong, Farrell and Maiguashca, eds (Cambridge: Cambridge University Press, 2005).

Hutchings, K. *International Political Theory* (London: Sage, 1999).

Ignatieff, M. *Virtual War* (London: Vintage, 2001).

Independent International Commission on Kosovo, *Kosovo Report* (Oxford: Oxford University Press, 2000).

International Commission on Intervention and State Sovereignty, *The Responsibility to Protect: Research, Bibliography, Background* (Ottawa: International Development Research Center, 2001).

Janzekovic, J. *The Use of Force in Humanitarian Intervention* (Hampshire: Ashgate, 2006).

Jett, D. *Why Peacekeeping Fails* (Hampshire: Palgrave Macmillan, 2001).

Judah, T. *Kosovo: War and Revenge* (New Haven: Yale University Press, 2000).

Kaldor, M. *New and Old Wars* (London: Polity, 1999).

Kaldor, M. 'Transnational Civil Society', in *Human Rights in Global Politics*, Dunne and Wheeler, eds (Cambridge: Cambridge University Press, 2001).

Kaldor, M. *Global Civil Society: An Answer to War* (Cambridge: Polity, 2003).

Kaldor, M. 'What is Human Security?', in *Debating Globalization*, David Held, ed. (London: Polity, 2005).

Kaldor, M. 'From Just War to Just Peace', in *The Price of Peace*, Reed and Ryall, eds (Cambridge: Cambridge University Press, 2007).

Kaplan, R. 'The Coming Anarchy', *Atlantic Monthly*, 2 February 1994, pp. 44–76.

Keck, M. and Sikkink, K. *Activists beyond Borders: Advocacy Networks in International Politics* (Ithaca: Cornell University Press, 1998).

Kennan, G. 'Morality and Foreign Policy', *Foreign Affairs*, 64, 2 (1985), pp. 205–18.

Knudsen, T. B. 'Humanitarian Intervention Revisited: Post Cold War Responses to Classical Problems', in *The UN, Peace and Force*, M. Pugh, ed. (London: Frank Cass, 1997).

Kouchner, B. 'The Right to Intervention: Codified in Kosovo', *New Perspectives Quarterly*, Summer, 16, 4 (1999).

Krauthammer, C. 'In Bosnia Partition Might Do', *International Herald Tribune*, 9 September (1992).
Kung, H. *Global Responsibility* (New York, Crossroad, 1991).
Kuperman, A. 'Transnational Causes of Genocide', in *Yugoslavia Unravelled: Sovereignty, Self Determination, Intervention*, Raju Thomas, ed. (Oxford: Lexington Books, 2003).
Kuperman, A. 'Suicidal Rebellions and the Moral Hazard of Humanitarian Intervention', in *Gambling on Humanitarian Intervention*, Timothy Crawford and Alan Kuperman, eds (London: Routledge, 2006).
Landman, T. *Studying Human Rights* (London: Routledge, 2006).
Lang, A. ed. *Just Intervention* (Washington, DC: Georgetown University Press, 2003).
Lang, A. 'Humanitarian Intervention: Definition and Debates', in *Just Intervention*, Lang, ed. (Washington, DC: Georgetown University Press, 2003).
Lemann, N. 'The Next World Order', *New Yorker*, 1 April 2002.
Lillich, R. 'Forcible Self-Help by States to Protect Human Rights', *Iowa Law Review*, 53, (1967), pp. 290–314.
Linklater, A. *The Transformation of Political Community* (Oxford: Polity, 1998).
Locke, J. 'The Second Treatise of Government', in *Two Treatises of Government*, Peter Laslett, ed. (Cambridge: Cambridge University Press, 1988).
Linklater, A. 'The Good International Citizen and the Crisis in Kosovo', summary in *Kosovo and the Challenge of Humanitarian Intervention*, Albrecht Schnabel and Ramesh Thakur, eds (New York: United Nations University Press, 2000).
Lu, C. *Just and Unjust Interventions in World Politics* (Hampshire: Palgrave Macmillan, 2006).
Lucas, G. 'From Jus ad Bellum to Jus ad Pacem', in *Ethics and Foreign Intervention*, Chatterjee and Scheid, eds (Cambridge: Cambridge University Press, 2003).
Lyons, G. and Mastanduno, M. 'Introduction', in *Beyond Westphalia: State Sovereignty and International Intervention*, Gene Lyons and Michael Mastanduno, eds (Baltimore: John Hopkins University Press, 1995).
Malcolm, N. *Aspects of Hobbes* (Oxford: Oxford University Press, 2002).
Malone, D. *The International Struggle over Iraq* (Oxford: Oxford University Press, 2006).
Mattews, T. 'Redefining Security', *Foreign Affairs*, 68, 2 (1989), pp. 162–77.
Mayall, J. 'Non-Intervention, Self-Determination and the "New World Order"', *International Affairs*, 67, 3 (1991), pp. 421–9.
Mearsheimer, J. 'Back to the Future', *International Security*, 19, 3 (1990), pp. 5–56.
Mearsheimer, J. 'The False Promise of International Institutions', *International Security*, 19, 3 (1994), pp. 5–49.
Medecins Sans Frontieres, 'MSF Condemns Violence in Darfur', *Medecins Sans Frontieres Article*, 8 April 2005. http://www.msf.org/msfinternational/invoke.cfm?component=article&objectid=2260FE2B-E018-0C72-09DACE85BB3176F8&method=full_html.
Melanson, R. 'Unravelling the Domestic Foreign Policy Consensus', in *Vietnam in Iraq*, Dumbrell and Ryan, eds (London: Routledge, 2007).
Mertus, J. 'Back to the Drawing Board: Human Rights Should Know No Boundaries', *Washington Post*, 11 April 1999.
Miller, R. 'Respectable Oppressors, Hypocritical Liberators', in *Ethics and Foreign Intervention*, Chatterjee and Scheid, eds (Cambridge: Cambridge University Press, 2003).

Molloy, S. *The Hidden History of Realism* (Hampshire: Palgrave Macmillan, 2006).
Morgenthau, H. *Scientific Man versus Power Politics* (Chicago, IL: Phoenix Books, 1965).
Moxon-Browne, E. 'A Future for Peacekeeping?', in Edward Moxon-Browne, ed. *A Future for Peacekeeping?* (New York: St Martin's Press, 1998).
Mueller, J. 'Legitimacy, Success and Iraq', in *Force and Legitimacy in World Politics* Armstrong, Farrell and Maiguashca, eds (Cambridge: Cambridge University Press, 2005).
Nardin, T. 'The Moral Basis of Humanitarian Intervention', in *Just Intervention*, Lang, ed. (Washington, DC: Georgetown University Press, 2003).
Orford, A. *Reading Humanitarian Intervention* (Cambridge: Cambridge University Press, 2003).
Pangle, T. and Ahrensdorf, P. *Justice among Nations* (Lawrence, KS: University of Kansas Press, 1999).
Parekh, B. 'Rethinking Humanitarian Intervention', *International Political Science Review*, 18, 1 (1997), pp. 49–69.
Parsi, V. E. *The Inevitable Alliance* (Hampshire: Palgrave Macmillan, 2006).
Perle, R. 'Thank God for the Death of the UN', *Guardian*, 21 March 2003.
Pugh, M. 'Peacekeeping and Critical Theory', in *Peace Operations and the Global Order*, Alex Bellamy and Paul Williams, eds (London: Routledge, 2005).
Reed, C. and Ryall, D. eds *The Price of Peace* (Cambridge: Cambridge University Press, 2007).
Rengger, N. 'The Judgment of War: On the Idea of Legitimate Force in World Politics', in *Force and Legitimacy in World Politics*, Armstrong, Farrell and Maiguashca, eds (Cambridge: Cambridge University Press, 2005).
Reus-Smit, C. 'Liberal Hierarchy and the License to Use Force', in *Force and Legitimacy in World Politics*, Armstrong, Farrell and Maiguashca, eds (Cambridge: Cambridge University Press, 2005).
Roberts, A. 'The Role of Humanitarian Issues in International Politics in the 1990s', *International Review of the Red Cross*, 81, 833 (1999).
Roberts, A. 'The So-Called "Right" of Humanitarian Intervention', in *Yearbook of International Humanitarian Law 2000*, 3 (The Hague: T.M.C Asser, 2002).
Roberts, A. 'Beyond Dictatorial Interference', in *The Empire of Security and the Safety of the People*, Bain, ed. (London: Routledge, 2006).
Robertson, G. *Crimes against Humanity* (London: Penguin, 2002).
Rockler, W. J. 'War Crimes Law Applies to U.S. Too', *Chicago Tribune*, 23 May 1999.
Roth, K. 'Bombs Report off Target', *Guardian*, 12 January 2000.
Said, E. *Culture and Imperialism* (London: Chatto and Windus, 1993).
Samuel, T. 'East Timor: The Path to Self-Determination', in Chandra Lekha Sriram and Karin Wermester, eds *From Promise to Practice: Strengthening UN Capacities for the Prevention of Violent Conflict* (London: Lynne Rienner, 2003).
SaveDarfur, 'About US: Frequently Asked Questions', (2007) http://www.savedarfur.org/pages/faq/#1.
Schachter, O. *International Law in Theory and Practice* (Dordrecht: Martinus Nijhoff, 1991).
Schmidt, C. *The Concept of the Political*, trans. George Schwabb (Chicago, IL: Chicago University Press, 1996).
Schnabel, A. and Thakur, R. eds *Kosovo and the Challenge of Humanitarian Intervention* (New York: United Nations University Press, 2000).

Seybolt, T. *Humanitarian Military Intervention* (Oxford: Oxford University Press, 2007).

Shaw, M. *Global Society and International Relations* (Cambridge: Cambridge University Press, 1994).

Sikkink, K. 'Human Rights, Principled Issue-Networks, and Sovereignty in Latin America', *International Organisation*, 47, 3 (1993), pp. 411–41.

Simma, B. 'NATO, the UN and the Use of Force', *European Journal of International Law*, 10, 1 (1999), pp. 1–22.

Simpson, G. *Great Powers and Outlaw States* (Cambridge: Cambridge University Press, 2004).

Slim, H. 'Dithering over Darfur?', *International Affairs*, 80, 5 (2004), pp. 811–28.

Smith, K. and Light, M. eds *Ethics and Foreign Policy* (Cambridge: Cambridge University Press, 2001).

Stromseth, J. 'Rethinking Humanitarian Intervention', in *Humanitarian Intervention: Ethical, Legal and Political Dilemmas*, Holzgrefe and Keohane, eds (Cambridge: Cambridge University Press, 2003).

Tanguy, J. 'Redefining Sovereignty and Intervention', *Ethics and International Affairs*, 17, 1 (2003), pp. 141–8.

Teson, F. 'Collective Humanitarian Intervention', *Michigan Journal of International Law*, 17 (1996), pp. 323–71.

Teson, F. 'The Liberal Case for Humanitarian Intervention', in *The Morality of War*, Larry May, Eric Rove and Steve Viner, eds (Upper Saddle River, NJ: Pearson, 2005).

Thakur, R. 'Intervention, Sovereignty and the Responsibility to Protect: Experiences from ICISS', *Security Dialogue*, 33, 3 (2002), pp. 327–8.

Thakur, R. and Sidhu, W. P. S. eds *The Iraq Crisis and World Order: Structural, Institutional and Normative Challenges* (New York: United Nations University, 2006).

Thomas, R. ed. *Yugoslavia Unravelled: Sovereignty, Self Determination, Intervention* (Oxford: Lexington Books, 2003).

Thomas, N. and Tow, W. 'The Utility of Human Security: Sovereignty and Humanitarian Intervention', *Security Dialogue*, 33, 2 (2002), pp. 177–92.

Todorov, T. *Hope and Memory* (London: Atlantic Books, 2003).

Tooke, J. *The Just War in Aquinas and Grotius* (London: SPCK, 1965).

Tyler, P. 'Threats and Responses: News Analysis; A New Power in the Streets', *New York Times*, 17 February 2003.

Tyner, J. *The Business of War* (Aldershot: Ashgate, 2006).

UK Government Strategic Defence Review, 8 July 1998, http://www.parliament.the-stationery-office.co.uk/pa/cm199798/cmselect/cmdfence/138/13809.htm#n263.

UN Commission on Global Governance, *Our Global Neighbourhood* (Oxford: Oxford University Press, 1995).

UNHCR, 'Report of the United Nations High Commissioner for Human Rights and Follow-Up to the World Conference on Human Rights: Situation of Human Rights in the Darfur region of Sudan', E/CN.4/2005/3, 7 May (2004), http://www.unhchr.ch/huridocda/huridoca.nsf/AllSymbols/863D14602AA82CAEC1256EA80038E268/$File/G0414221.doc?OpenElement.

US Department of State, 'The Crisis in Darfur: Secretary Colin Powell, Testimony before the Senate Foreign Relations Committee', 9 September 2004. http://www.state.gov/secretary/former/powell/remarks/36042.htm.

Waltz, K. *Theory of International Politics* (London: McGraw Hill, 1979).
Waltzer, M. 'The Politics of Rescue', *Dissent*, 42, 1 (1995), pp. 35–41.
Watson, R. 'Bush Deploys Hawk as New UN Envoy', *Timesonline*, 8 March 2005. http://www.timesonline.co.uk/article/0,,11069-1515816,00.html.
Weigel, G. 'The Development of Just War Thinking in the post-Cold War World', in *The Price of Peace*, Reed and Ryall, eds (Cambridge: Cambridge University Press, 2007).
Weiss, T. 'The Sunset of Humanitarian Intervention?', *Security Dialogue*, 35, 2 (2004), pp. 135–53.
Weiss, T. *Humanitarian Intervention* (London: Polity, 2007).
Weissman, F. ed. *In the Shadow of "Just Wars"* (London: Hurts and Co., 2004).
Weller, M. *The Crisis in Kosovo 1989–1999: International Documents and Analysis* (Cambridge: Documents and Analysis Publishing, 1999).
Wesley, M. 'The New Interventionism and the Invasion of Iraq', in *Beyond the Iraq War: The Promises, Pitfalls and Perils of External Interventionism*, Michael Heazle and Iyanatul Islam, eds (Cheltenham: Edward Elgar, 2006).
Wheeler, M. 'A US Political Perspective', in *The Price of Peace*, Reed and Ryall, eds (Cambridge: Cambridge University Press, 2007).
Wheeler, N. 'Agency, Humanitarianism and Intervention', *International Political Science Review*, 18, 1 (1997), pp. 9–25.
Wheeler, N. 'Guardian Angel or Global Gangster?', *Political Studies*, 44, 1 (1997), pp. 123–35.
Wheeler, N. *Saving Strangers: Humanitarian Intervention in International Society* (Oxford: Oxford University Press, 2002).
Wheeler, N. 'A Victory for Common Humanity? The Responsibility to Protect after the 2005 World Summit', Paper presented at the conference 'The UN at Sixty: Celebration or Wake?', Faculty of Law, University of Toronto, Canada, 6–7 October 2005. Available at www.una.org.uk/humanrights/R2P%5B1%5D.pdf.
Wheeler, N. and Dunne, T. 'East Timor and the New Humanitarian Interventionism', *International Affairs*, 77, 4 (2001), pp. 805–27.
Wheeler, N. and Morris, J. 'The Iraq War as a Humanitarian Intervention', in *Iraq Crisis and World Order: Structural, Institutional and Normative Challenges*, Thakur and Sidhu, eds (New York: United Nations University, 2006).
White, N. 'The Will and Authority of the Security Council after Iraq', *Leiden Journal of International Law*, 17, 4 (2004), pp. 645–72.
Wight, M. *The Three Traditions* (Leicester: Leicester University Press, 1991).
Williams, P. 'Military Responses to Mass Killing: The African Union Mission to Sudan', *International Peacekeeping*, 13, 2 (2006), pp. 168–83.
Williams, P. and Bellamy, A. 'The Responsibility to Protect and the Crisis in Darfur', *Security Dialogue*, 36, 1 (2005), pp. 27–47.
Zahab, M. A. and Roy, O. *Islamist Networks* (London: Hurst and Co., 2004).
Zakaria, F. 'Is Realism Finished?', *The National Interest*, Winter, 30 (1992), pp. 21–32.

Index

Breinigsville, PA USA
08 August 2010

243122BV00003B/2/P

9 780230 542211